Demystifying Strategic Thinking

Demystifying Strategic Thinking
Lessons from leading CEOs

Dr Tony Grundy

LONDON PHILADELPHIA NEW DELHI

Publisher's note

Every possible effort has been made to ensure that the information contained in this book is accurate at the time of going to press, and the publishers and author cannot accept responsibility for any errors or omissions, however caused. No responsibility for loss or damage occasioned to any person acting, or refraining from action, as a result of the material in this publication can be accepted by the editor, the publishers or the author.

First published in Great Britain and the United States in 2014 by Kogan Page Limited

Apart from any fair dealing for the purposes of research or private study, or criticism or review, as permitted under the Copyright, Designs and Patents Act 1988, this publication may only be reproduced, stored or transmitted, in any form or by any means, with the prior permission in writing of the publishers, or in the case of reprographic reproduction in accordance with the terms and licences issued by the CLA. Enquiries concerning reproduction outside these terms should be sent to the publishers at the undermentioned addresses:

2nd Floor, 45 Gee Street	1518 Walnut Street, Suite 1100	4737/23 Ansari Road
London EC1V 3RS	Philadelphia PA 19102	Daryaganj
United Kingdom	USA	New Delhi 110002
www.koganpage.com		India

© Tony Grundy, 2014

The right of Tony Grundy to be identified as the author of this work has been asserted by him in accordance with the Copyright, Designs and Patents Act 1988.

ISBN   978 0 7494 6944 3
E-ISBN 978 0 7494 6945 0

British Library Cataloguing-in-Publication Data

A CIP record for this book is available from the British Library.

Library of Congress Cataloging-in-Publication Data

Grundy, Tony, 1954-
  Demystifying strategic thinking : lessons from leading CEOs / Tony Grundy.
    pages cm
    ISBN 978-0-7494-6944-3 (pbk.) – ISBN 978-0-7494-6945-0 (ebook) (print) 1. Strategic planning.
2. Business planning. 3. Leadership. I. Title.
  HD30.28.G782 2014
  658.4'012–dc23
                                                                                             2013047711

Typeset by Graphicraft Limited, Hong Kong
Printed and bound in India by Replika Press Pvt Ltd

CONTENTS

Acknowledgements vii

01 Why strategic thinking really matters 1

Introduction 1
Who should be reading this book 3
The rationale for this book: the CEO and strategic thinking 9
What is strategy? 10
What is strategic thinking? 23
Content of the book 34

02 Moonpig 38

Introduction 38

03 APIL 67

Introduction 67

04 Samaritans 94

Introduction 94

05 Virgin Galactic 113

Introduction 113

06 Simplyhealth 130

Introduction 130

07 International Paralympic Committee 154

Introduction 154

08 Integrating important strategic thinking themes   175

Introduction   175
The key themes of strategic thinking   176
A recap on the nature of strategic thinking   201
The key research questions   202
Conclusions   207

09 Concluding lessons   208

Introduction   208
Reflections and lessons on methodology   209
An overview of what we know about strategic thinking   210
Understanding your own strategic thinking capability   217
The enablers and constraints of strategic thinking   220
Managing strategic projects   224
The role of toolkits in strategy cognition   228

10 Strategic thinking: visioning   237

Introduction   237
Strategic influencing: why not have a Halloween party?   237
Vision and thinking differently: an experience of Dubai   243
Postscript   247

*Appendix 1: Rethinking and reinventing Porter's Five
              Competitive Forces*   249
Appendix 2: How contingent should strategy be?   277

References and further reading   297
Index   299

ACKNOWLEDGMENTS

I would like to thank my wife, Dr Carolina Yepes, for shining her light and her love into my life, and for making this and my previous book such light work in the most challenging period of my life. I am indebted to her psychological influence in this book.

I also send all my love and my thoughts to Thomas, who is never far from my mind, and I hope that one day you will be able and wish to be a dearest companion in life's journey once again. May you enjoy *Alice in Wonderland* and never forget its inner lessons.

Why strategic thinking really matters

01

Introduction

> *Why is the future important? Because we will spend the rest of our lives in it.*
>
> **(ANON)**

'Strategic thinking' is often talked about as a sexy management process, but it is not so often defined and even less frequently explored. Similar in many ways to ideas such as 'innovative thinking', 'leadership', or 'transformational change', it is more often than not unclear and ambiguous what it is actually about. Even more of a mystery is what it entails and when one should do it, and on what topics.

Googling 'strategic thinking' brings up a lot of more general material on strategic management, but this tends to be thick with concepts and theory, but thin on cognitive processes. Essentially, therefore, to understand strategic thinking one needs to have some understanding of the practical aspects of psychology.

This is my 19th text on management (20th, counting my sole one on something rather different). These writings have evolved over 20 years and are a reflection on theory, research, experiences and insights and are very much concerned with practicality. This book is essentially about three things: strategic thinking, demystifying its nature, and practicality, and is a follow-on from my previous one, *Demystifying Strategy* (Grundy, 2012) which combined different perspectives on strategy with a very particular framework of thinking processes and tools, case studies and many practical do-it-yourself exercises. *Demystifying Strategy* set out to shed a practical 'I can do it myself' perspective on what in many texts is a somewhat exotic and esoteric subject. The result of the more abstract treatment is that strategy is positioned in managers' minds as being remote from everyday experience. In that earlier volume, the focus on demystifying was explicit and ruthless (even at the risk of upsetting colleagues at business schools). Its philosophy was that in the modern management world no one really has time for over-elaborate and mystical strategic concepts and ideas.

Most really good strategic ideas are actually quite simple, not elaborate, and so too it was with this book. I was on the beach at a five-star luxury hotel in Cancun, Mexico, the Grand Paraiso – on honeymoon (strategic heaven) – when the idea came to me. That thought was a true product of strategic thinking in that it combined ideas from disparate sources My previous book was an account of how strategy, as a more general concept, could be demystified, addressed from my perspective and from my experience. But my thought on that beautiful Mexican beach was: 'Why not explore how senior managers and directors actually process it cognitively? Indeed, even further, why not go out and ask some real CEOs how they see it, how do they do it, what is its value, and what are the challenges and constraints?'

I knew that when one explores a topic such as this at director level or above, it will generate a wealth of most interesting reflection and many insights. While thinking about it on the beach I then had the further idea of making the core material of this book not just straightforward answers to a series of open questions, but to actively engage with each CEO in a dialogue, and record and analyse that.

As I was not encumbered with the need to make this squeaky-clean methodologically this would not only produce rich insights but also ones of a unique nature. Unconstrained by some need to publish to the great and the good of the academic world to score some research qualification, I could probe existing thinking and stimulate some new thinking too. So I set out with the idea that the material would be much more a kind of Aristotelian dialogue. In that process I would also be taking the stance that while I was going to be alert to new themes and issues that CEOs raised, either explicitly or implicitly, I would also draw in my tacit knowledge. This has been gained not only through rigorous academic research but also in over 25 years of independent strategy consulting experience as a facilitator, and similarly as an executive developer and strategy coach.

Having already written *Demystifying Strategy* would also give me a tight framework to which I could relate these dialogues. Also, people could read this book first and if they decided that they need to get more familiar with strategic frameworks, they could go back and read the earlier one – or readers of

Demystifying Strategy could pick up where I left off and explore the practical world of how CEOs see it and do it.

Fifty shades of strategy...

In truth I was also inspired by two other things. First, one of my case studies that I have used in the past is Disney's acquisition of Marvel. The take from that was that Marvel Studios would do a whole series on the same thing: the fabulous four, one, two, three... The demystifying theme was too powerful to be left to just one book. Also were there to be more than one book – both being complementary – then that would help the sales of both. The second strand was that I had been reading the first of the trilogy *Fifty Shades of Grey*, a somewhat risqué set of novels that has become, it is claimed, the bestseller of all time. This proved that it was possible to develop a book theme in more than one volume (obviously there have been a number of earlier series that have accomplished the same thing).

This book, like my last one, is built around the notion that strategies and strategic thinking should be a little special: and that means searching for some kind of 'cunning plan'. And reading that *Fifty Shades* book was a most 'cunning plan' – to find out what its appeal had been (yes, I know, you don't believe me). I wanted to understand what was behind its phenomenal success: its gestation and thus market testing through fan fiction. Due to the spread of the Kindle, etc people could read it without anyone else seeing the cover. One of the lessons here on strategic thinking is that ideas often come from the most unlikely sources.

While *Demystifying Strategic Thinking: Lessons from leading CEOs* doesn't purport to be a comprehensive account of the whole topic of leadership, it does still give us many insights into the adjacent topic of strategic leadership – as experienced at CEO level. That is a secondary goal.

This Introduction is quite long as it not only tells us what to expect in the book but also links to *Demystifying Strategy* and has a number of practical illustrations of real strategic thinking. The latter are light and stimulating to read so I hope you will enjoy them.

Who should be reading this book

This book is intended for a number of key target audiences:

- Senior managers who wish to learn how to do strategic thinking and in particular to learn how CEOs do it and to understand the problems and issues they have in doing it, either because they would like to be CEO one day, or simply to model those cognitive behaviours.

- Students and graduates of management, MBAs or otherwise, who wish to learn how to deal with the practicalities of what they have been taught.
- Managers who might wish to do an MBA, but who either haven't got the time, the energy or the money to do so.
- Finally, all of those who may engage at CEO level, for example suppliers of services like IT, outsourcing, consultancy and professional services.

But why would or should any of the above read this book? The main reason is that, if done properly, strategic thinking adds a great deal of real value, even in hard economic terms to the business. This can be done in many ways, for example through:

- more effective strategic decision making that gives real economic value;
- avoiding making strategic constraints;
- avoiding time wasted getting there;
- reducing unnecessary difficulties and politics;
- influencing key stakeholders and building ownership;
- providing a frame of reference at an everyday level to resolve operational dilemmas;
- enhancing confidence and proactivity;
- dissolving anxiety about things like 'Are we deciding to do the right things?', 'Will I look silly suggesting this is an option?' and so on.

The following case study on strategic thinking at Tesco illustrates the perils of predominantly tactical management alongside the value of strategic thinking as a tool.

CASE STUDY Strategic thinking at Tesco Non-Food: from tactics to strategic thinking

In 1996 I was asked to design and facilitate a strategic workshop for Tesco's then fledgling non-food business. In the previous 18 months I had also worked on the very early strategic development of Tesco Express (when there were just two stores; now there are over 1,000), Tesco Metro, Tesco.com, Tesco Financial Services, and scenarios for the Extra format. At that time Tesco didn't have a formal strategy department, so I got lucky in being a kind of one-man task force they could call on when they were in a bit of strategic bother.

It was interesting that many of the strategies that proved so phenomenally successful were actually 'problematic opportunities' as Tesco had got into them very quickly without perhaps really thinking deeply enough at a strategic level. In the words of one of my very earliest books (Grundy, 1992): 'It is all about shoot – aim – load.'

Around that time I met Tesco's then Group HR Director who was very pleased to see me as she had heard about the work we had been doing together. I showed her some of the slides I was using to try to get people to think a bit differently. One of them was a picture of an Apache helicopter, to stress the need for us to maintain helicopter vision, and another was the rather whacky one of a man whose head seemed to be going down a rabbit hole in the ground – the antithesis of helicopter vision being that of rabbit hole thinking. I used to put up the rabbit hole slide to discourage unnecessarily detailed and microscopic thinking. (I still use those slides to great effect today though now scanned into my laptop.) The HR Director thought that this slide was very funny, and she said: 'That's just us! We are really good at digging ourselves into holes and then digging our way out of them!' This was very much my experience when we started on many of these projects: this is all the more remarkable considering that Tesco's huge success, at least up until 2011, was very much tied into these strategies to develop new formats like Express, Non-Food, and Dotcom.

Coming back to the story of Tesco Non-Food, at that time there were five major business areas: petrol, pharmacy, clothing, videos and CDs, and household. So the very first thing that we did was to decide that we would split the work into these fives streams, or teams, as it would have been far too unwieldy to try to do these all at the same time. In effect, we decided that we would do some more bottom-up mini strategies. Looking back we might have also looked at some new areas of investigation, such as telecoms, utilities, etc – these were picked up later. (That implies some later integrative work to sense-check the whole strategy).

The design of the workshop, a three-day offsite event, provided for:

- Some data input: eg on potential growth of the Non-Food market based on some analysis of its 'growth drivers' (which I did in the form of some pictures): this was informed by some published research from the (then) Henley Centre For Forecasting; also some input on the current relative profitability of the different product groupings.

- Some basic SWOT analysis: this was fairly raw and was used for further adding to and refinement.

- Some slides of a series of key strategic questions that were worked through systematically over the three days.

- Slides of the analytical process (as seen in *Demystifying Strategy*) such as growth driver analysis, competitor profiling, which compares one's own competitive strength against some key competitors.

- A process in the form of a one-pager of key questions for use in competitor analysis: we spent some time on day three to make a series of undercover visits to competitors (usually we were not spotted but sometimes the Tesco people wore sunglasses – at that time the film 'Men In Black' was very popular. On one occasion when we were exiting from Vision Direct, one of the staff taunted us by saying, 'We know who you are.')

- While we worked on the same key questions in parallel, with me facilitating the five groups, we also came together to 'challenge and build' the interim output.

At the very end of the process I handed over about 25 sheets of paper ready to be typed up, detailing the analysis, the debates, option evaluations, decisions, and list of implementation issues. In today's world it would have been even better to get that onto a PC in real time. Unless the output is documented very quickly its meaning can very soon be diluted. Other things that we might have possibly done were to:

- Do a full 'position paper' that would have added to the bullet point output and the completed strategic option grid evaluations.

- Do a more formal 'uncertainty analysis' of the key assumptions, maybe involving some deeper work eg to role-play competitors and thus to estimate the lags before they imitated Tesco's push into Non-Food and, given their mindsets, personal and strategic agendas (called the 'PASTA' factors (Grundy, 1996) because, a bit like spaghetti of different colours, they all get mixed up in an entangled mess).

- More in-depth customer research on what Tesco customers would most like to see them bringing into store.

- Piloting different elements of the strategy before taking it to the board.

- Doing some rehearsals of the kinds of questions Terry Leahy (then CEO) and his team might pose, like a version of the 'Dragons Den' TV programme.

- Doing some 'time travelling' to the future, say five years' time to sketch out that future competitive map, the shape of the terrain in terms of just how far would the supermarket non-food operators have eaten into the traditional retailers in the high street.

Interestingly, at the very end of what turned out to be a truly breakthrough workshop experience, I asked Simon Uwins, then Director Non-Food, two key questions: 1) what did you learn from the process (I put a stage-by-stage model of the process on the screen) and, 2) what are you going to do with this potential strategy? Simon Uwins answered the first question by saying that it was the first time that they had actually broken down the process into relatively discrete stages like 'diagnosis', 'option generation', 'evaluation', 'planning', etc. That had put a lot more structure and focus into the process.

When I asked them what they were going to do with the process they all went very quiet and exchanged nervous glances. I allowed a very long pause and then said: 'I am beginning to have an out-of-body experience. I am wondering whether you actually believe in this and are truly committed. You are Tesco, you could be awesome at doing this: so just go for it!'

The rest is history. Tesco's Non-Food sales which, other than petrol, weren't that significant, grew from the 1996 base by a factor of many multiples by 2012. If that growth was of the order of £8 billion and assuming a margin of around 6 per cent, that's around £480 million of net profit before tax: huge. While Tesco obviously had to invest to get those returns and also had to implement it all – a considerable effort – nevertheless there was a huge amount of value created on the back of this breakthrough.

If we take corporation tax off and the extra profit is say £360 million, on a price:earnings ratio of say 10, that is £3.6 billion. If we were to attribute only 10 per cent of that value (modestly) to the strategy (a kind of 'strategy rent') and there was as much value created in the follow-up work as in the original three-day workshop, the (approximate) economic value created would be:

£3.6 billion × 10% × 50% = £180 million, or £60 million per day.

Speaks for itself. Some key lessons from this case are that:

- Tactical thinking means that your accomplishments will not be great and thus can be easily copied by competitors, who will be encouraged and not deterred by modest successes.

- You need to do separate mini strategic plans for specific areas of the business where these are significantly different from each other.

- These can all be accommodated within a single strategic workshop, in parallel, and usually with a single facilitator.
- The workshop should have quite a detailed pre-design: key strategic questions, key tools, the process, pre-work, opportunities for playing back and testing options.
- It needs to be worked through stage-by-stage and not to have these modelled together.
- There needs to be sufficient marketing and operational data.
- Expectations need to be set up-front, eg that we are expecting helicopter vision not rabbit hole behaviour.
- Competitor data should be rich and dig down into intent: thinking about the future.
- It is very important to properly record (not just on a scruffy flipchart) the output as quickly as possible.
- It is usual to at least have a stab at estimating the resultant shareholder value.
- Quite often and especially at the end of such events there can be a disconnect between coming up with a clear plan and actually implementing it.

So having taken a quick look at the rationale of this book and seen what strategic thinking did for Tesco in its non-food businesses in terms of value added, let's now move on to some key principles of strategic thinking. In this first chapter we look at:

- The rationale for this book: the CEO and strategic thinking.
- What is 'strategy?'
- Strategy as the cunning plan.
- What is 'strategic thinking'?
- Strategic thinking as a process.
- Evaluation of options – the strategic option grid revisited.
- Content of the book.

The rationale for this book: the CEO and strategic thinking

This book will help you in three key ways:

1 To help you become a strategic thinker and to make you more deeply thoughtful.
2 To learn from the reflections, experiences and pointers of a number of leading chief executives.
3 To inspire you to begin to stretch your ambition as to what you can accomplish in business.

The core of this book is the interviews with a number of leading CEOs from a variety of businesses. It was felt that there would be some illuminating insights to be had in terms of:

- Are they always aware of when they are doing it, or when they aren't doing it?
- When they do it, what is it that they feel they are doing?
- How do they do it: what sort or recipes do they employ?
- To what extent does the particular business and organizational context influence what they think about (ie strategically)?
- Do they ever use any particular tools or concepts?
- Do they typically do it on their own, or do they do it with others?
- How much time do they spend doing it?
- What does it actually feel like: does it have any distinctive sensations?
- When they are doing it, what feelings are sometimes experienced, before, during and afterwards?
- How do they keep track of or record their ideas and insights?
- What value has come out of the strategic thinking they have done either solo or with others, in the past?

Looking at this little list my first thought is that so few books on strategy even begin to address these issues: they seem to be about a fairly surreal world of either competitive strategy or organizational theory. Also, research studies have rarely touched on how individuals cope with the practicalities, especially cognitively, and without gathering data from real CEOs. So, having given you a flavour of the particular focus and purpose of this book, let's move on to two definition of 'strategy', the second of which is most helpful for us taking a strategic thinking perspective.

What is strategy?

'Strategy' has very many possible definitions and this in itself can be highly confusing. I have always tried to take a pragmatic approach here, and rather than to get into long sentences with concepts like 'matching the environment' or 'inimitable competitive advantage' that can quickly put people to sleep, I will give you the first of my three useful definitions (Grundy, 1995): 'Strategy is how you get from where you are now to where you want to be – and with real competitive advantage.' There are five ingredients to this definition:

1 knowing where you are now;
2 knowing where you want to be;
3 knowing how you will get there;
4 the 'how' is based on competitive advantage;
5 this is real and not just in your head.

Strategy as being the 'how'

The strategy itself is to be found primarily not in these goals but in the 'how' itself. Any strategy needs to have form and colour and we must be able to describe it in specific terms. Often it is believed that strategy is broad; said by Mintzberg (1994) to be an 'umbrella strategy', or one that is a broad direction, or even something about 'what business/es we are in'. That might be so sometimes but generally speaking that should be by exception: it is unhelpful to leave it that broad and ambiguous unless it is labelled 'strategic intent', which isn't quite the same thing.

Applying the big test: do we have sustainable competitive advantage?

This leads us back to the search for a decent strategy, which must be one 'with real competitive advantage'. Here we aren't looking for average strategies but ones that are distinctive in some way. What is the point in having the average plan, which is probably what at least 60 per cent of most companies' strategies actually are? It would be a very real surprise if this were going to give us anything other than average returns. Probably 80 per cent of companies do not have significant competitive advantage/a cunning strategy.

A company with competitive advantage is one that adds more real or perceived value to its target customers than its competitors do, or has lower costs than its competitors do, or both (for more, see Grundy, 2012). This is represented in the 'three Cs' shown in Figure 1.1.

FIGURE 1.1 The three Cs (customer, company, competitor) analysis

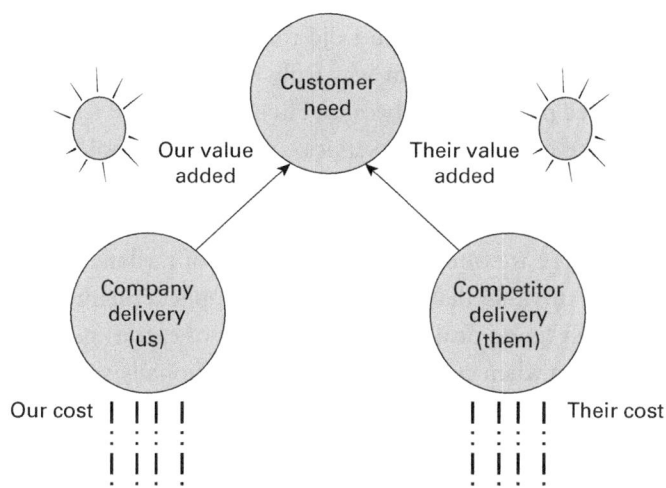

Companies that have achieved a very real competitive advantage more recently include Amazon, Facebook and Google. This has not just been through technology but through a deep appreciation of the emotional value that is generated, as well as giving customers what they 'really-really want' and at a reasonable cost.

'Competitive advantage' is now defined as: 'giving customers distinctive value relative to internal costs that are better than other competitors'. This distinctive value can be both real and perceived, but the proof of the pudding is in what customers think these are, and not what the company does. So that means that we must understand the value of products and services from the customer's point of view and not from our own.

Think about the last time you were impressed by the way that distinctive value was given – and without waste of resources. Can you remember that? Was this when you last had a car crash and had to leave your car for two weeks to be repaired, and not only did the insurance company treat you sympathetically in terms of not losing all of your no claims bonus (by Admiral), but had it repaired by a garage in Tottenham (by a Tottenham fan) who not only crafted the bodywork to completion, cleaned it inside, and even gave you a free estimate of its value? This happened to me in 2012. Or was it when you went to Brick Lane in East London to buy a new leather jacket and were running short of time but still managed to get the perfect one for £80, do a cash deal for £75 and then be offered a free reconditioning of your old jacket? In each case the experience gave me a warm feeling of satisfaction, of being truly looked after and was associated with a strong resolve to remember to get that service again for the same source when needed. (That's not to say that one would try to have another car crash!)

I found it interesting that when I did this bit of reflection it was a little hard to come up with much that was truly outstanding over the whole of 2012. I wondered perhaps if it's because I live in the United Kingdom, which is sadly not noted for its customer service – with rare examples of distinctive companies like the retailer John Lewis. Or maybe it is because we have been living in austere times so that customer service and niceties are cut to the bone, and suppliers are often predatory in terms of pushing 'value capture' (the proportion of value that ends up in the suppliers' margin rather than enjoyed as a truly 'good deal') too far in pricing of extras, penalty charges, differential pricing when customers are more emotionally vulnerable, as the funerals business has been sometimes accused of, and so on. But I do have an exception to tell you about, in the next case study.

CASE STUDY Truly distinctive competitive advantage at the Iberostar, Grande Paraiso Hotel, Cancun, Mexico, July 2012

A most distinctive experience of superior value-added was a holiday – actually a delayed honeymoon – in the fabulous all-inclusive five-star hotel, the Grand Paraiso in Cancun, Mexico, in July 2012.

The experience was excellent from start to finish. No reasonable expense had been spared to engineer a perfectly aligned business model, but the delivery of this value was something that all the staff truly cared about: one might call this not so much its 'competitive advantage' but its 'caring advantage'. The latter is something any other organization would find extremely hard to imitate. Someone clearly had not only done a lot of strategic thinking but this had been encapsulated in a true, strategic vision.

Compare this to all the examples of customer value destruction that one experiences on a regular basis. Banks are notorious for this. In 2013 one of the big UK banks that I had banked with for 21 years suddenly blocked me from making payments and told me that it was my fault as I had failed to input the correct security code three times – untrue. It would take three weeks to get me back on the system: meanwhile I had to pay hungry lawyers a very large amount of money to do a major court case. The bank suggested that I go to carry out a transfer of funds at another branch some distance away – and I found it had shut. After knocking on the glass window for five minutes and fearing that security was coming, I turned towards the High Street. Like someone from the bible on the road to Damascus I saw the sun glint off a red sign. That sign said 'Metrobank'. I went in and jumped on the chequebook and statements from that 'other bank'. Metrobank staff were not put off, sat me down, gave me a cup of tea and converted me.

Metrobank started in London only a couple of years ago with the strategy of offering a caring customer experience. It said it want its customers to 'love it as a bank'. It aims to create a revolution in banking. I now bank with Metrobank: it is cool. But if you were to ask me what the big difference is, I would say that my previous bank is about control and costs and Metrobank is about simplicity, slickness – and above all (caring) service. One senior manager in my previous bank had said, 'We aren't like Metrobank – we are so much bigger so we can't possibly be flexible', and another said, off the record: 'a lot of our people have gone through a difficult time as we thought we were going to be sold'. So behind the banking reality experienced by their customers there seems to be a lot of inner discontent and misalignment, ie behavioural factors at work.

To amplify the point about Metrobank actually caring, I visited to register for internet banking. I had to set up the password s and the numerical passcodes for both personal and business accounts. Now I am a Chartered Accountant and an MBA so you would have thought that setting all that up and getting it right would be a doddle: *wrong*. After 25 years of big-picture strategy work my attention span for random numerical detail kept getting lost. Time after time while Samuel Adetula of Metrobank guided me I failed to get it right. Six attempts and 45 minutes later I finally succeeded. Not once did Samuel ever show tiredness, frustration or impatience: he would smile no matter what! If I had been a 'mystery shopper' that day I would have been The One from Hell!

Worse is to come: I made a payment over the internet the next week while away from home and thought I had it cracked. Then a week later I tried at home and it wouldn't work! So back I went to the bank and oh – unlucky day – Samuel got me again! I remember thinking that I should have worn a bag over my head as I imagined that Samuel would be thinking when he got me as his next customer, 'Oh. not him again!' But I never saw his face drop, his eyes looked up and he still kept on smiling! He was even smiling when, almost as soon as we had sat down, I realized I was using some superseded codes that would never have worked! Again there was no glimmer of a look from Samuel giving away he might be thinking I was a little stupid. Please, please, Metrobank, hang on to that service culture as you get bigger as you surely will!

A point made forcibly in *Demystifying Strategy* was that often you just have to avoid competitive disadvantage that results from bad service, for example, to gain at least some competitive edge. Going back to our definition of competitive advantage, in terms of cost this doesn't mean price, which is a measure of economic value. It is about superior value or costs so it is possible to achieve competitive advantage by differentiating value, or through having a disproportionately low cost base. Finally, it is a question always of relative competitive advantage – and this needs to be formally evaluated. Having 'real' competitive advantage means that it is measurable in some way, or at least it can be observed. Also, we need to have some confidence that it is lasting, or more technically, 'sustainable'.

The advantage of the first definition above is that it helps us to think around a strategy in a very sound analytical and clinical way. But it isn't very inspirational. Strategic thinking thus means having the capacity to be highly objective, and to be able to take a fresh and detached perspective on your strategy and position.

Strategy as the cunning plan

Our second definition is that of strategy as a cunning plan, as follows:

- it works backwards from the result;
- it is fundamentally simple;
- it achieves its goals by a combination of obvious, and less than obvious, ideas;
- it isn't particularly easy to imitate.

Here I am going to take the liberty of using again a case study that appeared in *Demystifying Strategy*, both for the benefit of my new readers and as reinforcement for those with a copy of that earlier book.

CASE STUDY Blackadder and the 'cunning plan'

In the TV series 'Blackadder' – a comedy set in historical times – there was a character known as Blackadder, renowned for getting in all kinds of scrapes. His companion, a scruffy and disgusting character called Baldrick, often used to help him try to get out of these scrapes, usually with disastrously funny results. A constant theme of this immortal series was that they would usually come back to the 'cunning plan' to rescue them. While this was a humorous comedy invention it inspired me in my long quest to demystify strategy.

I would tell people the story of the millennium episode, 'Back and Forth' where Blackadder and Baldrick invent a time machine so that they can go back into the past and steal rare and expensive things that can be sold, like Nelson's boot, and also change the course of history in their favour. So they think that they have a 'cunning plan' but they don't implement it very well at all. In fact Baldrick falls by accident on the time controls and they get sent back in time but can't get back to the present because they have no idea what setting 'now' is on. This is the first example in this story of the need to always, when doing strategic thinking, to ask oneself the question: 'What is the one big thing we've forgotten?'

They arrive in Roman times and find that they have been reincarnated as Roman soldiers standing on top of Hadrian's Wall in Scotland. Unfortunately the wall is only three foot high, which is a metaphor in strategy for the importance of not spreading yourself too thinly. A key lesson of strategy is that you must choose and this frequently means saying 'no' to options.

The Roman general arrives to boost morale by announcing a retreat back to Rome, just as Blackadder and Baldrick spot something in the distance. The Roman general's assistant says: 'Is that an orange hedge moving toward us?' Seconds later his lieutenant says: 'No, it's the Scots!'

A hoard of crazed Scots with nasty looking weapons overwhelms the wall and surrounds the time machine where Blackadder and Baldrick have taken refuge. This is another important metaphor for the need in strategy to monitor signals in the environment.

There is another reminder in this part of the story about 'What's the one big thing that we have forgotten', too. When the Roman general appears on the scene he is almost fully armoured except down below where all he has got on is his underpants, echoing the story of the emperor's clothes.

At this point it is useful to reflect on what the options actually are for our two anti-heroes to be able to find out the setting on the time controls. Working backwards from the result one might for example get:

- some kind of truth drug;
- deep hypnosis;
- torture methods;
- shocks.

So here there is a range of options that need separate evaluation. But the really cunning one is yet to come... After many attempts at going up and down in time to try to get back to the present, Blackadder begins to show real frustration and reflects: 'So I am going to be cursed to spend the rest of my life being in a small wooden box with the most stupidest man in the world.'

Then Baldrick shows an unusual flash of intelligence: 'My lord, I think that I have a cunning plan. Well, you know that if you are at the moment of death that your life flashes before your eyes? Well, if we were to drown you we could take you back to the moment in your life when I feel on the time controls and just at that moment of death you would see the controls on the time machine, and then we would bring you back to life and we would all get back to the present' – with clever-looking grin on his face.

Whereupon Blackadder looks very thoughtful and then says: 'Well, Baldrick that is quite a cunning plan, but I think that I have got an even better one.' And with that he punches Baldrick unconscious and the next thing that we see is Baldrick's head being pushed down a loo to drown him. Each time he surfaces spluttering he gets closer to remembering and finally sees in his head the control settings saying: 'I've got it!' and then, as he stops spluttering: 'I wish that we had flushed the loo!' or, 'What's the one big thing we forgot?'

There are a number of important lessons about strategy that come out from this story:

- However good a strategy is, it will fail if implementation is bad.
- Always ask yourself: 'What's the one big thing we forgot?'
- Don't spread yourself too thinly: and strategy is about saying 'no' when necessary.
- Sense and interpret signals from the environment.
- Strategy is about options.
- We should seek out the 'cunning plan'.
- Even when it is cunning, see if it can be further refined with a last ingredient – to be the 'stunning' plan.

The actor who played Baldrick was knighted in 2013 for his services to charity and to politics – presumably as he gave them a 'cunning plan'!

Coming back to the idea of the cunning plan, in the Blackadder case this certainly arrived at by thinking about how one might remember something that one had forgotten: under what conditions might this actually happen? Having established that, it became easier for Baldrick and Blackadder to work out the cunning plan in terms of taking the near-death experience as a vehicle, and working out exactly how this could be done in a controlled way so it didn't turn into a real death. While this plan had some elegant simplicity, it wouldn't be that easy to imitate. QED.

Some cunning plans in everyday life

Strategic thinking isn't something just to be switched on when you are at work or when it is blatantly obvious that you are facing a particularly challenging situation: it is a fundamental human skill. It means having to deal with:

- complexity;
- choices;
- matters of some importance;
- some uncertainty;
- a context that needs to be understood in terms of time or space;
- a significant purpose.

Coming back to one of the strategic gems from Blackadder is the need, always, to ask: 'What's the one big thing we have forgotten?' You should also ask: 'What's the second thing that we forgot'? This is a quick and dirty check that you have reflected on all of the critical assumptions.

To further thaw the reader out in the process of demystifying strategic thinking and to illustrate its applicability to much of everyday life experiences, let's look at the following lively case studies.

CASE STUDY Free offer: take a strategic break in the English Channel

As I started to write this book I was on a free cruise, moored in a murky October (2012), tantalizingly three miles from St Peters Port, Jersey, along with 120 finance directors – the trip free on condition that I do some talks.

The opportunity had come up in the summer and I reasoned that there was a good chance of making contacts and getting some work, so the business case looked good. I did need to get some work from it: if you are on a cruise on your own there isn't much that you can do there that you couldn't do on land. In the latter case you can still eat, drink, sleep and exercise – and there is far less chance of drowning on land.

I had braced myself for a not overly exciting two days and three nights. As with all my projects I asked myself the really key question: 'What's the one big thing that I forgot?' Well, I got at least two. The first was 'Am I really sure that it sails on Tuesday from Southampton?' I decided to treble check this and indeed it wasn't actually sailing on Tuesday, but on Wednesday! So I was spared the disappointment of carrying all my luggage down on the train and trailing around the dockyard looking for a non-existent ship: a day early! Lesson here: strategists can't afford to ignore important detail.

The second one was that I was thinking about what could go wrong on such a venture: an obvious one was that there would be a lot of free booze and I might get too merry. Ships can be dangerous: accidents were possible. At the time I was e-mailing a prospective client about a strategic project that I might be involved in – for a funeral company. (Readers of *Demystifying Strategy* will be familiar with my compulsive fascination with the funerals industry.)

In an e-mail to my funerals client I jokingly mentioned that I would be away for a few days and I had definitely decided that I would try to avoid a situation of a premature funeral (of myself by burial at sea)! Well, when I got on board I discovered, a) that it was the norm for everyone to get plastered and, b) I had a sun lounge with a low window sill, from which it would be easy to topple into the cold Channel waters. (Apparently on a previous cruise a lady had got dunk and left her dress and shoes on the top deck, so there was a panic that she had jumped overboard!)

Returning to the 'one big thing we forgot', on the same cruise there was a fascinating story told in a keynote speech by ex-Royal Marine turned marine biologist and TV documentary maker, Monty Hall, who made 'The Great Escapes' series and 'The Great Barrier Reef'. He told us of his first media project which involved him spending weeks up in a wet area of Scotland at a time when there was plague of flies (which he called 'The Scottish Air Force'). While he was up in Scotland he spent quite some time with the Marines there, and they told him this story:

> *Once upon a time, two soldiers decided to go hunting for stags. They decided to do the hunt on a farm. One of them went to ask the farmer if they could hunt on his land while the other sat in the car. The farmer said: 'Aye, yer can go that. But could you do something for me too – my donkey is very sick and I haven't got the heart to kill it. Could you please shoot it for me, and put it*

out of its misery?' The soldier said that he could, but on the way back to the car he decided to wind his mate up.

The two of them set off to hunt and as soon as the first soldier saw the donkey he pointed his gun and shot is stone dead. He imagined that his mate would be shocked and he would then have fun saying that he was actually acting under instructions from the farmer. Unfortunately his mate, who had seen a nearby cow, decided to join in and shot the cow! It is probably unnecessary to point out that a cow is quite an expensive animal.

The one big thing that we forgot... never forget thinking about that in your plans.

CASE STUDY Conference with a difference: from 'cunning to stunning'

Back to my trip to the Channel Isles. I was enticed to do some talks on strategy and related topics to around a hundred finance directors while at sea. Here was the deal: as a speaker you get no fee but all expenses paid, ie a free cruise for two and a half days. In return there were the networking opportunities and possible sales that might be had.

Now while I may have an enlightened mind the concept 'free' doesn't easily sit with me, quite naturally. As a totally new experience I had to take a punt that even though FD's weren't noted for their buying behaviour (I can recall making a sale through an FD just twice in 22 years) I thought that, given I would be a speaker, could ply my books, and had a bit of a captive audience, there was a 50:50 chance of picking up one or two projects. I could also fill in the gaps with writing: I had an embryonic cunning plan. Two-thirds of the way through the cruise I had collected a potentially significant lead with a big police force, maybe two new things with an IT business entrepreneurial genius, a small piece of coaching with a young FD and a sniff of doing a short course with a major credit card company. So it seemed to be working. In *Demystifying Strategy*, I might have called this a 'deliberate-emergent strategy'.

Returning to the cruise, the conference company gets speakers to come on the experience for free, but unfortunately it ties up a consultant for a couple of days. Were a training company to hire him or her for a couple of days, the fees would be into thousands. So the 'value gap' between normal fees and the value of the free cruise needs to be exceeded by the (probable) value of the leads (or the probability times the pay-off).

All 'value capture' in that respect is thus down to the consultant. The exposure to possible clients can seem a mouth-watering, albeit possibly delusory prospect, as we are talking about finance directors here – who are not reputed for spending money. But behaviourally the conference company itself would seem to be onto a winner: a truly cunning plan. On the surface this appears to be a fantastic business model for the conference company. (We will see the importance of creative thinking about the business model in many of the CEO case studies later on in this book.)

I had imagined the ship would not be that special. It turned out to be an ocean-going ship operated to a very high standard indeed by P&O. The whole ship and the cabins were very luxurious – I even had my own balcony. There was also plenty of entertainment and the staff were excellent. I had been told that there were 800 people aboard and assumed that the rest were from other conferences, etc: it was October, a busy time for conferences. It transpired that the conference company had not just got the one conference but five! There was one for finance directors, one on logistics, one on marketing and also one on IT; in fact it had hired the entire ship! This didn't come cheap – someone hinted that the total cost was in excess of £1 million: that would be over £1,200 per head if we didn't deduct speakers, etc. So how did they make money out of it? How come it cost so much per head? These were all strategic questions for me as we went down the Solent.

So the take-away lesson here is that developing a strategy and a cunning plan is, as a general rule, very much tied into the business model and its economics. Well here is the real twist: the delegates go free. The revenue comes from a long list of people who are actually 'suppliers', let on board to sell their wares, like IT systems. So delegates can go to supplier meetings, talks, discussion groups, etc, drink lots, go to the gym and the outside Jacuzzi until 3 am in the morning, and try to avoid falling overboard or losing their clothes! They also get to have their CPD (continuing professional development) free, have a holiday, escape the office, socialize, and get tips on advancing their strategic advisory skills from me, and other expert input from explorers, leading economists and journalists. These suppliers pay not insignificant amounts for the experience: they may or may not get lucky – but effectively they are the main underwriters of this whole thing.

The event requires a huge project management effort, massive coordination and marketing effort, relationship development with expert speakers hunted down on the internet, and likewise nurturing of contacts with a large number of suppliers to part with a lot of cash. This means that the business model has very high barriers to entry and to imitation. Not just a 'cunning plan' but a 'stunning plan'. It has the characteristics of a well-developed near monopoly which, incidentally is also handled very slickly.

With some imagination and intent this models the possibilities of being replicated internationally. It's interesting that the organizations from which the FDs came were not particularly large: imagine what you could do in the United States sailing from Florida, or from the West Coast? And why didn't we see other conferences like financial services and banking, or pharmaceuticals, or energy? I wonder what the return on sales is for such a business model... maybe 20 per cent plus?

A potential flaw in the business model is the fact that the speakers end up all sat with each other over dinner. Instead of being able to circulate freely among the delegates as one does at a normal land-based conference, one gets cooped up with other people who are basically selling. What's worse, they are pretty well all consultants, who are individualists who would definitely get on each other's nerves. One in particular who rotated on my table really didn't like me at all: we were not at all on the same wave-length. The whole experience was something out of 'I am not a celebrity – get me out of here'.

Now I regret these two frustrations about not having free access to the executives at dinner and being quarantined with consultants. I decided quite categorically that I wasn't happy with the model, and told the company that I wouldn't be coming on board again, particularly as the incestuous nature of social seating arrangements was secretive and a fait accompli and diluted the value that I had expected to get. Now, as a strategic thinker by career, I try obsessively to surface as many assumptions as I can in a particular context.

A side issue is the sustainability of the business model: the organizers are unlikely to get repeat sessions from many speakers, thus pushing up the search costs and potentially having some speakers of lower quality. As we will see later in this book there does seem to be a greater prevalence of slightly dishonest business models around in recent times.

CASE STUDY Beware what you wish for – the really biggest thing that you have forgotten

We mentioned in both the Blackadder and the cruise cases the need to always think about 'the one big thing that we have forgotten'. This is not something that the strategic thinker asks randomly but as a habit and as a discipline. Take the following brief example from a recent holiday in Tenerife in July 2013.

Tenerife has probably the biggest water park in Europe – Siam Park. The rides are simply awesome and we survived all of them, including the sheer drop of the

Power slide and travelling through a tube at 50 miles per hour, taking you through a very large shark-infested tank (which is quite safe of course). Well, I did chicken out of that one but my wife, Carolina, made the drop: and she's so scared of heights.

The family got bored in the pool and on the beach so they wanted to go on something exciting: maybe the 'banana boat'. This cost €40 for 10 minutes or €240 an hour – not cheap but it would keep them amused, I thought. We had done this ride before and it entails clinging on for a while before everyone falls off. We were just booking up when we saw another ride called the 'Flying Fish'. It was €48. The kids were interested, so I put my valuation hat on and asked what extra value it added: what did you get for the extra €8? We were told it was also for 10 minutes and that it was 'more exciting'. We went for it without however asking questions like:

- What's the top speed?

- Do you have to be like Iron Man to stay on it?

- How far does it go in 10 minutes?

- What is it like to fall off?

- Should I not go on it if I have a heart condition or a back problem?

These turned out to be very strategic questions: these were the many things we regrettably forgot to ask.... We all piled on and there were two girls who joined us at the middle of the Fish – a huge lilo with flimsy handles pulled along by a powerful speed boat. We went out of the bay at around 10 miles per hour and then they opened up the throttle. We were soon up to 30 and the guy started to twist and turn. The Fish was at a 30 degree angle to the sea so we had to cling on and it was rocking from side to side – soon we were clinging on for grim life, just two minutes into the 'experience'.

It didn't get better, indeed it got much, much worse. After a mile and a half and with our arms getting very tired the boat turned round and really opened up to what seemed 50 miles an hour. The salt sea spray blinded me and my arms were being torn in two (I had been doing weights twice a week so I am pretty strong). My 'value over time curve' – see later in the book – was dropping like a brick. I wanted off. We all wanted off. We all had false grins masking deep discomfort. The driver on the boat was 30 feet ahead of us and couldn't hear a thing so the simple dilemma was: stay on or fall off.

My legs were absolutely killing me by then. We overshot the original bay and headed in the opposite direction up the coast: I calculated there were still four minutes of hell to come! Then the boat suddenly stopped dead. I looked around and saw a yellow and orange object bobbing up and down in the sea, 30 yards behind: I wasn't wearing my glasses, obviously, and couldn't make out what it was.

I then noticed that my wife, Carolina, was gone. She had fallen off when the Fish did its last jigs, unfortunately when we were going really fast. We went back for her. She was in a lot of pain. I managed to drag her on board. It appears that she had fallen off and hit the water on her bottom at about 50 miles per hour! I am not sure that I would call that an 'exciting experience'. I had to give her back an intensive massage for days to restore it to shape. Ten days later, back home, she had to see her trusty Chinese chiropractor, doubling the cost of the ride!

The moral is: never, ever, fail to ask the question: 'What is the one big thing that we have forgotten?'

So, having defined 'strategy' in a number of ways, let's turn to that mysterious concept of 'strategic thinking'.

What is strategic thinking?

We can now define 'strategic thinking' as:

> All the thinking processes that look at any complex situation from a variety of angles, and seeks out options and evaluates them and their implications – from differing perspectives, in a novel way.

Its key ingredients are therefore:

- Thinking: this a structured process that takes into account causality, the degrees of freedom and the constraints, and weighs the pros and cons of alternative decisions. It is also innovative and creative.
- Complexity: this usually occurs where there are many interdependent variables with uncertain dynamics.
- Different angles: this can be from external and internal perspectives, over short, medium and longer term time horizons, from different stakeholders' points of view, with different sets of assumptions, etc.
- Options: it distils possible choices into discrete and specific options.
- Evaluates them: it uses multiple criteria founded on evidence and judgement.
- Implications: it looks at things like the investment required, the implementation needs, the influencing of key stakeholders and the intended and unintended consequences.

- In a novel way: the end goal is to come up with some cunning (if not stunning) ideas; the process for arriving at these ideas might be itself novel, for example considering what a competitor might do with the same opportunity.

So, we can see that strategic thinking is qualitatively different from more routine thinking. One very important way in which that is so is through having both the intuition and the skill to ask the right questions.

Asking the right questions

Arriving at a novel way of looking at things is often not by analysis or deduction but by simply asking the right questions. In many ways this is more powerful than in evaluating position and obvious opportunities. For instance, fruitful strategic questions might be:

- Are we in too many businesses?
- How do we turn weaknesses into strengths and threats into opportunities?
- If we were a new entrant to our industry or a competitor what would we do here?
- How can we attack competitors where they are weak and would find it difficult to respond?
- How can we achieve a truly dominant competitive position in this particular market?
- What would we do if we had no position in this market at all and were a fresh entrant?
- What are our strategic assets and how might we exploit them in new ways, and where?
- If we hadn't got into this market would we not regret it and if we wanted to get out of it, how could we do this?

Asking the right questions is seen as very important to the CEOs. Indeed Nick Jenkins, former CEO of Moonpig (Chapter 2) articulates this as having a very clear 'hierarchy of strategic questions'.

Strategic thinking isn't just something that we should do when developing Corporate Strategy but at all kinds of levels, especially the everyday. For example, consider the comparison shown in Table 1.1. While operational thinking seems to be step by step (linear) and deductive (one thing follows from the other), strategic thinking frequently revisits its starting point (it is iterative) and its trajectory is less predictable. Also, operational thinking can be pre-planned while strategic thinking must have a creative spark. There are also much fuzzier boundaries with strategic thinking.

TABLE 1.1 Operational thinking and strategic thinking compared

Operational Thinking	Strategic Thinking
linear	iterative and unpredictable
deductive	inductive and intuitive
pre-programmed	creative
clear boundaries	ambiguous and fuzzy boundaries
safe	anxiety provoking

Finally, while the experience of operational thinking usually feels safe, strategic thinking can feel quite scary, especially for beginners. A high level of anxiety will make the thinking process very difficult as cognition will be impaired. Also, when managers discuss the issues this underlying anxiety can easily give rise to confusion, frustration and conflict. That is a good reason to have some facilitation on the process, besides it adding some structure.

One of the hallmarks of being an effective CEO is that far from being uncomfortable with that level of uncertainty and ambiguity, he or she finds it relatively comfortable, if not actually enjoyable. In identifying future strategic leaders that would seem to be something to look out for.

As an example of strategic thinking, during the writing of this book in early 2013 I had a strategic thought. This was all about asking the right questions such as:

- How is a product seen and valued from the customer's perspective?
- Is it seen as value for money?
- Is it in keeping with the times? If it isn't, how fast are sales eroding, and is that loss of sales likely to gain momentum?
- How viable is it going to be in the future?

- If we were to enter the market now, what optional positioning and business models could be adopted? How sustainable would that be, especially if the main incumbent tries to reinvent itself, or if other entrants are then attracted in?

See how well these map onto my intuitive thinking, below.

The UK's postal service

That night I e-mailed Moya Greene, CEO of Royal Mail.

Hi Moya,
My field is strategic thinking. I am a business school academic, management writer and from time to time facilitate strategic thinking in corporations. Over 15 years ago I gave some help to Royal Mail managers presenting some thinking on the impact of the internet to top management there, using scenario story-telling.

I had a strategic thought tonight that might interest you.

I happened to get sent out tonight to pick up my step-daughter Frannie from the bus. I decided that I could add some value to my walk by posting a cheque to my accountant for my self-employed tax return.

I walked 50 yards in the snow and began to think how inconvenient and antiquated this was – and expensive: 70 pence for a first class stamp and not a lot less for a second class one. Clearly economies of scale have been lost to the internet/e-mails, etc.

My next thought was: I hardly send anything this way. At nearing £1 a stamp that's a lot for a letter. And extrapolating past price trends so that you guys can break even/get a return, the £1 barrier might be breached in the next three to five years. The end game. Surely, in the words of Edward Bear in the first book of *Winnie The Pooh*, page 1, 'there has got to be a better way!'

I continued walking and as I did I reconfigured your business model in my head (in my work I call that the 'business value system'):

- You would continue to run the premium service for situations where urgency is important.

- It might be worth considering: why not have a parallel cheap service where the post is delivered only once or twice a week? You are guaranteed that it is delivered within seven days. You deposit your letter in a smaller number of more central post boxes as you drive past, minimizing collection costs. The rate per letter could be, say, 45 pence, depending on costs, elasticity of demand, etc. You then get rid of the

existing second class (a sub-option). This would use fewer people and physical resources and regain cost economies.
- You would use this system for all payments, posting of non-urgent documents, bank and other statements, birthday and Christmas cards.
- It could be branded the 'Think Ahead Post' or something like that.

These thoughts came together in about 25 seconds. It is fascinating how strategic thoughts crystallize!

Two cars pulled up as I had just finished posting the letter and I told one lady of my idea. It was cold so she got the idea quickly, agreed with me, jumped in her car and drove off. (I live in Croydon and one has to be a bit careful, so that wasn't a surprise.)

So where is this e-mail going?

Well, number 1, it is possible that you are already working on ideas that are along some lines like that, or maybe not – as this is too challenging a thought (?) Is it worthwhile having a strategic workshop on that?

Number 2, it shows that one can have potentially very valuable strategic thoughts with little time investment.

Number 3, the rapid intuitive process that I went through can be turned into an organizational process and taught and coached... I am sure that you have a Strategy Department but that doesn't mean that there isn't more scope for strategic thinking (often their bent is strategic planning – not quite the same thing). Royal Mail could absorb these processes.

Number 4, you might find my e-mail sufficiently intriguing to meet up with me: my most recent book *Demystifying Strategy*, published last October (attached cover) explains the process I have handed over to the likes of X, Y, Z etc.

I am currently doing research for a book on *Demystifying Strategic Thinking: Lessons from leading CEOs.* I can share some of the insights from that with you over coffee.

On the topic of 'one big thing I forgot' in the above: if you don't do this at some point in time and in price someone else will; maybe they are working on it now, and then you will be squeezed competitively from below. For example, when Moonpig was launched (the first of my studies in the book), the more traditional players, Clintons, etc appeared to do little as they watched their market share become eroded. Did you know that Nick Jenkins its founder/then CEO and his investors sold out for over £100 million?

Hoping to hear from you soon,
Tony

Dr Tony Grundy

The next night I was driving back home and passed by the same red post box. I thought, 'I don't think I will hear from them' (actually I was wrong), and it occurred to me that if they didn't come in with a more economic, cheaper model, then someone else might. Thirty seconds later I thought, 'What about "Easygroup, Easypost"', with orange vans, far fewer driving past orange boxes and deliveries on alternative days (like recycling is alternative weeks).

So I sent another e-mail to Moya: two for the price of one. One thing that I do find in strategic thinking is that without sheer persistence so many good ideas come to nothing: that's were entrepreneurs can be a good thing.

You will also observe the way in which the strategic questioning guided my thoughts, giving them a direction. Strategic thinking can benefit from brainstorming, but it isn't the same thing – it is more like a clever, guided missile: it just senses where to go. Strategic thinking, as Deborah Evans of APIL goes on to say later, can actually be very quick indeed, and not ponderous and long-winded: that is very good news.

Of course I always knew that even if I came up with an incisive diagnosis of strategic issues for Royal Mail or indeed for anyone else, and some interesting if early and prototype ideas for new strategic options, it could still founder on:

a   the lack of a political base to anchor that in;

b   whether that thought came up at a good time or not; and

c   whether many other distractions might have blown the interest off course.

Who knows where these ideas went in that great stream of corporate consciousness?

Postscript: in October 2013 Royal Mail shares were sold off for £3.30; the issue was heavily oversubscribed and the price rose to £4.50 within minutes of trading. There was press comment to the effect that the government had under-priced the issue to be absolutely sure of success. Readers are reminded that the short-term share price is a function of supply and demand, of expectations of future profits, dividends and underlying cash streams, based on the strategy, and of imperfect information. Scenario storytelling helps to give better information: who knows whether £3.50 or £4.50, £5.50 or even £2.50 is a fair price, without that?

It would have been really insightful to have done some story-telling scenarios for Royal Mail, perhaps using the techniques within *Demystifying Strategy*, for example, the 'uncertainty tunnel'. Here one might describe the secular trends of decline in the letters business and then posit circumstances in which this decline became accelerated by the stamp price going above £1 and a new entrant with a lean service taking market share, combined with a deterioration of service and adverse media coverage. The consequences then include the CEO having to resign.

As a final reflection on some of the things that we covered above I should say that strategic thinking can generate some discomfort on occasion as it will challenge mindsets and that can induce fear and anxiety. That fear can lead to denial and delay, But don't wait too long to decide to think about it – and actually do something about it! As we see in the APIL chapter there can be a 'time to die' ie the length of time over which the strategy may just about survive on the basis of 'do nothing' or 'do very little', before the viability of the business model implodes.

Evaluating strategic options

We now do a very quick recap to cover how strategic options were evaluated in *Demystifying Strategy*. I picked the strategic option grid from that book as it is perhaps the most fundamental in providing a framework for strategic thinking. I will also briefly cover its sister technique, 'Optopus', which can be used to generate a more creative set of options as means of creating the agenda of options.

The strategic option grid (see Figure 1.2) is simply a matrix of five really fundamental criteria for evaluating any strategic option. These are shown on the matrix down the left and the options along the top: four columns are shown here, but you can use fewer or more options to contract or extend the grid as you see fit. The key criteria are:

1 strategic attractiveness;
2 financial attractiveness;
3 implementation difficulty;
4 uncertainty and risk;
5 stakeholder acceptability.

Typically each criterion is scored as very attractive (three ticks), moderately attractive (two ticks), low attractiveness (one tick) or sometimes with half ticks. (Note that high implementation difficulty and uncertainty and risk are

FIGURE 1.2 The strategic option grid

Options / Criteria	Option 1	Option 2	Option 3	Option 4
Strategic attractiveness				
Financial attractiveness*				
Implementation difficulty				
Uncertainty and risk				
Acceptability (to stakeholders)				

<u>Score</u>: 3 = very attractive, 2 = medium attractive, 1 = low attractiveness.
* Benefits less costs, – net cash flows relative to investment

scores of one and not three ticks.) While each of these criteria normally has an equal weighting (for simplicity), they can be weighted if their importance varies a lot.

The strategic option grid can be used for:

- market development;
- product/service development;
- new technology development;
- sourcing decisions, eg outsourcing, off-shoring;
- acquisitions;
- divestment;
- alliance;
- turnarounds;
- strategic financing decisions;
- IT investment;
- organizational restructuring options;
- strategic projects;
- strategies in everyday life (even holidays, dating opportunities and so on).

Why Strategic Thinking Really Matters

Each of the criteria can be checked out/or supported by other, more specific techniques. These criteria are:

- Strategic attractiveness: this is the external market attractiveness and the relative competitive position. 'Market attractiveness' is based on things like the growth drivers, Porter's Five Forces and perhaps PEST analysis too. A simple technique which supports the judgements on 'strategic attractiveness' is the 'GE grid' (or the 'General Electric' grid) which has 'market attractiveness' on the vertical axis and 'relative competitive position' on the horizontal; see Figure 1.3.
- Financial attractiveness: these are the long- and short-term returns from the option (or possibly its economic profit); ultimately this should go in the value and cost drivers, and the financial model.
- Implementation difficulty: this is the sum of difficulty over time to achieve the strategic goals.
- Uncertainty and risk: this is the extent of the volatility of the assumptions underlying a specific strategic option.
- Stakeholder acceptability: this is the extent to which stakeholders favour, disfavour, or are neutral regarding that option.

FIGURE 1.3 The 'GE grid' (General Electric)

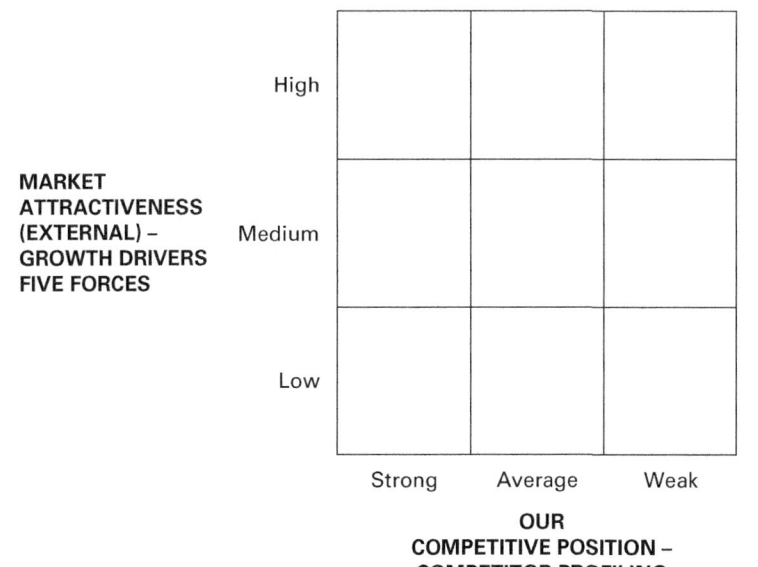

As a guideline, the totals indicate the following:

12 to 15: these appear to be attractive strategies on the face of it; they still need testing.

10 to 11: these need more refinement and are probably lacking cunning in some respect.

8 to 9: these need a lot more work and would be unacceptable at that level.

5 to 7: these are weak and unless they can be completely rethought are off the menu.

below 5: don't touch with a barge-pole!

The advantages of this technique are that:

- It encourages greater creativity as there aren't just spaces for one or two options but for more.
- It enforces a more structured approach to evaluating them as all the managers involved are using the same criteria.
- These criteria are aligned to five critical aspects of strategic decision making.
- The various boxes are discussed and completed one by one, usually vertically and then taking each option in turn: this concentrates managers' attention, and thus shared cognition, besides improving group dynamics.
- Once completed it is very easy then to stand back and debate them more objectively, eg to look at possible upsides and downsides and generally to challenge assumptions.
- It enhances openness and minimizes politics: where there is some of this at work this can be handled through stakeholder analysis.
- It is great for strategic influencing, for providing input to strategic position papers, for business cases, and for identifying new strategic questions to be asked, and also for targeting further data and evidence to be gathered, analysed and interpreted.

The 'Optopus'

In addition to the strategic option grid we may need to spend some time systematically looking at the sources of these options rather than just using random ideas generation or our intuition. To fulfil this role, the 'Optopus' (Figure 1.4) enriches the strategic thinking process by multiplying the number of strategic options available.

FIGURE 1.4 The 'Optopus' – for option generation

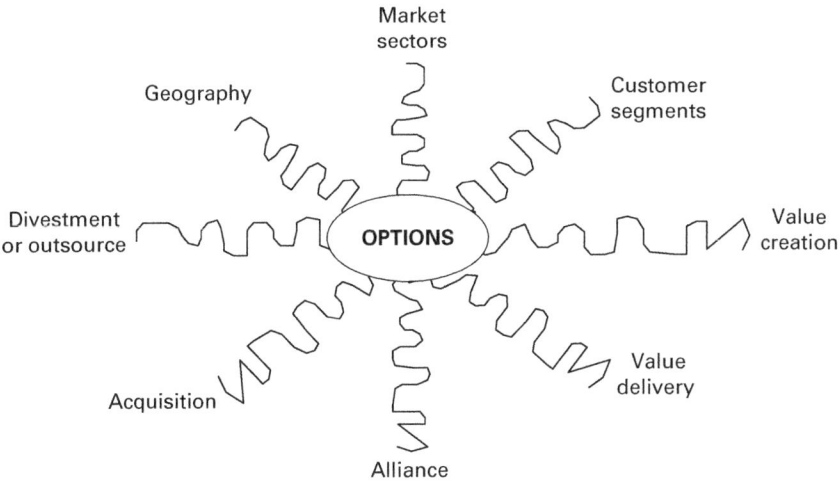

The 'Optopus' has eight generic dimensions of choice, or 'degrees of freedom':

1 Market segments: the different types of market that one might serve: private/public.

2 Customer segments: the different types of customer with different needs.

3 Value creation: the different ways in which value is added for the customer.

4 Value delivery: the technologies, media and distribution to take it to market.

5 Alliance: different partners and different types of alliances, doing different things.

6 Acquisition: different types, different targets, to do different things.

7 Divestment and outsourcing: alternative ways of configuring value adding activities/scope.

8 Geography: national, regional and global.

Each of the eight lines of enquiry listed here contains many branches and sub-branches, so a well-developed 'Optopus' could be quite large and easily cover a white board. Flipchart paper soon runs out. I show you the Optopus model:

- As an example of a pictorial technique that can open up strategic thinking far more than just a regular managerial conversation.
- Because in conjunction with the strategic option grid, you would have a very powerful mini system for strategic thinking to play with.
- Unless you are familiar with my previous work then both are likely to be new (I have found other strategy theorists prefer the more limited two dimensions of new product versus new market development (the Ansof grid), or they expect managers to do all of this intuitively.
- It appears in a graphically illustrated way in the case study on Virgin Galactic (see Chapter 5).

So, there definitely needs to be some process and structure for evaluating strategic options and these twin techniques are definitely worth a look. They have been used and adopted in numerous SMEs, and blue chip companies like Microsoft and Tesco. Tesco used the strategic option grid, for example, to develop its Non-Food, Dotcom, Express, Metro and Services businesses. In addition to scenario techniques, these two techniques are precisely the things that I would have got Royal Mail to use in the earlier example.

Content of the book

The main part of this book consists of six substantive case studies of dialogues with CEOs from:

- Moonpig: a pioneering internet retailer selling personalized cards and other merchandise (Chapter 2);
- APIL: the Association of Personal Injury Lawyers (Chapter 3);
- Samaritans: a leading charity dedicated to helping prevent suicides (Chapter 4);
- Virgin Galactic: an international business delivering sub-orbital space flight to members of the public (Chapter 5);
- Simplyhealth: a private health care organization offering affordable high quality, personalized service, dedicated to inspiring people towards better health (Chapter 6);

- The International Paralympic Committee (IPC), whose task is to plan, coordinate and deliver the Paralympic Games and to facilitate the progression of athletes to compete at that level (Chapter 7).

The choice of organizations was partly by design, intuition and opportunity. I wanted most of the organizations to be 'on the map', brand wise. I got that. I also was interested in one or two not-for-profit organizations to provide a perspective of non-commercial strategies – I ticked that box too. I also wanted some entrepreneurial companies in there: Moonpig and Virgin Galactic were start-ups, but both either substantial now (Moonpig) or on a major growth trajectory. Finally, my sampling criteria were that they needed to have two out of the following three:

1 complexity (Moonpig, APIL, Virgin Galactic, Samaritans, Simplyhealth, IPC);
2 challenge: either of a competitive or change nature (Moonpig, APIL, Samaritans, Virgin Galactic, Simplyhealth, IPC);
3 diverse stakeholders (APIL, Samaritans, IPC).

In addition the CEO needed to see strategic thinking as a significant issue in his or her role. Even in the IPC's case, where that was more tacitly recognized, the interest was very strong.

I would go on record as being disappointed that the CEO of Arsenal Football Club, Ivan Gazidis, declined to be interviewed on account of 'not so good timing': that was a shame! I did calculate that an hour of his time would have cost around £1,250, but I pointed out that if he was like the other CEOs spending 30 per cent of his time on strategic issues that was an annual investment of around £700,000, so an hour's reflection on that with me was not a big deal! No doubt reticence was due to media sensitivity – some other time, Ivan.

Once we have gone through the six case studies I spend Chapter 8 comparing and integrating the outputs to examine common themes, to answer our research questions and to look at the implications of what we have found. In Chapter 9 I distil some key conclusions for the book and go back to the original questions that I posed to the CEOs. I also link back to what is in my sister volume *Demystifying Strategy*. I then give some personal thoughts on the future of strategic thinking (or 'the future of the future') and suggest some concrete and practical ways of moving that forward. I also give you some psychometrics so you can rate yourself (and others) on your strategic thinking capability. I then synthesize the top-level findings of the book in a new framework: the 'strategic thinking wheel', and end with some ideas on how to apply the principles of strategic thinking more generally (Chapter 10), for example in strategic influencing.

During the course of writing Chapters 2–7 I realized that it would also be useful to include some material in the Appendices on the concept of a more fluid form of strategy: 'contingent strategy', which is a means of dealing with acute uncertainty, whether due to threat or opportunity. In addition I thought that given the far greater competitive pressure that we have seen in markets post-credit crunch (hyper-competition) that I should make more widely available my work on rejuvenating Porter's Five Forces, as optional reading, in Appendix 1. I think that these elements will be very helpful in refreshing a theory that has been relatively static for some time, I believe.

SUMMARY KEY INSIGHTS

We end this chapter with a summary of the insights of value that have come out so far:

- Strategic thinking is far from purely random: it requires some process.
- After any strategy event the outputs need to be captured very soon afterwards: it is a kind of 'strategic washing up'.
- It usually requires collecting some data, some evidence and, if possible, some piloting.
- If done both imaginatively and thoroughly it will increase confidence.
- Competitive advantage is often transitory: sustainable competitive advantage is much more difficult to secure. Tesco achieved some of that through innovation, speed, and then mass, the Iberostar hotel in Cancun through complete alignment with perfect tranquillity and customer care, the conference cruise company through a very novel and hard to imitate model with high entry barriers.
- To provide true innovative focus the challenge is to come up with a genuinely 'cunning plan'.
- Strategic thinking is applicable in all spheres of life and not just business, as is the notion of the 'cunning plan' – but 'cunning' doesn't mean dishonest or manipulative.

- Always ask: 'What's the one thing we have forgotten?'
- Strategic thinking entails looking at things from many angles and creatively identifying as may options as you can, evaluating them and understanding their implications; and thus asking the right questions – in the right place and at the right time.
- This is normally a long way from being a linear process; it is iterative, fluid and at times fuzzy. Especially when dealing with big issues, there may be too much fear to deal with them as things stand, so one might have to wait for the right political circumstances, the right prioritization, and the right timing.
- Don't let the time for decision and action run out!

02 Moonpig

Introduction

In this first case study we take a look at an internet retailer, Moonpig, which pioneered the design of personalized cards on the internet. Moonpig was an incredibly successful internet business started up by an entrepreneurial MBA, Nick Jenkins, becoming a household brand.

In this chapter a whole range of themes are covered, including:

- intuition and strategic thinking;
- a hierarchy of strategic questions;
- strategic jargon;
- business models;
- strategic data and evidence;
- entry barriers;
- business and financial model;
- future change;
- feasibility studies;
- the CEO's role as a strategic thinker;
- economic value;
- strategy versus tactics;
- exiting a business;
- strategic energy;
- strategic implementation;
- strategy tools and concepts;
- perfect competition and economic value;
- imitation and copying;
- formalization.

Here and in the other case study chapters, each theme is highlighted as it arises, and there are conclusions drawn at the end. I also add in some independent commentary in italics to extract any key thoughts and insights, and to link back to the theory.

Intuition and strategic thinking

Tony:
I decided to do a book on strategic thinking as I wanted to find out from chief executives themselves how they saw it. Was it very analytical or was it rather more an intuitive process?

Nick:
Yes, I have never taken that view (that strategic thinking is very analytical), I suppose that working within a very small business you take a more seat of the pants view of it (strategic thinking), rather than a very formal view, and having gone through (the MBA) and done the strategy at Cranfield, the full-time MBA there. And it was sort of interesting.

It did seem to me a rather long-winded way of expressing common sense, really. And my impression was that it was always best to stand back and to look at the bigger picture and the context and then work from there, working out a hierarchy of decisions that may need to be taken, because otherwise you can end up fluffing around sorting out all kinds of detail when the reality is that you are doing that with detail that you shouldn't be involved in at all. That's one of the issues that I had when running Ark (a charity), you can look at it and spend a lot of time working out what kind of people we need to do what we are doing at the moment, when the big question should be 'Should we be doing this at all? And you might as well ask that question first, before you get into the detail.

A hierarchy of strategic questions

Nick:
It is a hierarchy of questions if you don't answer the questions in the right order; it makes life complicated. So that's my approach. But business wise it is quite obvious why you are doing it; when I set up Moonpig and what I wanted to do with that. And then strategically there were other questions like did we want to stick just with greetings cards or go into other areas, did we want to get into the business-to-business space, and a lot of those sort of questions that needed to be sorted through logically, and what does that mean for us in terms of infrastructure, what does that mean in terms of any exit from the business. But they were quite straightforward, and I think we developed a fairly clear strategy from the beginning.

Tony:

Do you think that that training at Cranfield helped in any way?

Nick:

To some extent, but I think a lot of it is quite basic common sense. What I learnt on my MBA was that most of business is common sense dressed up in some jargon. But it enabled me to have more of a framework in which to think. I think that I probably set up a better business as a result of having gone to Cranfield than if I hadn't gone there, possibly partly because the way you put together a business plan, and having the structures that other people have worked on, saves a bit of time.

Strategic jargon

Tony:

In relation to the terms that you used, I was lecturing on the MBA at Cranfield the year below and we were using terms like 'core competencies'. I am not sure that you would regard those kinds of words as helpful expressions or as something that you think about but you wouldn't actually use in meetings.

Nick:

Jargon is useful because you can say in a couple of words what otherwise you would need five words to say… but things like core competences, that's absolutely critical. We had to work out at Moonpig ultimately what we are really good at and what's at the heart of it: the bits that we should keep in the heart of it and the bits that we can farm out.

And we had some strategic questions at the very beginning: should we source out all of our production or not. We probably could have done that but I felt that actually, I knew that at a level of production it would be cheaper to have our own, and also when we got to that we would need to have resources internally in printing software and printing technology to be able to do that job properly. If we had outsourced it for several years and brought it in then we wouldn't have any competence in printing. So it probably cost a lot of money in the beginning but it was well worthwhile later.

Tony:

So that was a strategic investment.

Nick:

Yes, yes. So the printing side was a core competence that we needed to have and software development was a core competence that we needed to develop. Marketing, product development, software printing – those were the sort of things that are absolutely key.

Tony:
It seems as if you had a picture in your head of what sort of system that was. The expression that I have used is that of a 'business value system': you have maybe three or four activities and they feed off each other.

See Figure 2.1 for my original model, taken from the football industry; basically the original business model or 'value system' of the game itself, game takings and limited revenue from terrestrial TV up until 1990, has been transformed by growing merchandise sales, satellite television, sponsorship, higher prices, and, not shown here, internationalization.

FIGURE 2.1 The business value system – football clubs

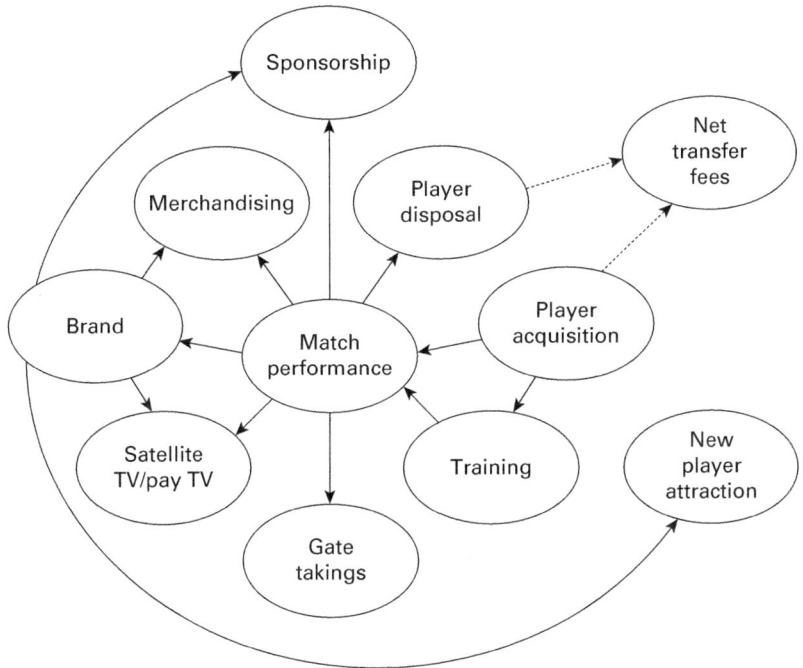

Nick:
Mmm.

Tony:
It seems as if you had that even if you never had that on paper.

Nick:
Possibly yes; I always saw the most important thing was the end product, and then it was, 'What do we need to consistently produce?'

Business models

Tony:

So how did the idea for Moonpig come about? If you say the word 'Moonpig' people will take notice. I have been working with a team of young entrepreneurs in Croydon who are 16–17 and they came up with a name of 'Fringo' for a fun device for kids to encourage them to brush their teeth and it just jumps out at you. A bit like a soft toy, sounds a bit crazy though. So how did 'Moonpig' come about?

Nick:

I had been working in Russia as a commodity broker and I wanted to come back to England and set up a business and I didn't want to be a commodity trader any more so I needed to think of a new business, so I looked at all the different kinds of things that I could do.

So I could have, say, sold digital cameras online, and I looked at everything quite strategically – in a sense – so I thought ok if I sell a digital camera online then it is something that could be bought somewhere else so that at some point somebody is going to work out a bit of software that is going to be put in the Fujitsu 220 and work out how much it is going to cost in this shop, in that shop, so ultimately it is going to squeeze down my margins, because I am not offering the camera at the same price, so you could have bought it from me, but you then you buy it from someone somewhere else. So I figured that that was one of the downsides of the internet as a retailer.

One of the upsides of the internet is that the internet allows a level of personalization that strips out a lot of admin when it comes to order processing of a personalized card. If I wanted to order a personalized card in a graphic design shop it would take hours and a few hundred quid, whereas someone could go online in their own time, on their own computer, and they could go on it as many times as they like and it doesn't cost me anything and they are happy as long as they end up with a card. And the card that they end up with will be exactly what they have ordered. There is no margin for error, there is no interface where there are instructions by someone on paper that get picked up by someone at Moonpig and has to write those down again and copies them badly. Whatever they put in they get back out again.

So it stripped all of the administrative costs out of doing personalized printing on a very, very, small scale, down to the level of the single card. But that can't be unique because the designs were unique to us. So you couldn't buy that card anywhere else, so therefore you are not going to make that comparison between how much you are paying for it at Moonpig and how much you are paying for it at Clinton cards.

Tony:

And it was still very cheap.

Nick:

Well, it is good value for whatever it delivers and when you get it right you can add an enormous amount of value with the personalization, and this doesn't cost us an awful lot more.

So when I had narrowed it down I didn't want to sell a physical product that you could buy in the shop. I didn't just want to sell a digital product that you could just download because everyone was just giving that away for free. So the personalized card was a way of creating a product that was unique to Moonpig, it eliminated price competition and enabled me to charge more than what that product would be in the High Street, because it was personalized.

Tony:

So it added better value all round?

Nick:

It was looking at what the internet does and the internet is very good for… it is wonderful for allowing anybody anywhere to order a niche product. We have an enormous selection of cards for niche subjects, but it is difficult when you have to supply those cards to niche customers across every card shop in Britain, in order for that person in Dumfries to buy it then you would have to produce far too many of them….

So there was a lot of logic there to work out what I should be doing in the first place. That comes back to my 'big picture' principle which is: 'The more that you think about the high level decisions the better the chance you've got. If you ignore the higher level decisions and start going down the wrong route, then you've got a handful of decisions at this level and this will be limited by your poor decision making at the top level.

Tony:

After 10 years of teaching strategy all over the place through my own business I used to get so fed up that I used to give them (managers) the polarity of you are either in the helicopter world or you are in the rabbit hole world. That, very simply, had such an appeal to thousands of managers. They just found themselves drawn to the detail. A lot of people tend to go that way (into the detail), and I used to hypothesize that it gave them a sense of security, given that they were actually producing something and they can master it, whereas the bigger picture stuff for many people seems to be too big for their heads to cope with.

Strategic data – and evidence

Nick:

Yes, whereas I tend to get very frustrated doing anything with too much detail if I don't feel I'm in the right game. There is just no point in putting time into that if I haven't got the first bit right.

Tony:

Yes, I find the detail increasingly irritating… but I do feel that sometimes in strategy we have to examine really important detail; that can be hugely important in terms of the strategy. For instance, at Tesco Express (when it first began) they were selling on average things worth only 10 quid… and this was in the petrol stores, things for only 10 quid; you are never really going to make money out of it. So that little detail was quite important.

Nick:

Yes, the detail came in the fact that online you collect an extraordinary level of detail about all transactions that a new customer makes. You can log where they come from, how long they are with you, what they do when they are with you, and what they do over time, in a way that you couldn't possibly do at Clintons, where they wander into the shop and then wander out again. They are not measuring the conversion rate… they just don't do that, whereas online you can do that. And that was the start; that was what drove it. But you have to be fairly confident that you are heading… and I think that the strategic thing is about you just generally heading in the right direction. It doesn't matter how fast you are going unless you are heading in the right direction.

So that bit has always been quite important – the confidence of thinking that you are doing the right thing. If I am happy with that, now we can look at the finer detail, the next level down. It's a hierarchy of decision making. You need to take the decisions at the next level when you have made the right ones here.

Entry barriers

Tony:

So you got this futuristic business model and you have good economics and presumably you have built some entry barriers so that other people can't just come in….

Nick:

No, there were no great barriers to entry, other than the fact that we had swept up most of the decent publishers. Publishers were reluctant to engage with anybody else after we had done a deal with them. That was always something difficult to resist when Funky Pigeon got involved. Funky Pigeon then said, well if you don't supply us then WH Smith won't buy your cards. For anyone who didn't own a card shop, anyone coming into the game and trying to set up a version of Moonpig, the card publishers would say, 'To be honest that would just annoy Moonpig', whereas when WH Smith said, 'Well, we are not going to stock your cards on the High Street any more' they had to come back to us and say: 'We will supply to Funky Pigeon' which was annoying.

But similarly I didn't try to waste much time trying to protect the idea or anything like that because it is very hard to protect it, and you can waste an awful lot of time thinking that you are protecting it. Actually we put all our effort into just getting big, and that ultimately was the protection. I think that we have still got about 70 per cent of the market and Funky Pigeon has about 15.

Tony:

Sometimes, for example in a book on competitive strategy by a certain Michael Porter, competition can be good. When I was doing my MBA I thought that that was interesting – that competition was bad – it helps to give comparatives in the market place... it grows the market too.

See Figure 2.2 for Michael Porter's Five Forces, explained at greater length in Grundy, 2012, and at even greater length in Appendix 1 of this book.

FIGURE 2.2 Porter's Five Competitive Forces

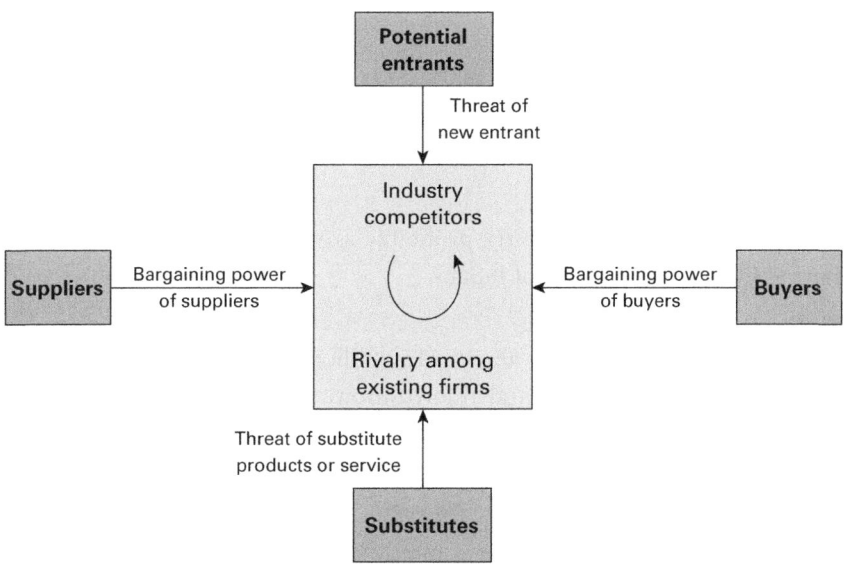

SOURCE: Competitive Strategy, Porter

Nick:

I think that it does. To some extent they (Funky Pigeon) grew the market, and to some extent they took business from us. We have grown consistently every year so they haven't taken a great deal of business from us. Maybe we grew 20 per cent and they took 10 per cent off us, I don't know, but we are growing at around 10 per cent.

Tony:

It sounds as if you tracked your relative market share. I now teach somewhere else – at Henley – and the students are actually terrible at thinking about their position relative to competitors and maybe we just don't teach them somewhere and they assume projections without thinking about modelling the market, their relative market share what is actually driving market growth; the external dynamics are not really modelled through and they delude themselves that they are very good strategists by thinking about their own strategy.

It sounds to me as if you were able to think about the competition, the market place more, then maybe….

Nick:

We were always conscious of what might happen. We were left on our own for a while. There were tiny, tiny start-ups. By 2007 we were pretty big – by that point with £20 million turnover – and Funky Pigeon were beginning to crank up a bit, and I was a little bit concerned because there was nothing to stop lots of companies from coming in and simply copying what we have done. And we had paved the way and that's a more expensive route. We made all the mistakes. On the one hand we got in there and got the customers, and on the other hand we were concerned about what that would do for our sales, but overall the market has grown.

Business and financial model

Tony:

I presume that you were pretty profitable around that time. You seem to have sold for a decent sum of money.

Nick:

I think that we peaked at about £15 million EBITDA (earnings before interest, taxes, depreciation and amortization), which is pretty good and we were making a lot more money than Clintons were. We had a hundred people working for us and Clintons had about 3,600.

Tony:

(So these were) two different types of economic model. One thing that fascinates me is the dynamic of strategy. Sometimes a company can get really successful and they seem to freeze the business model because it has all worked out, their architecture is all self-consistent, so they then begin to get resistant to changes and so they are susceptible not only to market maturity but to mindset maturity.

Nick:
That's an interesting one because at Moonpig our biggest issue was where do we grow from where we are, and I looked at it and I thought at the moment we are trying hard to sell as many cards as we can. Other than that there wasn't an awful lot more that we could do but to sell cards. So where are we going to go with the business? At one point our competence was online retail. We understood online retail and those customers, so we could start acquiring online retailers and run those and expand them and add critical mass. If we bought someone with a £3 million turnover then we could probably use our fulfilment centres and we could make those businesses more profitable.

The other thing that we looked at was doing more gifts: we are selling cards, so what can go with cards? We decided not to acquire any more online retailers mostly because I suppose that we didn't know online retailing better than almost anyone else but there was no leverage in the brand, and one of the most valuable things that we had was the brand.

So we thought we would put all our effort into expanding what else people would buy from Moonpig, and we thought that it would probably stretch into flowers and maybe chocolates and maybe personalized bottles of wine, and T-shirts and mugs. So these were the products that were most similar to Moonpig's and now we do around £10–£12 million, which is definitely the bit that has kept our overall sales growing.

Tony:
What's turnover now?

Nick:
About £42 million.

Tony:
That's quite significant. So the model has evolved.

Nick:
The model has evolved. We started doing flowers around 2006. Up until that point I had been quite keen to just focus on cards and getting that bit right, and to get us really, really good at cards. We could always do other bits later on but I wanted people to remember us for the cards. It got to the point where everyone knew about personalized cards, so we could afford to expand into other things so they would think, 'I know that they do cards, but they also

do flowers', as opposed to, 'I know that they do flowers.' I didn't want to confuse the public.

Tony:

Well, going back in time I happened to once do some work for Tesco with Tesco Direct and at one (very early) stage they were just selling a few flowers and chocolates and they said, 'What do we do with this?' Now in terms of process, which is one of the things that I would like to find out about, they said, 'Well, we know some guy who does strategy so let's do a day's workshop.' So I went there and we used some (strategy) processes and we went for example 'time-travelling' into the future, and my God, there was a potentially very big business. We did some scenarios; we actually told some stories about the future, and the limitations of not many people (then) being on the internet, and what the price point of computers would need to be to be plausible (so they would get one) and do internet purchases.

Nick:

What sort of time was this?

Tony:

That was around 1996.

Nick:

So it was well before… one of my Moonpig investors was the MD of Flannigan Supermarket Direct, which was the first online supermarket; then Somerfield bought it and cocked it up and shut it down. That was the beginning of that sector.

Tony:

We had some formal processes and we had (strategic questions) and subgroups and things like that and there was creative analysis but there was also a structure in it. So what did you do? Did you get people together on an away-day? Or did it all just come out of your head?

Future change

Nick:

It was a sort of benign dictatorship really. Every year we produce a business plan. And there was a formal presentation. Every single year I would produce a strategy document to the board and we would say, 'This is the strategy next year. This is where we are going.' It wasn't so much the strategy for the next 12 months; it was, 'This is our strategy for now, which is looking forward, and that might change next time.' The strategy document in 2010 would be for the next five years.

Tony:
So for the next five years, but it depends on a lot of other things.

Nick:
If it changed by 2011 then we would say that we have actually changed it. But a lot of it would remain the same. I would look back at the (last year's) strategy document and I would think, 'Does anything need to change? Has anything happened in the last 12 months to change that strategy?' I am a year into the five years so if I got most of it right then most of it should remain the same.

Tony:
I am thinking about not just the changes that may have happened but also, given that new point in time, what future changes might be coming through?

Nick:
I suppose what I am saying is, 'Has anything changed in what I know?' When I wrote it last year, my view of the future would have included what I think is going to happen in the next five years. If anything had changed in my thinking about the next five years, then if anything had changed – future or past.

Tony:
Conventional thinking is that you change the strategy when there have been changes in the past, which is historic, but what we are talking about here is the second zone of change which is perhaps more important – the future change.

Nick:
Well, I suppose that I didn't think of it (separately) but I was thinking about it as I am looking at it today and if by looking at it today I think... actually I think that we have got a bigger problem with the competition than I thought we had last year, and I think that in two years' time we will be suffering from this, that and the other. That would be something that has changed.

Tony:
You see, what I am doing here is to say, I know all this stuff that is written about (in the theory). By talking to you, you might be structuring the problem in a way that isn't written about in research, it is not in there, and actually that was a success. We actually did generate new linkages in knowledge rather than assume that everything that goes on has already been written about. There are subtleties that go on in such a dynamic world about how people think, about how they think about these things.

So that was part of the thought that I had on the beach in Cancun, which was, 'Wouldn't it be interesting to find out about how CEOs think about strategic thinking.' I had written a lovely little book, called *Demystifying Strategy*, which has all these self-contained frameworks and is screaming: 'How can we demystify these', and I thought, what better place to find that out but from the horses' mouth, from CEOs?

Because what you are saying to me is that you actually need as light a luggage as you need to do the strategy journey. Ok, we do need a document that says, 'We do have a strategy' but we don't have to have the all-singing, all-dancing strategy department with all that work going on all the time. It is much more fluid and intuitive, informed by some facts, as well.

Nick:
It's a small company and I guess that it's the CEO's job to think of the strategy. When I became Chairman that was my job; my only job was to stand back away from the fire-fighting. As a Chairman it was slightly easier as I didn't have to make things happen. I just needed to work out what needed to be done.

Tony:
Were you tempted to get back involved in the detail?

Feasibility studies

Nick:
Not after 2007. But my thing was to push the boundaries back a bit and ask, 'Why aren't we in America?' Let's look at that. There were strategic questions that came up over the years. One was: 'Do we break into other countries?', and in the end the conclusion that we came to was that all the circumstances that allowed Moonpig to thrive in the UK such as the fact that people buy lots of cards and there is a very efficient postal service that didn't exist in most other European countries. They only really existed in English-speaking countries, and Holland, bizarrely, so we did Australia and that worked.

Then we did America; with America I had the view, 'Let's try it.' It is much better to have the answers. So we set up an American site. It was going to cost (something) to produce the content. We would run some advertising and it would (all) cost a few hundred thousand pounds in America. So in order to work out what we needed to do, we needed to know what it would cost us to bring someone to the site in America, and how many of those people would convert and how many of those people would come back. Those were the critical things: the cost of (acquiring) the customer and the life time value, just those two things.

And we did that in America and what we worked out was that the life time value was poor and the cost of the customer was high, so as a result of that we haven't tried to expand in America. And we understand the reasons for that, that they have got a quite slow postal service and it's a big country. They have a higher propensity to buy e-cards, and the other thing is that the British like taking the mickey out of each other. There are cultural things that work much better in Australia and the UK.

Tony:
The number one though, is that you needed to pilot the strategy and there is not a lot about piloting strategy in any of the literature. It is something that retailers do and there's no substitute sometimes for actually getting into the water....

Nick:
Absolutely. With television the plan was, once again, to test. If you test something, it is much easier to get an answer. It is much easier. So with television we risked £80,000: you spend £30,000 on the TV ad and £50,000 on the media and I figured that at least, after £80,000, we would know whether TV was likely to be an element of growing the business or not. But it is not something that you could guess about.

Tony:
In the management literature it's about the economics of information. Taking decision trees and saying what's the probability. Like drilling for oil: you do seismic studies and on the basis of that you drill a test hole so that you get a better steer on where the oil is but it's all a gamble. But you systematically spend money just to buy information. But outside those particular areas it is not so central that you actually have to do a thing like that and put the time and money and effort into that investment to actually buy strategic information.

The other thing that occurs to me is that one of my '55 ways of being creative/innovative/or cunning' (see *Demystifying Strategy*) is that you might imagine that you are doing psychic market research – as if you were to say, 'We are not going to let you do that pilot and save you money.' Now you kind of project yourself into that market place and say, 'If we were to do that exercise, then if we were to do this pilot and setting all of this up, what sort of behaviours would get in its way and what sort of things would really help it along, and things that we haven't even imagined?' It is like storytelling: you can sometimes get that sort of market alignment or misalignment from doing it.

What is interesting here is that you said that we the British love taking the mickey out of each other – in some ways you could 'psychically' have done that, and said perhaps if we do some comparatives on psychological drivers of buying cards in the UK versus the US, and collected just a bit of market research, and tried to understand that. So in some ways it may have been possible to have acquired some of that data without a pilot.

Nick:

Yes, there's nothing like testing for real (he paused at this point)... testing your assumptions about what's going to happen and then you prove them badly wrong. I would have thought if you had asked me if TV advertising is going to work, I would have probably said 'No' before October 2006. We had a small competitor who was doing some sort of advertising on television and we had been measuring their performance by buying a card from them every week and recording the order number and then deducting the previous week's order number, and that would tell us how many orders they had taken a week.

So we realized that their sales had shot up thorough advertising on television and sales stopped (growing) and dropped back down again when they stopped advertising. From that we were able to work out what their cost of customer acquisition was. We knew how much they had spent and we knew how many customers they had got in the course of the month. And that's what led me to believe that actually that might well work for us.

I noted from this that in the strategy literature there is relatively little said about the role of data collection. Besides the role of innovative thinking in the generation and evaluation of strategic options (and of 'cunning planning') there can be an equally 'cunning' take on collecting the strategic data itself, as in this particular example.

Pure fluke that, because if they hadn't done that I would never have thought about advertising on television, I thought that it wouldn't work, I don't know why. It wasn't based on anything intelligent. I just assumed that it wouldn't work and then the evidence led me to think about it again. Even if we had known the answer, even if we had spent £80,000 on it. Our assumption was that we would need a £10 cost of customer acquisition and if it had ended up being £20 then we would have wasted £40,000; that £40,000 would have bought us the answer so we would have known that that was not a route that we wanted to go down. Buying information.

Tony:

Some people don't seem to think that you need the data.

The CEO's role as a strategic thinker

Tony:

In terms of strategic thinking, are you actually aware of when you are doing it?

Nick:

No, not in business, it is just very logical. I definitely found it more difficult in the charity sector: there you have to consciously think of strategy. In the first place you have to ask yourself the question: 'Who are we?' and then: 'Why are we doing the things that we are doing?' We didn't ask that question in business – we are doing it to make money, to put some food on the table. But in charities there are all kinds of other angles, we have to really understand that. I am doing this because there is some kind of problem that needs sorting out. And unless you answer those kinds of questions, it is very difficult to move forward; much, much more complex.

Tony:

I have done some work in one charity organization and it was so enmeshed in stakeholder issues.

Nick:

And you have got trustees who haven't really taken the time to examine their own motivations. There are a lot of illogical things that come into it like people wanting to be seen to be doing it, they want to be feel that they have changed the world; and also you have got the bigger issue of thinking and standing back and asking, 'Are we right to think that we have the answers?' So we can go to all of these countries and tell them how to run their lives and does that work?

Economic value

Tony:

There's this theory in management called 'economic value' or 'economic profit', whatever you would like to call it, and it really helps the strategy process and makes it a lot simpler.

Nick:

Yes, at least we all know what we are focused on, and we have got an end result at the end of the year. Are we bigger than we were last year? We made more money that we made last year. That is simple. Whereas in a charity, how do you measure? How do you know the contribution of the charity did improve, make a necessary improvement in human happiness? Because you could say that last year we raised lots of money but if last year we spent the money badly on a project that was unnecessary it is a waste of time. So it's not about how much money you raise that is the measure of success. If you don't manage to raise any money then that's a disaster, but it's not all about raising money: the measurement is what you do with it.

Tony:

In terms of a 'value chain' it is much more sophisticated and difficult to judge.

Nick:

Very difficult to judge and the criteria are set by the person who is trying to justify their existence so a CEO would say, 'Well, we did this and we did that', but actually these are the criteria that were set to justify his own existence as opposed to... it is just very difficult.

Tony:

But organizations/companies also have welfare benefits to society. If I look back at my last 23 years (of independent consulting) I think of the personal value of people that I have worked with at chief executive level who have conquered this gap of (strategic) confidence. It is not everyone who is like yourself – who hit the ground with the ball of strategic thinking running, and who had not had (previously) much of a clue as to what it (strategic thinking) is other than that it is moving from where you are to where you want to be, and so the greater confidence and capability and satisfaction that have arisen are quite separate from what GNP increase was a result of that.

It is obviously so much more tangible with something like the Samaritans where you can actually save somebody's life; the implication of that is the huge fallout of unhappiness – when someone committed suicide when that could have been avoided. So that is a no brainer in a way, that that will have a high welfare benefit.

Nick:

Yeah, yeah.

Tony:

In terms of charities, if one could think a bit more about the kind of value that is added to all kinds of different stakeholders – I was speaking to someone who has worked in the police force and it is so much more complicated there because there are a whole variety of people being influenced by a particular process.

Nick:

Yes, one of the differences is that I was looking at it from the perspective of someone who was doing it for free, so I am happy to be... so my general view is that I am only interested in the general good. I don't want to be wasting my time working for a charity if it isn't actually adding to the general good, whereas a lot of CEOs of charities are thinking that I am undermining my existence here so my message at the beginning was that you can only say to everyone in the organization that there are two ways that you can do good in the charity sector. One is that you can increase the pot and the other is that you increase the value over and above the money that you could have just given away; or you can do something better than the next best alternative with the money.

So if all you are going to do is to take money that was already put into a charitable trust and spend it, then you are not really increasing the value of that money and all you are really doing is reshuffling it, and so therefore you have to be pretty confident that whatever projects you have chosen to invest it in are better than the 'next best' alternative. If you take money from the Gates Foundation and spend it on a project that is just a waste of time then all you have done is caused harm. Some people struggle a bit with that. They just feel that if they work for a charity then everything that they do is good. It is an interesting comparison though, between charities and business.

Strategy versus tactics

Tony:
So, coming back to these general questions that I asked, in terms of strategic thinking, is it any different to thinking generally?

Nick:
I don't think so. It is good to write it down, and it is just a constant process. I tend to try to keep strategy separate from tactics. A lot of people don't make the differences they don't seem to have one.

Tony:
How would you explain that?

Nick:
For me strategy is levels one, two, three and tactics is levels, four, five, six, and it is just the higher level decisions that question your existence. You have got to answer those before you can answer those.

Tony:
To give you an example, supposing you got your company to a size that you wanted to hire a high calibre FD and while that might have been a tactical decision not one, two, three, just hovering below that for me, within

that particular decision you have got something that is complex. There is a market environment and there are some ambiguities about what the criteria are that are we looking for in the future, what kind or resources. There is also uncertainty, they might not fit in very well if they are from a big corporation, they just can't get that it is fluid and stuff like that. So would that be a tactical decision within corporate strategy – but still be something worthwhile thinking strategically about?

Nick:

The strategic element of that is, 'What kind of an FD do you need to get to where you are going?', and if you think that where you are going is a flotation, then that would govern the kind of person you would hire. (There is) a very big difference between an FD who makes sure that everything adds up and someone who has a different kind of thought process, a more creative corporate finance type. We had an FD; everything added up – he was brilliant (at that), but he wasn't going to be the sort of person who was going to say, 'This is what we actually need to acquire in order to expand, this is how we are going to acquire these companies and this is where the money is going to come from', and so forth.

So the strategic part is showing that you know where you are going before you set about deciding who you are going to hire, so it is a tactical decision based on your strategy. But ultimately it is about whether you want to sell or float because whoever buys you will probably stick their own FD in, and....

Exiting a business

Tony:

But presumably that decision is kind of strategic?

Nick:

Yes (hesitatingly) we actually had lot more flexibility than we had at the beginning. Had we raised VC (venture capital) money at the beginning then it would have been a forgone conclusion because they need an exit and as it happened I couldn't raise any VC money and it was all private and all of my investors were saying to me once we were making a lot of money and we were paying it all out, we were paying 100 per cent of our profits out in dividends, so as far as our shareholders were concerned they didn't really care. They said, 'If we are getting £1 million in income or £10 million in sale proceeds it really doesn't make much difference.' If we take the £10 million and invest it to try to get £1 million out of it – that's going to be tricky, particularly after I have paid 28 per cent capital gains tax on that.

Tony:

Well you can't tell what the real value of a business always is, can you? The possibility was there. A year ago I was working with a major chain of retail food shops and they had the VAT added to pasties and their share price dropped 5 per cent just because of that. That possibility had been there for years.

Nick:

Well in a year we made £15 million EBIDA: and after we sold I had to ask, 'What do you want to do with your own life?' Do I think: 'I want to start another company, do I want that challenge? Or do I just want to stay in my comfort zone and be the man who runs (Moonpig)?'

Tony:

Well, that was a strategic decision.

Nick:

Well, it wasn't a company-level strategic decision but it was a personal strategic decision for me.

Tony:

I have a friend who is in a similar position who is in health clubs but he seems to be driven by what he wants to do in his life, which means that that might sub-optimize on the disposal decision and the (best) timescales.

Nick:

Well, you get past 40 and you think life is not infinite and you can't faff around for another five years and get a slightly better price. If you want to do something else there are a lot of ways you can do that. I had decided, I could have kept that I was Chairman, I was working two days a week and with other stuff I could have fitted that in and my main thing was that I had 90 per cent of my assets tied up in one company and so I felt a little bit exposed. And I was clearly quite right on that. It was, 'What do I want to do with the rest of my life?' And also I had built up a wonderful team of people, really great people and, er, I quite enjoyed the camaraderie, it was good fun. I still get enjoyment out of that.

Strategic energy

Nick:

It took a huge amount of energy and many years to build that up; it is difficult to recreate that.

Tony:

There must be a sense of loss.

Nick:

On the other hand there is also a sense of challenge, when you think, 'Right, I am going to do it all over again' and redefine myself. You could easily get pigeon-holed as, 'Before I did Moonpig I was the man from Russia… and then I was Mr Moonpig so now I will be something else.'

Tony:

Do you ever spend a day doing something that we call 'white space', where you just sit down to think? What could you come up with if you had a blank mind? Where would you go?

Nick:

Well, I do a lot of personal strategic thinking which is: what kind of life do I want to have? Where do I ultimately get satisfaction from? What things do I find frustrating? What am I good at? And what am I good at now as compared to what I was good at 10 years ago? Ten years ago I would have been a lot more prepared to get involved in the nitty gritty, but now I would probably pay someone else to do it. Although that is a real problem: often when someone has sold a business people come along and say to me, 'Oh, you could be a CEO of this charity because you did that', but because you have done that you have probably less tolerance for the usual garbage that goes with running any organization. The personal spats like having to get rid of people that are underperforming and those kinds of things that are quite tiresome…. Those are the kinds of things (that I think about) – what am I good at, what do I enjoy doing?

Tony:

Well, maybe you would hire a CEO to do that.

Nick:

Well, that's almost certainly what I would do. I almost certainly wouldn't be a CEO from day one. I would be executive Chairman from day one and I would employ a CEO to make sure that it all happens.

Strategy implementation

Tony:

From what you have said, there has been nothing about it being hard to implement strategy. Why do you think that that has been so in your case?

Nick:

(After a long pause.) It was a smaller, flatter structure. I had a board. I did have to get things through the board as well and that wasn't absolutely a 'slam dunk'. There was at least one of the shareholders that used to ask a lot of questions. But we had a fairly sensible strategy.

Tony:

A sensible strategy but not all of the large company paraphernalia that goes with that, and not an awful lot of politics, presumably?

Nick:

No, there was always some politics that you would get, but nothing that would get in the way of the strategy. So we would chat about it and inevitably there would be differences of opinion: for example, should we be doing gifts or not? For instance, a typical one would be: should we be selling remote control helicopters?

Tony:

Those things are cool.

Nick:

If you looked around, a lot of companies were thinking about gifts; you need an entirely different infrastructure from what we had. A day's production started off with a pile of paper in the corner of the room of the factory and then went out of the door. To hold stock of those things that may or may not sell, was quite a risk for us. It requires a different level of space and also why would we necessarily be that good at it? There were lots of people doing it and not making any money. I looked around all the other companies that were doing it and worked out if they were making any money, and they weren't: it was quite a competitive business. The only advantage to us was that it would be going out to existing customers already acquired for greetings cards, so it was all marginal....

Tony:

Well, maybe that's the test then: you shouldn't just be selling things because you can sell them to customers that you have already got.

Tony:

Are there any other things you would like to tell the readers on how you feel about strategic thinking as a process?

Nick:

I think that it's absolutely central. It is absolutely the foundation on which your business is based.

Tony:

So clearly in your view it adds value.

Nick:

I don't see how you can do without it. It is so central, it is about ensuring that you are pointing in the right direction. It is absolutely critical to any business, as opposed to people who say, er, we make these things, so how do we sell them? I would always start from one stage back and say, 'What should we be producing' before you start worrying about what you are selling. What you are actually producing should be based on what you are in a good position to produce competitively, and whether or not people will actually want it, and when you have worked that out, the next level down is: how do we sell more of them?

Tony:

For me it's a bit like the 'Dragons Den' approach (on TV). They have a relatively small number of questions in their book, 30 or so questions, but no one seems to read it before they go on 'Dragons Den'. Then they always look shocked when someone asks those questions, but unless you do you will be going off half-cocked.

Nick:

Yes, I look at everything, when the strategic process starts, when we come up with the business plan in the first place. Everything starts there. Once you have started a business you have somehow got to keep it alive or take the decision to shut it down gracefully. But if you can't answer those questions before you start then just don't start.

So I would look at, I am looking at a new type of business at the moment, and the first thing that I am going to do is work out is how big the market is. There is no point in investing a lot of money if you are ultimately looking at a market that is only this big, and it is going to cost you that much to set yourself up, and so, I suppose my strategy started with my original business plan, which looked at the size of the market and the opportunity, and worked out why I was in a particularly good position to do anything about it.

Strategy tools

Tony:

Would you do anything as crude as a SWOT analysis, or not?

Nick:

Those make me laugh actually. I see them so many times from people who are looking to do an investment and they do the SWOT analysis, using Porter's Five Forces (laughing a bit). It is the reference to it: (as if) it must make sense because we have used the name of the great Porter. I don't consciously use that framework. I try so hard not to use any kind of business jargon, but ultimately I am going through that framework, I am thinking, I don't tend to think of it as SWOT, strengths and weaknesses... I don't think of it as that, but I do have my own framework of thinking, and when someone comes to me with a business plan and they want investment I just think:

1) how big is the opportunity, 2) why are you in a particularly good position to take part in it?

Porter's Five Forces is actually one of the frameworks that would help make sense of the strategic context of Moonpig – see Figure 2.2, earlier. Basically these five factors influence the inherent attractiveness of the industry and reflect the changing level of perfection versus imperfection in market forces. They play a major role in determining margin, return on capital and economic value creation. I call these 'competitive pressure' – which uses less jargon. Adding to that rather static picture one can also project or track how these change over time, either separately or together, on the 'competitive pressure over time curve'; see Figure 2.3.

FIGURE 2.3 Competitive pressure over time curve

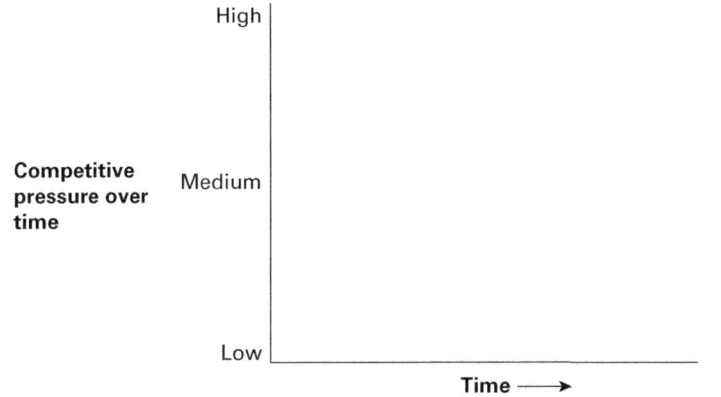

Tony:
Well, those things would be spot on what is called the 'GE' or General Electric grid/the directional policy matrix (see Chapter 1, Figure 1.2), which has market attractiveness against competitive position, which has a much more technical meaning than a SWOT, which is fairly superficial. I sometimes call it a 'Superficial Waste Of Time' (SWOT).

Nick:
Yes, I see lots of stuff in people's embryonic business plans. I was looking at a presentation that someone was doing on watches, saying the watch market is worth about $12 billion. So what? Actually, what I really want to know is: the market for cards is worth £1.3 billion and the market for individualized cards that are bought for people's birthdays is probably worth about £200 million, and all of the cheap cards that are bought,

and we are not even going to compete with cheap cards. I am only really focusing on: what do our cards compete with? If someone is prepared to pay £1.50 in a shop then that's probably a part of the market that we are concerned with. So then you have got to ask, 'How big can you get within that context?'

A lot of people have a formulaic approach: people do the boxes in a kind of 'How to write a business plan' way, but actually, it is as if their heart isn't in it. I really want to know the answer when I write a business plan. But I write about the stuff that is actually relevant.

Tony:

It seems somewhat analysis-driven. Sometimes I say MBA means 'More Boring Analysis'; it seems so involved in, so magnetic to the analysis. Where is the 'so what' in it? Does this mean that this is a great market, or is it a rubbish market?

Nick:

It comes to testing. When I started Moonpig, I think it was a good product. So I just didn't bother. Also, you can ask those people those questions but there's nothing quite like having a live audience. And the real test of the business was after we had launched and we had got people we didn't know who were buying cards and were coming back and buying another one. Then you think ok, they like the product, the product is good; the question then is, 'Can you make enough money out of it?'

Actually getting the business model right was quite important. It was: 'Is it a product that people really want? Yes.' You buy greetings cards and I know from my own experience that if it is personal then it is much more relevant. So the second question is, 'Can you make enough money out of it?' The gross margin is about 70 per cent but it is quite small. The question is: how much does it cost to get a customer and what is that customer going to spend with you over time?

Imitation and copying

Tony:

It is interesting about the margins on cards. I buy cards and I think: why is this two quid? Seriously, for some of this stuff, it is ridiculous. It is very, very expensive, and it is because of all the waste you are paying for and ultimately the margins in this domain are buoyed up by the fact that, relatively speaking, this other stuff is expensive, and it sends a signal of what you can charge the market.

Like if I am honest about it, people at Cranfield (formerly my business school) did 'private work', and what they were saying was, 'Do you know what? It would cost you nine grand a day through Cranfield, but it will cost you, two thousand, sometimes three thousand and you are still getting 6,000 quid off (a day) – aren't you lucky!' So you are thinking about the inefficiency of an imperfect market, to buoy up your margin. But if you take that far enough into the future, which goes back to your exit decision, if everything went online because these places died off then people wouldn't buy cards from retail shops as it was ridiculous, then someone may just the drop the price (of online cards).

Nick:
Well, I have always worked on the principle that in a mature market ultimately you will get squeezed out to the point of an acceptable profit.

Tony:
It is based on a 'perfect market'.

Nick:
Super-profits are dangerous, they are vulnerable. And that's another reason (for exiting): we were making 30 per cent net profit.

Tony:
So it worried you that you were making that kind of margin. And that should worry you.

Nick:
Definitely, it is not sustainable. Somebody ultimately will take it off you. There just comes a point where you are making a 10 per cent net profit. It is acceptable, but any less than that and you wouldn't be doing it, and it keeps the competitors out. Everyone is always looking at you and saying: 'That looks fantastic, let's copy that.'

Effectively Nick is alluding to the fact that competitive pressure has a tendency to change over time, which we might draw as a curve on Figure 2.3.

Tony:
I don't know who taught you corporate finance at Cranfield but they might have said that eventually you will only just get your (zero) net present value as you have just covered your cost of capital. You are in a perfect market. And if people had just learnt that theory then they ought to get it in their head that that is an unsustainable very high margin. Unfortunately a lot of the students that I teach don't get it.

Nick:

I always thought: we are making amazing money here but that's not going to last. Also with the growth rates that we were getting, we were going to get a cracking multiple on the super-profit. So get out while you can, otherwise you end up with so many other retailers and they turn over £200 million and they are making £3 million. That's not attractive at all. I don't look at that and think, I will put a lot of money into that kind of business.

Tony:

I was hoping to have an interview with Ann Summers, they should actually have very high margins but they don't, not really, unless they have come back a lot recently; 6 per cent I would imagine.

Nick:

Well they have a strategic advantage in the sense that it is attractive – it is a good business – and (would-be entrants) think: 'Do I want to tell my grandchildren that I am in the dildo game, so the very nature of what they do, that's a business that puts people off – it is good business, very profitable.

Tony:

You took the words out of my mouth! A bit like funerals.

Nick:

You have got a strategic advantage, because everyone is put off by the thought of formaldehyde.

Tony:

Are there any last big things that we have missed?

Formalization

Nick:

No, no. I think it is ... I must admit I haven't really thought about it before; maybe I did have a semi-formal sort of strategy (process). I thought that it was always seat of the pants. Well it wasn't quite as bad as that.

Tony:

Well, my reflection is that you did have a tacit process, internalized from somewhere else. There was less necessity for exposing it in formal structures that were visible to other people – considering the size of your organization, the relative simplicity of the strategy, the fact that you were more or less telling people what to do.

Nick:

Well, I had a board who were also investors in the business so I needed to be able to express a strategy to them and secondly it is useful in terms of getting everyone on board and saying: this is the general direction that we are going in.

To some extent, as we got bigger I used to spend a bit of time with the marketing department where I would say we need to come up with some (new) ideas and to put it into one coherent document that starts with this and then works out: this is who we are and what we are doing, and this is what we are going to do from a marketing perspective. So they would all have an input to it. There is always the danger that if you sit down with them as a group and you disagree with what they have come up with… and I think that sometimes there is an advantage in coming up with a single vision.

Tony:
One of the things that I have found useful is to represent things visually, even if this is just in the written form. It makes it so much easier to be reflective, and to manipulate ideas and to ask, 'Have I missed something?'

Other things, some of the frameworks that are useful, are good for putting down the mental maps that are (otherwise) far too complicated. Human beings are not good at holding very complex mental map in their heads.

Nick:
Whenever I write a document I write a skeleton plan of the document and then I flesh that out. I think, if I am writing about the market, here is the overall market, the competition and, hang on, should I write about the UK, and then the US market, and the UK and the US competition? That's different… in merely putting that all together it makes you think about it fairly logically.

Tony:
So you are exploring the potential structure of your actual business model?

Nick:
Yes, it does help. For example, our marketing strategy in America is very different from our marketing strategy in the UK, because different things work in different ways over there. But when you are talking about the size of the market, the size of the global market for cards… but we have decided that we are not going to do anywhere other than Britain. It was just a useful process. In any business I would do the same: start with business plan before you start the business and every year renew it.

Tony:
In my book *Demystifying Strategy* I call it a 'position paper', which is similar except that it is just an outline sketch of the overall shape of the plan, but only as far as your ideas take you, but then it gets expanded. I find that very helpful.

CONCLUSIONS

Some really useful lessons came out of this interview:

- Strategy theory gives us useful frameworks to think strategically about complex business issues, but shouldn't be worshipped for its own sake.
- It is often about formulating a 'hierarchy of questions'.
- The end goal of strategic thinking is to make the best strategic decisions.
- The competitive forces, especially barriers to entry and imitation, are what should keep the CEO awake at night; strategic anxiety is no bad thing.
- Sustainable competitive advantage and sustainable value creation are inextricable.
- Strategy development is all about evolving the business model (or the 'business value system') to create and capture value.
- We saw that in evolving businesses the competitive pressure over time curve (Figure 2.3) will change, and that's one of the key things that should be on the CEO's mind. Indeed, closely related to that is the idea of economic value creation, which again will shift over time, not just through the effect of Porter's Forces, but also the market growth drivers, shifts in relative competitive position, and also in the effectiveness of strategy. This could be represented as the (economic) value over time curve; see Figure 2.4.

FIGURE 2.4 Economic value over time curve

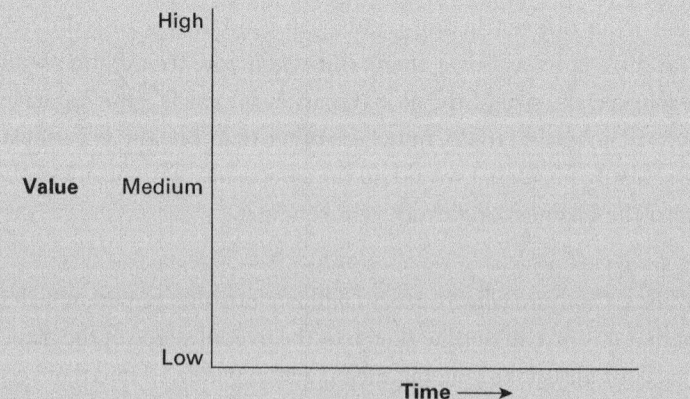

APIL

03

Introduction

This chapter is based on an interview with Deborah Evans, CEO of APIL (The Association of Personal Injury Lawyers), which has been fighting for the rights of injured people for 20 years. A not-for-profit organization, APIL's 4,700 member lawyers (mainly solicitors, barristers and legal executives) are dedicated to changing the law, protecting and enhancing access to justice, and improving the services provided for victims of personal injury. Over the years APIL has grown to become the leading, most respected organization in the field, constantly working to promote and develop expertise in the practise of personal injury law, for the benefit of injured people. APIL's offices are in Nottingham in the United Kingdom, although it has reach throughout the UK.

Deborah was previously the CEO of Legal Complaints Service, and this chapter draws on her some of her experiences there. The themes we covered were:

- strategic thinking in a group context;
- the 'time to die' strategically;
- storytelling;
- strategic leadership;
- changing business models;
- strategic communication;
- thinking and decision-making processes;
- value of strategic thinking and decisions;
- stakeholders;
- uncertainty;
- time spent on it;
- training in strategic thinking;
- scenarios and contingent strategy;
- strategic tools;
- strategy implementation and change management;
- doing it in practice.

Strategic thinking: in a group context

Tony:
Strategic thinking – what do you think that is?

Deborah:
Well, strategic thinking is something that you consciously do. It's not something that just happens. You have to allow time in your working day to think, and that's quite a mind-shift for some managers, who actually think that they always should be doing something. Stopping and thinking may make them feel that they are not busy. But it is the most important thing that you do.

I don't like to do my thinking and planning alone. I like to put several minds together so generally I would like to invite two or three members of the management team to come in and explore ideas and start putting the plans together, rather than thinking in isolation.

Tony:
How does that help and how much?

Deborah:
It helps enormously. Obviously it means that they get to input to the strategy as well. There's never, ever, been one occasion where they haven't come up with something different to what I thought about and that ends up in the final plan.

Deborah emphasizes here the value of not confining strategic thinking to the CEO's own thoughts but incorporating the ideas and insights of others in the organization. This is somewhat in contrast to the case of Moonpig. This is not to imply that a more open style of strategic thinking is beneficial or essential in absolutely all cases – it is likely to depend on the situation. In Moonpig's case this was a very entrepreneurial context and its CEO was the founder who had thus always been with the business from inception, while Deborah joined APIL in 2011. Also, it is likely to be a function of personal style. Nevertheless the extent of, and the habitual nature of the way in which Deborah set about strategic thinking, might be an example to CEOs and potential future CEOs elsewhere.

So it's not purely that you go through an exercise so they know what you are thinking, and so that they feel a part of it. It is about getting a better final decision, and quite regularly we come out of discussions with me having gone with what they have said, rather than what I have said, and I am thinking: 'Well, let's see how it pans out, and is it right', but you have got to trust other people, and let them be able to shape strategy, as well as yourself.

So I find that absolutely essential. And certainly, the market that we are in here is constantly shifting. Now, we are in professional services, and the biggest impact on us is governmental reform. They are really trying to shake-up the professional services market, and they are bringing in cost competition, different business structures, that sort of thing. So these are massive reforms, they are not little tweaks. They have massive effects.

The 'time to die'

Deborah:

So it is actually more forward looking, most of the time. We are trying to work out things that will be imposed on us from the outside, and then you work out how you respond to those changes, how you keep one step ahead.

So it is very much forward looking. If we weren't forward looking we would die in under 18 months. That's the long and short of it. You cannot afford not to do this (strategic thinking).

Tony:

It is an interesting thing to think about: the time to die-strategically.

Deborah:

Well, it's 18 months for us, but at the moment you have got to change and flex and evolve. If we stood still and did nothing the business model would be unsustainable.

This is an interesting discussion: particularly the way in which it generated the idea in my head of 'the time to die-strategically'. This would be the expected duration of an organization without strategic thinking – and thus organizational adaptation – before it either failed, got taken over, or at minimum had to go through radical surgery and turnaround. In Demystifying Strategy *I explained the competitive advantage over time curve: this is a representation of the decay in competitive position that might occur precisely through strategic inaction (as well as how it might shift with more proactive input, of course). The time to die strategically is thus the limit: the situation where strategic thinking is switched off.*

In the context of extremely rapid external change as in APIL's case, this would seem to be a very short time indeed. While most organizations have much greater latitude in strategic response time, this is a reminder to CEOs not to be complacent. Only where competitors' strategic thinking has been similarly switched off is there likely to be a respite. Clearly, strategic thinking is not an optional activity for the CEO, nor should it be intermittent.

Tony:
So I am sure that in our past experiences (working) together we have talked about the idea of scenarios or storytelling: is that something that you weave into strategic thinking, or do you anchor yourself in the present, looking forward?

Storytelling

Deborah:
We do quite a lot of storytelling. If we do this, what impact will that have? What will they say, what impact will that have further down the line? And because there are so many interlocking changes going on, we need to look forward at how the sum of how each of these things will impact. Actually storytelling when and how changes will impact on our members is a really good way of seeing it through, allowing you to travel with your vision, rather than just staying in one place.

Tony:
That sounds to me as if, when you say you travel, that you go into that future. Do you find that you just talk, use words to represent that, or anything else?

Deborah:
I spend a lot of time scribbling on pieces of paper, and I tend to draw a lot more pictures than words. So if I am thinking strategically it is always about drawing pictures; strategic thinking isn't just about writing lots of words on a piece of paper. Maybe the final business plan might look like that, but that doesn't aid the thought process.

Tony:
And does that feel different, when you are doing the pictures?

Deborah:
It feels a lot more creative and imaginative. It really stretches both sides of your brain, and I actually write with both hands at once when I really get into it, because your brain is completely engaged.

Tony:
It is a bit like doing artwork and slapping paint on it.

Deborah:
It looks quite similar: it is very visual when you have finished it, but it is much easier to digest and understand it. You get far more on a piece of paper.

Here Deborah is describing quite distinctively intuitive cognitive processes that are associated with right brain activity. In more detailed planning and also in data analysis this would be more left brain. Different people have differing biases to which style of thinking and thus which parts of their brain they use: in pure strategic thinking they might need to engage in routines and activities that stimulate their right brain.

Also organizations are primarily geared – except during formation or in periods of huge disruption – to engage in routine activities that are more left brain, so it may be a struggle to get into the right brain mode, unless there are similar routines to those described by Deborah, for organizational play.

Tony:

There are some people, possibly people like accountants – I was an accountant – when you start talking about strategic thinking you can see them getting stiffer, and they think it is going to be really difficult. But what you have described is a quite pleasant process.

Deborah:

It is particularly satisfying, yes, and it is pleasant even with a particularly difficult problem, because it is about finding ways forward. You do get a lot of job satisfaction seeing that you have options. You are unlikely to hit conflict when you are doing strategic thinking because it is all options, so really nothing can be said that was wrong. So when you are having a discussion with your managers it's just ideas, it's not an argument.

Tony:

I think that often CEOs are frightened of being proved wrong, and they want a definitive discussion and want to push forwards and it seems to me very much that you have a vested interest, some sort of investment in a particular set of decisions. You (yourself), seem to be able to change your views as new evidence comes up.

Deborah:

I think that the job of the CEO is to facilitate the decision, because if you don't then you are making that decision entirely on your own, and then it is a less well-informed decision. But it is certainly about driving the decision making and thinking and making sure that it happens.

Strategic leadership

Tony:

My publishers were quite keen on the leadership theme, and I am aware that there are close relationships between leadership and strategic thinking, but from what you said it sounds as if you were in that (leadership) mode, you are behaving not as if you are a 'strategic leader' in the sense of one who says: 'This is the direction', but actually harnessing the thinking and then evolving the direction.

Deborah:

I have obviously been a manager for some years and developed quite a lot in that time. One of the early lessons that you learn is that if you make decisions solely on your own they will never be as good as they could be. Sometimes it is a brave step to start encouraging others to contribute. But then the results will speak for themselves.

Tony:

In *Demystifying Strategy* we talk about options, and the different slices of options: the options for what you might to, how you might do them and when. When you say you have the input on decisions, would you say that it is mainly about the implementation? It is mainly about the formulation and the sort of direction to go in?

Deborah:

It is the formulation. It is the basic choice of 'What do we do about this?' and it may not always come up with one clear answer. Quite often it will come up with two or three things that we can do. You then start looking at the resource analysis, the costings, etc. Or sometimes it can be tactical – the outcome. But you always have choices, so the first thing is to understand what your choices are, get the options on the table, and then decide which road to take.

Tony:

So how do you get as many options as you can?

Deborah:

Generally, by getting a group of people around you, sit and brainstorm, call it whatever you like, just basically throw as many ideas on the table, and then have a look at it.

Tony:

And then how do you sort them out, how do you evaluate them?

Changing business models

Deborah:

Well, it's going to depend on what the particular choice is: what's important? So, for example, at the moment we have a scenario which is a potential train crash. There are a lot of reforms, all going on simultaneously, but independently, and not in a joined-up way. But they are all actually happening in the same month. And as a consequence as yet we have got no detail, because it is all being done at the same time, and this slows everything down and makes planning impossible.

Now if you are a business, in this case, a law firm, trying to plan for all of the changes, the detail of these changes is only revealed at the last minute, you can't flex your business model to respond. So we then start discussing with the government how we can get a more sensible approach. What are your objectives as a starting point? Our objective is that we want changes done properly, not at breakneck speed, but we are not anti-change, quite the opposite. We are however anti-business changes that will cause instability. To cope with change you do need some form of evidence-based decision process so that there is some idea of what is coming.

It may be that government are firm in their policy and the result is court action, which is the route that Richard Branson had to go down (with the Virgin Trains franchise). So you look at the scenarios for options that may or may not work. Tactically you resource them, you cost them, you work out whether you are doing all of them, or whether you are going straight for the bigger option, etc, and you plan and you think it through.

Tony:
So it sounds as if there is an awful lot of manipulation of the architecture of choices, which is driving a lot of what you do. Because, in a way, you are the one that sees ahead for the many, many members that I saw listed downstairs (in your Registry) which is a substantial membership.

Deborah:
We have about 4,500 personal injury lawyers as member and yes, it is substantial. Equally we campaign for the rights of the injured person, and it's not all about money; this is about people having the opportunity to get compensation when they have been injured through no fault of their own. A lot of the agenda at the moment seems to be about making those people go away, even though they are genuinely injured through no fault of their own, because they cost money.

Strategic communication

Tony:
Yes, now in terms of what it (strategic thinking) gives to people, something that I highlighted in earlier research (Grundy, 2002), one of the areas of value is personal self-confidence. I saw you on TV twice that day when you were making your case that you were doing everything, going everywhere – this was like someone who was very, very clear on where they were at, very clear on what the perception of all these injury claims was, and I wonder to what extent having thought about it strategically it helped you to do such things, because it is not the kind of thing that is easy to do – to go on

TV and to talk as you did for over two minutes. It is quite unusual to see an interview that long.

Deborah:

Well, part of the strategic thinking is not just to think about what you are going to do but also why you are doing it. It is about why you are making those choices. It means that you start developing the messages in your head about why you are doing it so that you can then communicate this to your members or to your staff and to the outside world. Normally when I am doing strategic thinking I would have our communications manager involved, who has a really strong steer on the impact of action we take on the outside world and how it will be perceived – and perceptions are often quite different to the reality.

Deborah here is underlining the significance of being clear on organizational purpose. This doesn't seem to be anchored in abstract mission statements bit in more specific strategic motives/objectives. In APIL'S case there seem to be: to protect the rights of legitimate claimants who have been wronged/hurt by organizations through accidents who otherwise might not pursue legal cases because of the cost and the risk; and to help ensure that the lawyers that do the work in supporting them have an adequate incentive and stable enough business environment such that they will continue to do that work: ie it is worth their while.

While such strategic motives or strategic objectives may be explicit in an organization's strategy they are often not; they seem to lurk as more taken for granted assumptions. They may therefore need explicit articulation from time to time in the strategy.

So that input is there right at the start of the process. When we have considered what action we are taking we have already defined what we will be telling the outside world about it, and what we will be telling our members. Our messages are quite interesting because sometimes we are talking to lawyers and they are quite technical, but a lot of the time we are talking to the general public – what happens if you are injured, and what will these changes mean to you, that your damages will be reduced, and we have to be quite clear about the separate groups that we represent – and how each message will come across.

Tony:

A lot of this involves looking at stakeholders and another thing that comes out is that while you describe strategy as being complex – all these different choices – and also about uncertainty, but equally you are focusing on some ingredients that are actually quite simple, and it is going back to the simplicity of that process, dealing with that complexity at the same time as actually trying to get some simple stuff out and hanging onto that.

Thinking and decision-making processes

Tony:

So how do you actually recognize that you are doing it? Is there paint all over the wall, or...?

Deborah:

Well, when I am making a decision, I would plan to sit down and think about it. I will invite two or three people to come and join me in that process. If I am on the train I will do it on my own, obviously. I do actually decide to do it – and I do start thinking differently. It is not something that I will just mix up in other work. You make choices all through the day and those are the little choices. For the big strategic decisions you do put time aside.

Tony:

So when you do start to do it, what emotion creeps in? Do you get a shift?

Deborah:

Yes, it is quite a rush of thinking because lots of options start coming out at once and it can all go off in different directions. It does get the adrenalin going, definitely, and it is that shift into being imaginative and creative, so it does feel different.

It would thus seem that right brain activity associated with strategic thinking is quite pleasant – a clear enabler.

Tony:

When I was at Cranfield, I probably trained 1,500 managers in this, and they have this sort of guilt that they should be doing it but they are not. The more they don't do it the more guilty they feel, and so in a way, and this is something that I have myself, when you start to do it you suddenly seem to alleviate that guilt – look: I am too busy doing this, and this and this.

Deborah:

Well, it's quite quick as well: you don't have to do your entire strategy for your whole business in one go, you can do it in chunks. You can get a decent amount of strategic thinking done in three-quarters of an hour. So you can just take a topic and do it well. And I also take the whole management team away for a day of strategic thinking where we concentrate on nothing else – outside the office, and everyone puts onto the table ideas on things that they want to discuss.

Here Deborah is highlighting the important process of breaking down the material for strategic thinking into manageable chunks or slices (as in the 'mini-strategy' process), rather than working on the whole thing all in one go.

Tony:

So, probably, by the sounds of it – you mention the 45-minute cycles and stuff – a bit of the sort of thing that I was teaching the group, is it less structured than that?

Deborah:

It could be either. It does have structure to it and it does depend on what the topic is, but we do use a lot of those tools. I think it is the usual thing. If you plan to do something it will happen. You put the time in the diary to do it. The more that you do it the more valuable you see that it is, and you keep repeating it.

Value of strategic thinking and decisions

Tony:

So in terms of the value that comes out of it, you actually do see a value pay-off?

Deborah:

Well, it stops procrastination for a start. A lot of managers suffer from the inability to make a decision, because they don't know whether it is right or not. Well, if you start thinking it through, seeing into the future, this can give you an indicator of what may or may not be right, and it just enables you to make a better decision more quickly, I think.

Tony:

Deborah, do you remember when you were CEO of Legal Complaints Service that you worked on a Regulatory Strategy and I think that you made some savings through avoiding a fine by the Regulator – it would have been around a quarter of a million pounds. Do you remember how long you actually worked on that for? Was it a long time?

Deborah

No it wasn't. We started working on it on one of the strategy days that we had with you. Then I had to task my team to cost the options without me as I was out of the office, and I think that they spent about another two hours on it. Interestingly it was the costing of the options that actually defined the strategy. There was one option that was going to deliver a much better reward and at less cost than the others. But having done the (strategic thinking) training they were able to do that on their own – and they just delivered me the result.

For the record, Legal Complaints avoided the fine.

Tony:
It sounds as if they were using the five criteria of the strategic option grid, strategic attractiveness, etc but that they were drilling down into financial attractiveness here.

Deborah:
They did all of that detail – it was such an important thing to do. That obviously reaped dividends but there were other bits of decision making that delivered results as well. We did a lot of work to recover compensation for miners who had deductions from their damages taken by their solicitors incorrectly and we did the thinking around that very much as a group. Because while we could see what needed to be done, because this abuse had happened on such a large scale it was going to be almost impossible to resource solving the problem, because we only had so many staff who could work on it, we sat down as a group and we realized that we could get firms to sort out their own problem so we wouldn't need to resource it. And it is that sort of 'outside the box' thinking that can really deliver rewards. Sometimes you are constrained by your own resources or your own time whereas if you can harness other people's resources as well then you can do bigger things.

This was a good example of developing options to implement the strategy, rather than with the actual 'what' of the strategy.

Stakeholders

Tony:
You mentioned seeing things from a different perspective when you are doing the PR, the communications side. You remember the idea of the 'out-of-body experience' that we used to talk about (laughing) – is that something that you use intuitively or do you explicitly say 'let's have an out-of-body experience'? Or maybe it's not that specific?

In an out-of-body experience (for more, see Demystifying Strategy*), one literally puts oneself in the mindset – the thoughts, feelings, agendas, beliefs and assumptions – of the other stakeholder.*

Deborah:
We do regularly try to see things from others' point of view, as you can imagine. We have a lot of debates about the insurance sector. They are the compensators – they pay the claims. We regularly try and see how an insurer would react to proposed changes and quite often it is the polar opposite of how we would react because they are trying to get their books to balance, trying to get their premiums down. So from their point of view fewer claims and lower damages are very good things.

So we do think about things quite regularly from others' points of view. As a general rule we try not to antagonize the other stakeholders, because it is quite easy to say things that may be aligned to your principles but fly in the face of another stakeholder strongly so that it creates conflict where there needn't have been any, and if you can find the areas of overlap it makes things much easier.

Tony:
Are you saying there that it helps a lot with influencing?

Deborah:
It helps a lot with relationships and negotiation and certainly influencing. For example, at the moment the changes will benefit the insurers but they are going to be struggling as much as we are with the chaos, the uncertainty and the lack of detail: they can't set their budgets, they can't set their premiums, so even though they may see the changes as largely positive they and we are both feeling the same ill-effects that the disorganization is producing. It is finding that common ground. So I spend a lot of time to talking to insurers about their viewpoint – because that really helps.

Tony:
So a lot of the stuff that you are doing there is actually collecting strategic data about the environment. There is a theme in strategy which is about sensing weak signals. It sounds as if you were doing a lot of that. Whether we call it 'strategic thinking' or not I don't know. What's your view on that?

Deborah:
We do a lot of data collection. Firstly we do research; also I go around the country talking to people. I will go to conferences and our regional meetings. I will talk to as many lawyers as I can and I will find out what they think and what the personal impact of these changes is, because our members have different business structures and they feel things in a different way. You can never assume that you know how a change will impact everybody, so you have to go and find out and that's again one of the most important parts of the job.

Tony:
In terms of the work that I have done in the past – particularly with accounting firms, they will tend to see clients and that's it, that's a given – a lot of the work that I did was to help them to understand the business model of their clients, because if you could do that then you can actually align what you can do for them. That turned out to be an application of strategic thinking that you don't read about in the textbooks. If you look at corporate strategy and some theorists it's all about the market and we need to do this for our own

plan, to plan our own strategy, but there is not that much about the strategies of customers and of other stakeholders and their business models.

Deborah:
Yes.

Uncertainty

Tony:
It feels like your bread and butter.

Deborah:
Well it is, because personal injury lawyers have over the last few years become far more commercial and they have had a lot of competition, from all the claims management companies that have come into the market. Clients respond very well to things like TV advertising, so even if they have been the client of a law firm for years, they may still decide to ring one of the companies that advertise on the television. They are very open to being persuaded. There are lots of ways now to decide to use a service. The internet is a common way that allows clients to shop around. So it is about being alive to the ways that claimants think and understanding their route to market, really.

Tony:
So, the markets that your members are in do seem to be changing quickly, and that seems to mean that you have to do strategic thinking on behalf of your members, and that is a big part of your job, then?

Deborah:
Yes it is huge. The reforms have a massive impact on how they do business. One of the things that we do is keep members informed. We also put on conferences to get them up to date really quickly – we do the thinking on their behalf. And we can communicate so that they can absorb it and concentrate on their day jobs. They are dealing with people and sorting out their cases and they haven't necessarily got the time to keep up with the intricacies of all these reforms. So we do that thinking for them, but they still have to do their own business planning, and that's the big challenge because at the moment the detail is yet to be announced.

Time spent on it

Tony:
So if you looked at your total time in a week, could you estimate approximately the amount of time you spend directly on strategic thinking – or indirectly related to that?

Deborah:

I would say that between a half a day and a day a week is going to be spent on strategic thinking. It will be pure thinking time, sensing the environment, talking to people, doing the influencing and negotiating and doing the messages; all of that sort of thing.

Tony:

And how much is all that sort of thing?

Deborah:

At least another two days of the week.

Tony:

So with all the talking too we have got at least a half (of your time) minimum – it is half a day at least plus two days – it is half of the week, closely involved in strategic thinking.

Training in strategic thinking

Tony:

In terms of anything else that makes it (strategic thinking) easier, we talked about having more people involved etc and you also said that you had those thoughts on your own – are there any things that enhance that, or make it any easier?

Deborah:

Well, firstly having the management team thinking the same way makes a big difference, which is why we have done training in strategic thinking. A lot of them have had previous training but it is also about thinking the same way and having the same thought patterns and models so that everyone knows what you are talking about. That makes a big difference. It means that we make progress a lot quicker.

The other thing is talking to the management team very regularly. It is quite easy with modern technology when you are out of the office to do a lot of things by e-mail, but what you can discuss in a 5- or 10-minute conversation can take half an hour to type and you don't get that exchange of view. I think that a lot of people shy away from having a good conversation and talking it through.

Tony:

It may be that the emphasis on e-mails is actually one of the factors that is driving out strategic thinking.

Deborah:

Well, it is, because it's mainly one-sided communication where you put your thoughts down and you wait for someone to come back, whereas if you were talking to somebody it is far more intertwined. I do like the more old-fashioned ways of dealing with things, talking to staff at least once a month, talking to the managers as a group at least every two weeks and also seeing individual managers independently. We do the same with groups of lawyers to formulate our policies and strategies as well as using the experience of those 'at the coal face', and we would never deign to think or assume that we know what suits everyone until we have that input. A lot of it is conversational.

Tony:
In terms of how long it takes to train someone up who has not done very much before, could you have just got the one day of input, or two? Would one day ever have been enough?

Deborah:
No, I think you need two days, That's not too much time though, at the end of the day, to invest in your management team just to get everyone running the same way. Basically it didn't cost that much for what it delivered. Some people think you need to do a six-month course. You don't really.

This was an area I was interested in asking about particularly as I have done training interventions of a variety of forms and durations over the past 23 years: three-, two- and one-day – even a couple of hours – and in large groups, small groups, pairs and individuals. The longer programmes have sometimes been en bloc and other times split into two days with a day later (the latter does seem to be about the best option). Typically the first day is needed to tune into the different thinking process and the tools, the second day to gain greater confidence, and the third day to crystallize the desire and the commitment to adopt the new habits. In APIL's case, to date there have been two separate days of formal training, mainly working on APIL's live issues, supplemented by many separate sessions orchestrated clearly by Deborah.

Tony:
Especially if you don't have to go to a big business school.... What about constraints? What sort of thing holds you back from developing a robust strategy?

Deborah:
Sometimes it is the unknown. We have had this problem quite a bit, where we are trying to base a strategy on what's likely to happen – but the majority of it isn't within your control. For example, when you are dealing with government reform you don't know what they are going to decide and when they are going to decide. Quite often there is a lead-in time, so we develop

our thinking around that – I can't remember what you called it – the 'funnel of uncertainty'.

Tony:
Yes, the 'uncertainty tunnel'.

The uncertainty tunnel is a dynamic model that begins with the antecedent conditions to a particular change, the changes resulting being subject to things that amplify or dampen their impact, and then the first-, second- and third-order consequences, shown as a funnel shape. Maybe I should rename it 'the uncertainty funnel' – thanks Deborah!

The uncertainty tunnel is depicted in Figure 3.1, which shows a change from state of the world 1 to world 2 initiated by precursor trends, events and discontinuities. These forces are either amplified or dampened and then give rise to consequences. This is a very dynamic framework, and can be used to help with storytelling.

Scenarios and contingent strategy

Deborah:
Basically you decide your strategy by guessing some of those decisions on their behalf and that at least enables you to get to the end point, but then you have to revisit your strategy when those decisions are actually made. Otherwise their indecision would become constraints which would stop your progress, and you can't have that.

FIGURE 3.1 The uncertainty tunnel

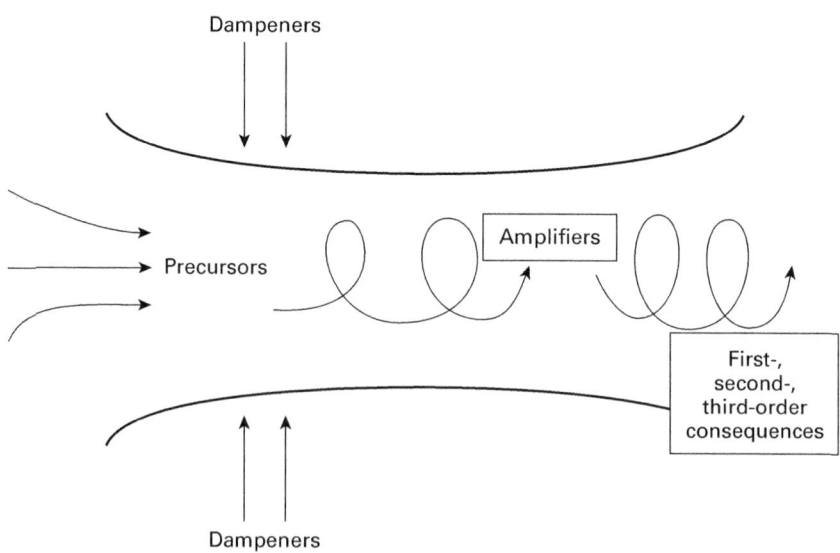

Tony:
Did I ever show you... explaining the story of Pearl Harbour and how that was anticipated in some detail in the controversial and fictional book *The War in The Pacific* published over 15 years before the date of the actual attack? This recounted the events leading up to the surprise attack including the geopolitical, economic and military forces that built up to it, the way in which the surprise was mounted, the detailed casualties and the knock-on effect of Japanese victory. The point of this case was to illustrate the power of storytelling and scenario development in the sphere of strategy.

Deborah:
No, but I have seen the film.

Tony:
The author must have role-played the key players and pinpointed the conflict over natural resources such as rubber and oil in the Far East which triggered this. I know that we did some work (together) when you were at Legal Complaints Service at the very time that the government was changing and do you remember that people (at the workshop) were actually listening in (via Google) on the changes that were coming and we were role-playing them because there were some big issues in terms of the duration of the organization that were very uncertain?

Deborah:
Yes, we had to close down the organization without knowing the end-date. It was a very difficult thing to do because you have obviously got to give notice to suppliers, you have to sell the building, you have to make your staff redundant, when you don't actually know when you are going to be closing; it's hard to do that. And these things take time: you can't do them in a couple of weeks, they take months, and it was quite clear that we wouldn't get a date out of the government but also that we wouldn't get adequate notice. So we defined a strategy around that which involved us setting our own date of closure but then keeping a contingency operation that could have been extended if needed – and that was all we could do. We had to take control of the unknown because otherwise we would have failed.

And I am now coming to the conclusion that life is like that all the time and you have to fill the gaps, and then decide what you are going to do. Obviously you won't be entirely right and far better to make the decision to do something rather than to leave it until it is too late to do anything. So it was a very good exercise to go through.

This gave me the thought that where many organizations need to deal continually with a rather 'foggy' future it might be useful to think along the lines of this being a kind of 'uncertainty gap'. This is where, ex ante, there is considerable uncertainty ahead, and some thought and research is done to close the gap between desired knowledge of the future and actual knowledge of it. This gap might be closed by, for example, research, scenario storytelling, role-playing the key stakeholders and environmental modelling and also by actual events as they crystallize.

Clearly the Legal Complaints Service was doing what it could to close this uncertainty gap for itself and for its members: the problem was that that there would be inadequate time to respond to events once they had happened. This necessitated as much closure of the uncertainty gap as was possible and a reduction in the reaction time through developing contingent strategies and tactics, and minimizing the lag in implementing them. For example, it is conceivable that a law practice might have to tell its staff that should a particular regulatory regime be decided there would need to be some redundancies, so that this implementation lag could be cut down.

While this may seem to be an unusual case it may be more common, given organizational turbulence, than one might think.

Tony:
What you were doing was quite logical: to have built-in flexibility. There's an unpublished paper I wrote on the art of contingent strategy: the idea was that if you are going around an obstacle, you have one strategy for one world and one for another one, so you have a whole set of contingent strategies. In that paper I asked: 'How do you explain that to people because they would say: "What do you mean: on the one hand you do this, and on the other hand you do that?" Isn't that difficult to say in that kind of situation, that we don't know which way we are going to go? How do you deal with telling them? There is no singular plan.

As a result of this interview and the fact that at times the other CEOs also faced situations not amenable to more linear planning (like the International Paralympic Committee) I decided to include some material on contingent strategy in Appendix 2 in this book.

Deborah:
Well it's like a football match basically, you know what you are going to do but you don't know what the other side is going to do so you have to respond to moves on the other side. You are not the only person who is in control of this environment and as long as everyone appreciates that that's the way things are going to be and that when every decision is made you sit down and you review your strategy again, that's fine.

Everybody can understand that, really. With the reforms going through at the moment, one of the things that we can't do is to finalize our budget for next year but that hasn't stopped us from setting one. We have done an interim budget that we will then review when each decision is made. We have at least got planning in place and contingency built into that. But you should never use the fact that there is uncertainty not to do anything. Contingent planning is the way forward.

Strategic tools

Tony:
Speaking of tools: if you had lost some of them, which ones would you love to have back?

Deborah:
Well, we love the strategic option grid (see Figure 1.2), it goes without saying. We love generating ideas with the 'Optopus' (see Figure 1.4) and we like the models with the arrows going up and down.

Tony:
I think that you mean the force field-type diagrams.

Deborah:
And one that we have definitely used a lot of is the stakeholder analysis (see *Demystifying Strategy*, Figure 3.2), we have used all of those.

Tony:
Do you use the uncertainty grid at all (see Figure 5.1)? I ask because sometimes people have a struggle getting their heads around that one.

Deborah:
I don't know if we do use that very much.

Tony:
To prioritize which assumptions are most important and most uncertain.

This grid has certain/uncertain as the vertical axis, and relative importance on the horizontal.

Deborah:
When everything is so uncertain....

Tony:
I once used it ironically to identify that it was very important and also very uncertain that I *wouldn't* be hit by a car in or around London, some years ago. I was in the habit of dashing across busy roads and this voice in the back of my head kept telling me that I should be more careful. I think I actually

used this in a workshop semi-humorously to illustrate what was meant about a 'taken for granted' assumption of a strategy going well – I put that assumption amongst others in my life on the uncertainty grid and lo it was in the 'danger zone' – both very uncertain and very important: then.

One night later I was watching a Second World War film and a tank was coming down the road and this soldier leapt out of the way. I thought it would be a really good idea for me to try that with a car – especially as I happened to have very strong tendons in my feet through doing the 'awkward posture' of Bikram Yoga. That week I was going to a sales meeting with Honda in Swindon, which makes a lot of four-wheel drives, and on the way I stopped off in Farnham Common Post Office, I think that it was. I realized that I was running a bit late so I accelerated up to about 8 miles per hour back to my car. Unfortunately a four-wheel drive car came out of a hidden entrance to a shoppers' car park – also at about 8 miles per hour – at 90 degrees. In a split second I realized that at a combined trajectory of around 12 miles per hour (because of the side angle), there was no way that I could avoid impact. So I leapt into the air and, like a ninja warrior, I bounced off using my bottom on the car bonnet and I landed perfectly on my hind feet. My words were: 'I have been hit by a four-wheel drive – but look! Just a scratch – no real damage!'

Deborah:
That's very specific to you!

Which was a polite way of saying that I often use examples from my personal life to illustrate the use and applicability of strategic thinking, and that this was a little whacky. While this particular example seems somewhat extreme it actually did happen and could have been a very serious situation had I not practised strategic thinking as I did. People certainly remember it.

Tony:
When you were at Legal Complaints I think that you got to use the idea of scenarios.

Deborah:
Yes, we did. And that was incredibly useful in dealing with that redundancy situation, because the managers were committed to the organization and put their own future on the back burner. But by taking time out of the business to look at what was going to be happening to them next, and how they could best prepare for that change, to give an investment in that, it enabled them to perform better in their job as a manager. Then there isn't that thing in the back of their mind that would keep them awake at night. Quite often

in someone's life there is something that they should be doing but they are not – if you can focus on that with them that is very helpful.

Strategy implementation and change management

Tony:
Many of the books focus on the problem of turning a strategic plan into a reality – the curse of implementation. Is that something that you feel is bad or maybe not?

Deborah:
It has never seemed to have been a big issue. We are always planning for something that is going to happen, so implementation hasn't been so much of a choice which, perhaps, puts us in a different environment to where you are maybe making proactive decisions to do something unusual like launching a new product.

Tony:
Or change management.

Deborah:
We have done a lot of that, change management. Again, it was a road to go down.

Tony:
But you still did it. A lot of change management is about tackling the more difficult aspects of the strategy.

Deborah:
Well, maybe that's true but I have never seen in your strategy an option to jump off and not see it through to the end. We have never sat and looked at a strategy and asked, 'Well shall we or shan't we?' Once you have done the thinking then you start to do it.

Tony:
It's not an analytical problem then, it sounds like?

Deborah:
It's a leadership issue, as to whether people are hesitant there. But if you have done the thinking properly then you can see it through to the end and you are not going to be hesitant about it.

Tony:
So to blame the strategy for the implementation issue is probably not the problem, it is not the strategic thinking.

I must say that what Deborah says here is pretty obvious: there is so much written in the strategy literature emphasizing the problem of strategy implementation that one is left thinking that this is an inevitable constraint. Deborah reminds us that much if not all of this is due to leadership/commitment failure. Obviously in very large, hierarchical and complex organizations there are likely to be other process and stakeholder issues but these should be manageable if leadership and commitment are aligned.

Deborah:

It's about getting the right strategy so that you can actually do it and then about the leadership to see it through. But there is nothing wrong if you try something and if it is not working to sit down and think why, and then flex your strategy. If something doesn't work immediately it shouldn't be the reason to stop. If people are expecting perfection they won't get it.

As an example, we obviously did a massive redundancy exercise (at Legal Complaints), but we didn't do it all in one go; it was phased. The first time we did it we learnt lessons. We got all the staff in the same room and we told them all at once and it obviously wasn't a surprise, but no one was expecting it to be happening that day. What we learnt from that was that there would be value in telling the managers that the message was coming in their area, so that they were equipped to deal with their teams. Because if they discover the news at the same time as their teams they would then be processing it from their point of view and coming to terms with it at the same time, and they were not necessarily able to give their team members the support and counselling they might need. So we instantly thought 'we could do this better' the second time round.

So the second time round we called all the team leaders the night before and said, 'Look, this is what we will be telling you, so that you are in a position where you are able to assist tomorrow.' That was a big improvement. You don't have to stick to exactly what you have decided. You are constantly improving it.

Tony:

If you were having what I call a 'strategic amnesia' and went back in time, what were the processes that could have been used… this whole thing about 'What is the one big thing I have forgotten?' When that happens to me I think, 'My God, I don't think that I asked that question. At least of I had asked that question then maybe I would have got that.' Maybe this is unfair to do that, but just for the readers it may be worth raising that.

Deborah:

Well that's a really good question. But again you can't necessarily see it sometimes. So the one big thing that we forgot was that the staff would look to their team leaders for their emotional support, and that you have got to ensure that the team leaders are in an emotional place where they can deal with it themselves.

Now I know a lot of organizations that are almost on the verge of doing redundancies by e-mail and text and staying as far away from people as possible, whereas actually we found that it was the personal relationships that made a redundancy scenario a lot more healthy, because we wanted every member of staff to feel valued and not to feel that it was a personal reflection because the whole organization was closing down. So we looked at it from the point of view of staff health; we wanted them all to perform until the day we shut. It was a sensible decision to make.

Tony:
Yes, it was a very tough stage for you.

That reminds me of another tough situation when, I think it was in the second workshop in Spring, where we were looking at some changes you were going to make, was it around some website or something? Some stakeholder issues that came up that were semi-visible and when we examined them they changed the way you were going to do that. Do you recall?

Deborah:
Yes, we have a members' forum (online) where the discussions are very free-ranging, and some of those discussions would have been much better in a private arena than in a public forum, so when we analysed it one of the changes we decided was to introduce pre-moderation, which meant that we would look at each posting before it went on, and where there was a posting that was more suitable with the Chief Executive or with the Executive Committee it went to the appropriate place. And this avoided the problem with calls on the forum for the Chief Executive to come and respond, which is very hard when you are out of the office for perhaps several days at a time, and obviously discussions on electronic blogs are fast moving.

So it was a very positive change. It meant that conversations were happening in the right place, and we only saw that by having the time to sit down and think it through, and to think about what impact it would potentially have.

Tony:
There was something about the sensitivity of your original way of doing it.

Recalling that we discussed the stakeholder issues at length on that issue and did some 'out-of-body experience' type of thinking.

Deborah:
Well, we were concerned that the members would feel that perhaps we didn't want them to speak as freely, even though they were able to speak as freely

as before: it was just different avenues for choices. In reality they have been quite happy with the options, because actually they are still getting replies but we have just defined separate routes, one leading to management discussion and one leading to members' discussion. So it was a really positive change. It was really about thinking through the handling of the change.

Tony:
So it was about thinking strategically about the implementation, where one might argue that there should be as much thinking about the how, rather than in the bigger formulation picture.

Doing it in practice

Tony:
In terms of any other, really important insights that we can give the readers, we have looked at what it feels like to do it, what value it has, its processes, the things that help and the things that get in its way, things that block success, uncertainty, tools, training, spending time (on it), enjoying the process.... What other things would you say to someone who is perhaps just starting to make that transition into strategic leadership: how do they start to do this with their team, get themselves more skilled in this? I am trying to think of the sort of things that might occur to you as someone involved in strategic thinking.

Deborah:
Well, the best way to start is firstly to pick your topic: what is it that you need to think strategically about? And there is going to be a myriad of options, but just pick a topic: it could be about getting a better relationship with other stakeholders. So, if you wanted to look at something like that then you would sit down and get everyone round the table, and if you were a new CEO you would get the benefit of their experience and in that scenario, they would have known those people longer and they would chip in and answer on what has happened in the past. Then you can start thinking about what has happened differently, and you can get lots of options and then you analyse those options.

Beforehand you need to pick up a couple of models and decide when to use them. And you need to be careful that you team can keep up with you, so that you don't run at a million miles an hour. Make sure that everyone is on board, and then just see where it gets to. There is not necessarily going to be any wrong answer. But just see where the team takes that decision. You need to avoid anyone being overly dominant because you don't want any conflict in this; just see what happens, and I think that they will all be pleasantly surprised.

Tony:
So, basically, you need a process and you need that step-by-step, to create the right conditions (for thinking), and just be open.

Deborah:
Yes, just be open, literally: take a leap of faith and see what comes out, and if you are concerned then start with something small.

Tony:
Pilot it.

Deborah:
Yeah. Just see whether you are getting quality output or not, and if it doesn't work and some of the team aren't sure and don't know where to go then you need to start with some training. But I have always found it amazing that staff can contribute to this as long as they feel comfortable, as long as you don't put pressure on them.

Tony:
An odd question occurred to me. I absolutely loved that hotel that we went to – it may be a minor thing, but I think that it just finished the job off, because it was so comfortable, it was so nice, I thought that just put the icing on it. Do you think that….

Deborah:
I like to take the staff out for the day, particularly for strategic thinking. We take all of the staff out to a slightly bigger hotel once a year to talk through the business plan, the budget and the like, but taking the management somewhere out of the office so they are not rushing back to their desk, it puts you in a different mindset: you know that you are supposed to be acting and thinking differently, and you do need to get a comfortable and relaxing environment, soft settees and all that kind of stuff, so make it somewhere nice. It is all part of that different mindset.

Tony:
I must say that there was an overwhelming over-supply of deserts, but that was fantastic, it sent a signal.

Deborah:
It was. The biggest vote goes for starting the day with bacon sandwiches – that's the real win.

Tony:
Bacon, yeah, yeah.

Deborah:

But it's that sort of thing that makes it a fun day.

Tony:

So you start up grounded in bacon and end up in enormous cakes.

Deborah:

Particularly as the first time that you do it you are going to be a bit nervous, so you need the ice-breakers such as the bacon cobs; that is interesting. You can get these very flat, boring conference rooms but you might feel on edge in there.

Tony:

Deborah, thank so much for this hour: that's given so much but I have also been given a new idea, the idea of 'strategic cuisine' – that's the 'one big thing that I missed' in *Demystifying Strategy*.

Deborah:

Yes, 'Management-by-chocolate'.

Tony:

Wonderful!

> **CONCLUSIONS**
>
> Deborah has given us an excellent account of the issues involved in dealing with acute uncertainty and also change in two very dynamic organizations that while not being fully 'commercial' have a lot of those pressures and a myriad of stakeholder interests. Her contribution to our understanding of the practicalities of strategic thinking is considerable and some key points that we can take away from this are:
>
> - Don't just do strategic thinking alone – do it as a group.
> - Apply the idea of the 'uncertainty gap'.
> - Storytell the future using scenarios to help close that gap.
> - Where there is a lot of residual uncertainty, use the idea of the 'contingent strategy'.
> - Do a lot of stakeholder analysis, ongoing.
> - Use the strategic option grid – create options.

- Understand why you are doing things.
- Concentrate on a few tools you find most useful.
- Make it playful and draw pictures: switch on the right brain.
- Do some training first.
- Don't look for excuses in implementation.
- The end product is likely to be very valuable indeed – you are not wasting your time.
- Break it down into chunks.
- The CEO must spend a lot of time on it.
- Even very difficult dilemmas and uncertainties can be resolved and at least partly dissolved.
- Create a congenial climate and environment for it, attending to little things like the bacon baps!

Having completed our second case on CEOs' takes on strategic thinking we now move to a pure not-for profit organization in the form of the Samaritans.

04 Samaritans

Introduction

Our next case study is from an interview with Catherine Johnstone, CEO of Samaritans. Samaritans, based in Ewell, Surrey, in the United Kingdom, has a remit that is essentially to discourage people from taking their own lives. It was founded in 1953 and is a not-for-profit organization.

As in the other cases this one is very wide-ranging in terms of strategic thinking themes, spanning:

- organizational context;
- planning time horizons;
- learning to do strategic thinking;
- organizational constraints;
- evidence-based planning;
- planning processes;
- emergent strategic thinking;
- playful strategic thinking;
- stakeholder involvement;
- strategy communication;
- strategic training;
- helicopter thinking;
- avoiding jargon;
- 'strategic excitement'.

This case study is especially interesting as Catherine gives us rich insights into the very special factors that come into play in doing strategic thinking in the not-for-profit sector. Here, organizational objectives are much more complex than in a strictly commercial setting, where they tend to focus on the financial side. Also, there is a very wide set of stakeholders whose interests need to be thought through. Finally, the definition of 'what business we are in' is much more fluid and keeping a focus while at the same time developing and growing the organizational model is a key balance to maintain. Samaritans' situation is very similar to the International Paralympics Committee and also has some parallels with the legal organization, APIL.

After a 10-mile drive across South London I began by explaining to Catherine that my inspiration to contact Samaritans was partially because my wife, Carolina, works with severely traumatized clients who frequently have suicidal tendencies. This carries a very heavy responsibility – for example when we go on holiday she thinks: 'I do hope that they will be alright when I am away.' Samaritans exists to be available 24/7 to offer a safety net for people who are struggling to cope for whatever reason. It was set up in 1953 and now has over 20,000 unpaid frontline volunteers who work in shifts to listen to the problems of those whom are feeling emotionally distressed and potentially suicidal.

Organizational context

Tony:
So where do you want to start?

Catherine:
Depending on what organization I am the CEO of, I have to define strategy and strategic approaches in a slightly different way. For me, changing the way an organization works, changing its approach, is about looking at establishing: 'This is what the beneficiaries need from us, that's our market, our market segmentation is this, the organization strategically needs to position itself here, and it needs to follow these areas of work.'

Tony:
So what is your starting point on this?

Catherine:
Organizations approach strategy development very differently. Some don't have a strategy, some organizations choose not to have a strategy, and they deliver. Others choose to have a published strategy; they say to the outside world: 'This is who we are; this is what stakeholders can expect from us.' So if I had my way I would always ask the organization to publish some form of strategy document, because it is important for our beneficiaries, donors and other stakeholders to understand who we are, what we do, how we do it, and what you can expect from us.

My preferred model is to go the whole hog and to consult within the organization on the strategy, so that the organization has ownership. At Samaritans I have got more than 20,000 stakeholders, so that's an awful lot of people who can get behind the strategy but equally it would be very difficult if they think that the strategy is rubbish.

Tony:
There's quite a scale to this organization. I am sat here in your offices, and we have got the sound of water going, the mill at the back – which is very good for (drowning) my tinnitus as background noise; you turn up in the

car park and you wouldn't think that there are all these massive organizational tentacles going out all around the country doing stuff, and hopefully minimizing the risk of suicide from this (smallish) office.

When designing a strategy process there needs to be a hard look not just at the strategic agenda and the issues it faces, but also at the organization's structure, culture, processes, capabilities, its mindset and its adaptability.

Catherine:

Samaritans is 60 years old this year and it is still bang on the mission that it set out with – to reduce suicide. It is a federated charity, so it has a central charity, and it has 201 branches that are all affiliated to the centre, all called Samaritans.

We have a 'strategy', a document, which means that all the 202 charities in the federation deliver our core services as one organization. My job as Chief Executive is to coordinate all the 202 charities to deliver with one voice through volunteer effort (21,000 volunteers), day-to day service from those centres, and a range of other services to include work in settings such as prisons, the railways and local communities. These services are provided across a whole range of channels to include telephone, SMS, e-mail, letter, face-to-face.

Suicide is quite a 'scientific event': people generally think that it is a random act. There is a lot of research and evidence that gives us huge insight into suicide prevention and the risk factors.

We do a lot of different forms of work, for example with big companies where there has been a high profile suicide, or with celebrities, and we are often the organization working with the family and friends. That's the stuff that people don't know goes on at Samaritans.

Tony:

How many suicides are there a year (in the UK)?

Catherine:

In the UK there are about 6,500 suicides per year. However, there is not an even geographic spread across the UK so it is important to understand the reasons for higher incidence of suicide in certain locations or settings in terms of taking a lead to reduce suicide.

I was wondering at this point what the lost economic value to society the 6,500 suicides a year represent. If the economic value of the average life were, say, half a million pounds (that would need unpacking in terms of the inherent value of a life and the effects on others of a suicide) – assuming that you could ever value a life – then the value destroyed each year would be of the order of £3 billion.

Tony:
In effect, you are defining 'what business are we in', and you are trying to do that (prevent suicides) but in fact all the activities around that could be quite diverse.

Planning timescales

Catherine:
That's why it is really important for the Samaritans to have a published strategy as it does. We are currently working on a six-year strategy. That's the other thing that I have learnt: don't ever write a three-year strategy – it should be a six-year strategy.

Tony:
So what's wrong with a three-year strategy?

Catherine:
Three years is too short and too quick. Again there is a scale issue here organizationally, but if you are trying to run a large organization, whether it is not-for-profit or not, by the time you have consulted on it and written it, with three-year time horizons you almost have to start again with the next strategy.

The first year is about everyone going, 'Oh look, we all have a strategy.' The second year (of activity) you usually get some quite good work going on, it is all bedded down, you might have all the funding in place, and have done the more creative stuff. And in the third year you are then looking at what you will get done in the next year of the strategy. So (at that point) you are forced to go into the strategy cycle again.

This raised thoughts in my head as to the impact of the inherent lags in an organization that make it hard to go through a cycle of issue recognition and diagnosis, options, planning, evaluation and justification, stakeholder management, mobilization and implementation. In some organizations these in-built lags might be much longer, and perhaps this is a characteristic of the not-for-profit sector: this raises the issue not just of the optimal planning horizon but whether these lags can be shortened. Clearly there are choices here in adopting timescales for plans, which are affected by the foreseeability of the external environment and the time horizons of investment decisions, and in strategy dissemination and organizational change lead times.

Learning to do strategic thinking

Tony:
Who should steer the development of the strategy?

Catherine:
So, that's one of the other things, coming to your last question. It's kind of: don't think that you have to follow what's in the book. Lots of people make lots of money doing strategic planning in organizations. I actually think that you should learn how to do it yourself. The chief executive shouldn't be allowed to be the chief executive unless he or she understands planning. You can't understand how to run an organization unless you understand how to do planning. By all means have people in your senior teams, or have a consultant to do the development of the strategy but for heavens' sake sort out what it is you are trying to do first. I think that it is imperative that the CEO as a key leader of an organization must know where the organization is trying to get to otherwise mission drift, wasted resources, frustrated staff, volunteers and stakeholders have a high degree of probability.

I made that choice as a CEO: I had to go and make sure that I understood what the nuances and the options were and what sort of skill-sets would be good at planning, and what wouldn't. For instance, I am quite good at identifying whether someone is good at strategic planning, operational planning, or financial planning, and they are three different skill-sets. At chief executive level, because you have to oversee the budgets, you have to be reasonably good at financial planning and understand it. You should really be good at the strategy stuff because otherwise what are you doing advising the board? And regarding the operational planning, I just need to know once the strategy is done, what we need to do to translate that into what I call a 'corporate plan'.

My own initial training was in finance, and before my MBA I very much saw strategic plans as extended financial budgets with a SWOT analysis stuck onto it to incorporate some non-financial factors. But this doesn't tell you how you are going to accomplish the plan in any kind of novel or effective way, let alone in a 'cunning' way. Where the task of developing a strategic plan is given to what I often call 'escaped accountants' (as I was once one myself) it will be doomed to being average. Catherine clearly discriminates here between a range of quite diverse skills associated with 'planning'.

Organizational constraints

Tony:
There's a charity I once worked with where there was great potential for growth – beyond what they had ever imagined prior to doing a strategic workshop.

Catherine:

Samaritans has that potential to continue to grow and develop its services but the issue is about how you are going to grow Samaritans using volunteer effort. This has to be done very, very carefully, because you can't tell volunteers that you are taking on a new project and therefore instead of four shifts a month you need to do five.

We have grown a lot. Increasing the reach of the service is very possible. We are very keen to do that, but the caveat has to be that it is done within a big capacity and capability assessment and an impact assessment of what the demand is likely to be, and what it might do to other services.

In my book Value-based Human Resources Strategy *(2003a), I emphasized the two-way and interactive role that HR strategy (or as I would prefer to call it, 'organization strategy') should play in supporting the external (competitive) strategy and in enabling new strategy development in its own right. Both of these might open up 'lines of enquiry' for Samaritans.*

Tony:

In the strategy books there is very little mention of the most limiting constraint. There was a book written a few years ago by Goldratt, called *The Theory of Constraints*, which made the very simple point that you should address the most limiting constraint first, like in an exam where you do the hardest question first.

Catherine:

Because when you do that, then, the rest just flows.

Also I say (to myself) pick your battles carefully. Just because an organization has the potential to do something really exciting, (that) doesn't mean that's right. If it is culturally abhorrent to the organization or it is generally going to be a real fight to get everyone to agree that it's a good idea, it may be better to present a different option, to do some development work on it for a period of time to warm everybody up for a later time.

Unsurprisingly, as we saw in our first two case studies, it is crucial to see strategic thinking embracing strategic influencing and stakeholder management.

Catherine:

Before we wrote the strategy we actually did a lot of research. We looked at what people thought about Samaritans' services, so in setting a direction for the strategy the trustees had to come together to approve an evidence base. That said, the board thinks that these are all really important things that Samaritans should be focusing on.

I found it interesting that Catherine was using the idea of 'evidence base' as a key part of strategic thinking. Clearly this is the same thing as the long-standing notion in strategy development that you need to find out your current position; add to that the need to collect data on strategic trends and discontinuities. We see particular emphasis on this at Moonpig, APIL and at IPC.

Tony:
So, what is 'strategic thinking?'

Catherine:
I have got that it is the 'bigger picture', it is focused on the beneficiaries; it requires some research to underpin the creation of a strategy. (You should) do it over a longer period than three years, because in my view, just over three years has never worked. Don't get bogged down with the jargon. Learn to do it yourself first before you start to get others to do it for you so at least you don't get ripped off, or get taken down avenues that are not appropriate. If you choose to bring in additional support for your strategy development you must stay at the forefront of this development and maintain oversight.

So how do you know when you are doing it? Well in an organization the size of Samaritans, you are never in any doubt (laughing) that you are doing it – if you are. Samaritans is a very operational frontline service charity and I think that it is easier to put that delineation between when you are doing operational and strategic, because we are doing operational all the time. Operational things change and there is a service day and night and there is always a lot of effort going into that going on.

Planning processes

Catherine:
At Samaritans we plan to do strategy systematically and have an ongoing schedule. The board has a strategy away-day annually and we agree at the beginning of the year what that is going to focus on. The board's annual strategy day is always externally facilitated to enable a degree of objectivity and the senior management team are full participants in the day.

So because of the operational nature of the organization strategic planning has to be scheduled in.

Tony:
Do you find that that is enough time to cover all of the material?

Catherine:
At Samaritans we have a variety of approaches but for all strategic planning we avoid ad hoc discussions and decisions. Increasingly we start with an evidence base and a clear idea of what we are trying to achieve.

So for instance I try to present early concepts and ideas (warm-up), well in advance of strategy decisions being required. The worst decisions in my experience is a board having big strategic issues bounced in on them and you have not got enough time to understand the strategic issues and the implications of them to make sensible decisions.

So *Catherine stresses the need to 'ease into' strategic thinking on more complex issues – it can't just be switched on.*

Catherine:
So at the beginning of every board meeting there is a session about strategic issues so sometimes there are three items, sometimes there are three papers, or they might be only one paper.

Tony:
So they normally have between one and three issues. Why is that the magic number three?

Catherine:
I think because we all have got a limited attention span and you also have a limited ability to take on new information in a constrained period of time.

Tony:
So it is a cognitive constraint?

Catherine:
Yes, it is a cognitive constraint.

Tony:
Well that's interesting because in Hoshin, or breakthrough thinking, you don't try to do more than three really big things at any one time (Grundy, 1995). And that goes back to Miller's Law of 'five plus or minus two', which means that if the average person can just about hold five things in his or her mind at any one time, a genius would hold seven, and a not so bright person, three. As organizations and teams are collectively more limited cognitively than a single individual, you have to go for just three.

It would seem from this that Catherine has apparently arrived at Miller's Law quite independently. This is reassuring in the sense that it shows that CEOs frequently discover for themselves what is best practice. But the fact that this tends to occur through serendipity might also a bit concerning at a general level as it is very much a 'hit and miss approach'.

Catherine:
In terms of planning, if you talk to my executive team, they can tell you what they need for their areas in terms of strategic issues and decisions, at least six months or even a year in advance. If you go into their rooms they have

whiteboards like mine. It is much calmer as the leadership team know what needs to be planned and agreed in advance and therefore the preparation of papers is an ongoing planned process.

In Demystifying Strategy *these are called 'strategic position papers'.*

Tony:
So it is a continuing, rolling process.

Emergent strategic thinking

Tony:
It could sound from the outside as if we are still taking a lot about strategic planning (primarily). There is obviously strategic thinking going on but is there strategic thinking that transcends, or happens in moments when you are parking your car, for example?

Here I was trying to get us to think about the different ways strategic thinking can set itself off – not just as part of a 'deliberate' process, but also as an 'emergent one' especially as so far we had focused most on the deliberate variety. Having started us off with the more tangible and formal processes of strategic planning Catherine is now moving into more fluid territory commonly associated with strategic thinking.

Catherine:
Oh God yes, all the time, yes. I will be at a meeting or at an event and I will think: 'Oh that's really interesting' or, 'I haven't thought about that strategically from that perspective.'

Tony:
So do you actually identify that specifically as a strategic thought? Do you label it as a 'strategic thought'?

Catherine:
Yes (in a serious tone). It has got a light bulb with it: I think 'Oh'.

This sounds like a particular kind of thought process where a single new thought that connects other thoughts which were separate comes suddenly and intuitively – similar to an 'Ah Ha' moment, but that is slightly different as that is more diagnosis than synthesis.

Catherine:
So I think: we need to think about that at some point, where in the strategy can I get it into? What is it akin to? Is there something else that is going to the board in the next six months that I can attach it to, or is it new? Like the online stuff is completely new but it came out of an opportunity, so you don't want to pass the opportunity up. You don't want to be marking time while you preposition it.

The daily routine of a CEO can make it hard to get a good run at strategic thinking on an issue because of its fragmentation.

Catherine:
If you are a chief executive, you are never not busy, so I work quite hard to reflect on how well we are doing, assimilating all the things that come across my desk, because I could be doing this interview with you now, and I have got a telecon at 4 o'clock with our biggest project provider, and then I have got to review the latest draft of the corporate plan that is going to the board on Friday, with all the associated budgets. In any one day I have mixed up strategy, operational delivery, fire fighting, media and external engagements.

Tony:
Even in that meeting tonight there might well be some strategic thinking.

Catherine:
Yes, there could be, the strategic issues come up all the time and the trick is to recognize them as exactly that – strategic issues.

I have always been fascinated in the impact that management style has on strategic thinking: most senior managers dash from meeting to meeting and when they are not doing that they are machine gunning each other with e-mails. Managers taking time to actually reflect are very rare sights. When becoming a CEO they will typically find it hard to disengage and step back from functional/operational concerns and adjust to a role of conductor rather than instrument player in the management orchestra. Yet Catherine seems to have learnt the knack of maintaining a state of strategic mindfulness wherever and on whatever she is working on, which is quite a skill. From my experience of coaching senior directors, this is at least a partially learnt skill: it has to be deliberately acquired and continually worked on.

Tony:
Deborah Evans (of APIL) was able to come up with the percentage of time that she spends on strategic thinking; I was surprised that she could do so.

Catherine:
I would probably say on the combination of strategy development, implementation and thinking it is about 30 per cent of my time.

This was almost identical to the APIL CEO's estimate of the proportion of time that she took.

Tony:
In terms of implementation, is there strategic thinking there?

Catherine:

Oh (laughing) yeah. Sitting beneath that organizational strategy we have a plan that picks up on all of the inputs for the delivery of the strategy. So that plan has five major outcomes, which synthesize down to the five key things and then sitting beneath that are a range of projects which contribute towards delivering those outcomes. So it is a hierarchy, yes. That's the way it works.

Having a hierarchy of strategies or of strategic questions (as at Moonpig) does seem to be a common element in CEO thinking about strategy.

Catherine:

You have to think strategically about the implementation of anything you do, because there will always be a strategic element.

Tony:

How much do you think the demand for your services has gone up?

Catherine:

We estimate approximately 30 per cent but it is difficult to be precise due to the nature of our service delivery.

Tony:

Wow! Government, are you listening?

Playful strategic thinking

Tony:

Sweeping up the other things on the agenda, what is the value of strategic thinking?

Catherine:

The value, tangible and less tangible… I think that the value is self-evident. We have got 20,000 people who understand the journey we are on, my volunteers understand the 'new look' Samaritans; it is based on an evidence base from callers. So there are loads of tangible outputs from a strategy that people understand and subscribe to.

I think that the less tangible thing is where someone is confused in thinking that a strategic discussion is where it is blue-sky thinking or where they think that it is just Catherine thinking outside the box: you know (they are thinking), let her just play over there. Again you have to be quite mindful to make sure that you have the strategic conversations; you have to flag this is 'strategic': it is a strategic paper, there are implications therefore for the organization, otherwise if you don't you will find that in six months' time that people say 'Oh, we thought that you were having a bit of the 'out-of-the-box moment'. That's where it is less tangible.

There are hints here of differences in cognitive style that the top echelons of an organization bring to their strategic debates – we will see this too with Des Benjamin, CEO of Simplyhealth later, where you have a naturally visionary CEO and some of the board share that style but others are more operational and 'now' focused: a mix is needed but that mix needs managing.

Tony:

Deborah Evans of APIL majored on the playfulness of strategic thinking. But that is not to say that it (strategic thinking) is not about the real world.

Catherine:

Oh, absolutely, it *is* about the real world! And for us it is *really serious*, because, if we get our strategy wrong, *people can die*! If we design a project that goes wrong then potentially more people will die.

What I do use strategy for is to get the whole organization to come back together as one organization: if there is something that we are going to do and suddenly people are not liking it, I will often stand up and say: 'Hang on, this is what we agreed, and you were consulted…'.

Stakeholder involvement

Tony:

How would you do your job without strategic thinking?

Catherine:

Having a strategy allows people to do what needs to be done, define ourselves better, and to broaden horizons…. But what the strategy has done is to harness the whole organization in the same direction. Without strategic parameters I would be sunk.

We would never do anything new. But ultimately one of the biggest challenges is to stay relevant, particularly in terms of its channels, because the younger population use the phone but they text, they e-mail, and if they want a conversation they go on Facebook: increasingly they don't actually talk in the traditional sense!

Tony:

Do you think people need to be trained in it?

Catherine:

I think it is all pretty straightforward. It is not so much the training in doing it; it is getting people to see the benefits as well for the beneficiaries, because that is actually the motivator for a chief exec and senior teams to spend time on it, because why would anyone do anything if there's not a difference to the beneficiaries, because you are just turning out a strategy. If you don't focus on the beneficiaries it is going to be a miserable experience.

Strategic training

Tony:

Yes, in some ways strategic planning can sometimes be a bit like having a Christmas tree. I saw a dead one outside just lying around. I was trying to park and there was this dead Christmas tree lying in my way and I just couldn't get round it. It is just like a strategy: they have one once a year and unless you are real Christian it's just a bit of decoration.

Catherine:

You have to recognize that there are different types of skills needed for different kinds of strategy. I have worked with people who can produce a strategic budget but fall on their face in a strategy plan. It is fantastic: all the numbers add up and all the Is are dotted, but actually, 'Does it relate to the strategy?' You need to get the right people to do the right parts of that production, and actually you need your own head-space. If you don't think about it, it doesn't work. Therefore that strategic thinking thing is really important.

Tony:

Is it any different, then, from just the thinking, or is it strategic thinking?

Catherine:

I can think about multiple things but if I want to think about really important stuff – that is about changes in directions, the future, potential challenges, issues – I actually have to have a quiet space, for instance on a Friday morning when I am working at home I will turn the phone off, and I will sit down with my pad of paper and ask, 'Why is this bothering me?' and I will draw visuals, because you can put as many things as you like in a picture.

I use pictures, yes. And it might not be every Friday but I know, when I have got lots of things in my head, that I have got to do it.

Helicopter thinking

Tony:

When I was at Cranfield and used to do an awful lot of executive development, I used to call it 'helicopter time' or 'helicopter vision'.

Catherine:

It is; that's why I have a helicopter on the desk.

Tony:

I had one! I was thinking of getting one of those that take off, but people would be worried about the health and safety issues of flying it around their atriums.

Catherine:

In my experience executives can *hate* that helicopter at times. They come to me with all kinds of stuff and I will pick the helicopter up and I will stick it on the table: and say to them: 'You tell me what your strategic issues are and I will go away and work on them.'

In a busy frontline charity such as Samaritans it is very easy to get sucked into the operational delivery and finding time as an executive team to focus on strategy can be very challenging.

I wish that I had asked Catherine why they hated that helicopter (we were running out of time): her take on that subsequently was that they are 'very pressed for time delivering against the existing strategy and keeping the show on the road in a 24/7 service'.

Tony:

I used to also use pictures of a man with his head down a rabbit hole to emphasize that we should be doing 'helicopter thinking', rather than going down the rabbit holes.

Catherine:

Well, you can just drop in a cartoon. Or I use a lot of 'Yes, Ministers': I do that with my chair. Yes, humour is important.

Catherine:

It's (about) finding a different head-space; get the views of all the people around you, don't get sucked into the jargon. But, you know, you can swallow as many management books as you like, but....

Tony:

Would you see 'competences' as jargon?

Catherine:

No.

Tony:

Would you see 'resource-based theory of competitive advantage' as jargon?

Catherine:

Yes, I think I would. What I mean by jargon is: don't use it, I might understand it and you understand it, but the people who you are working with may not understand it.

Catherine:

We had an example of someone who used 'boiler plate' in a technical project and we spent 40 minutes in this steering group meeting before one of the volunteers asked, 'What does "boiler plate" mean?' Don't use it (jargon) because it slows things up, people feel inferior (echoing Nick Jenkins, CEO of Moonpig).

(Also) don't have multiple strategies and don't use terms like 'competitor analysis'; for me, always use plain English and boil it down. I know what 'competitor analysis' means and half of my trustees would know what it means.... For example, in a recent initiative we tried to imagine which of the charities would like to sit in the hot seat and coordinate it, so we said we needed to look at the 'competitive nature' of the charity sector. We needed to look at where the challenges will come from these agencies, so therefore I wanted to do a little work on that; that's actually 'competitive analysis'. But then if I had gone in and said it was going to be 'competitor analysis', I would have lost everyone.

'Strategic excitement'

Catherine:

So, in summary, don't use too much jargon and don't get too carried away with yourself. I come up with some *fantastic* initiatives, but I have learnt to live with my excitement, and I actually try not to get people too excited before I work out whether it is fair to introduce that into the thinking. I and my executive throw these things around for some time before we get anybody else involved.

I found that a particularly interesting comment as I have observed in strategic workshops that sometimes managers will experience a 'strategic high' and come up with the elements of an idea, sometimes successfully shaped in a strategy and sometimes just part of one. The effect can die away rather rapidly and nothing ever really gets decided or implemented. Managers not involved in the process may be alienated. These sessions thus generate some interesting cognitive and emotional dynamics buoyed up by endorphins from the creative process. Perhaps a naturally visionary CEO must control the release of endorphins rather than get carried on a high not shared by more operational colleagues. In the world of meditation practice it is taught that we should make sure that when we return from very high energetic spaces we 'ground ourselves': absolutely the same thing needs to happen in strategic thinking.

Catherine:

Before I came to Samaritans I probably wasn't that good at it (strategic thinking), because I would be so focused on the stuff that I knew we were doing, not what we weren't doing: the stuff that was off-the-page, I didn't necessarily spend much time about what we should or might be doing.

Because we are such a frontline organization there is so much stuff all the time, all the time we are scanning the horizon. So here I have been forced into that (strategic discipline) and I like to be focused. So that constantly being dragged away (by operational issues)... I now force myself to be constantly dragged away to look outside the page but it is not my natural trait.

I am reasonably good at strategic planning and I can assimilate the evidence as I am good at that, all those peripheral things that we should be thinking about, but doing it on a regular basis. I have done it much better here than anywhere else but I think that some of this stuff comes with experience and, dare I say it, age.

CONCLUSIONS

Catherine has given us a very rich account not only of how she tackles strategic thinking but also how that nests within the strategic planning process in Samaritans and within not-for-profit organizations generally. She has given us insights into her visionary cognitive style which she applies in a very pragmatic and grounded way in the cause of preventing suicides.

By her own account, without the focus put on strategic thinking it would be very difficult to manage an organization of its size, especially as it is growing and becoming more complex. It is certainly not just 'a nice thing to do'. Even though there are great pressures and temptations to become absorbed in the operational, she deploys an impressive proportion of her time in that direction.

Catherine has put in place a clear strategic architecture, including vision and strategies for Samaritans, which is then supported by a quite solid and tangible strategic programme. This is all anchored in research and position papers and has a set process. But alongside all of that 'strategic thinking' is what stimulates it and moves it forward, in fluid and at times emergent ways. If the strategic plan were seen as the 'car' then strategic thinking would be both the oil and the petrol.

Catherine has given us many insights of great value, particularly:

- Design your strategy process not just around the strategic agenda/issues but for the organizational context.

- Publish your strategy to the key stakeholders: get its content right and pre-owned, first.

- Don't just make the time horizon three years: think about the range options you could go for and their pros and cons.
- If there are long lags in the process to release its value, why are these there and how can they be reduced?
- Resource and organizational constraints are a strategic issue: there may well be options for challenging them.
- Assess the economic value of the strategy.
- There are huge differences between the styles and types of planning skills: remember it takes all sorts and manage the mix. Some are very analytical or practical, some intuitive, and some creative and visionary.
- Learn to do it yourself before buying in skills, either planners or consultants.
- The strategy must be properly based on evidence.
- Limit the jargon to what people know or can grasp.
- Hold strategy events, have enough of them, and get them professionally facilitated.
- At strategic meetings don't try to deal with more than three issues/decisions: keep a tight focus of attention and debate.
- Write 'strategic position papers' to prepare the thinking ground, the options, and the supporting evidence base.
- Do enough preparation work on complex issues before starting to debate.
- Don't try to work on an entire strategy at once: make it issue-focused.
- Be alert for 'light bulb' moments.
- Thirty per cent of time spent doing strategic thinking is, at CEO level, appropriate and healthy.
- Don't get too intoxicated with 'strategic excitement': ground it in practical activity and turn ideas into possibilities, prioritize them and then draw up plans.
- Be strategically mindful whatever you are doing in the role of CEO, even when doing tactical stuff.

- Use the analogy of 'helicopter thinking' and any other mechanisms and signals to people to engage more in strategic thinking.
- Senior executives are under a lot of time pressure as they are, a) delivering against the existing strategy, b) overseeing day-to-day operations, and c) being asked to think about and develop future strategies, which can stress them quite a lot and might explain when they may not be bursting with enthusiasm for c.
- Recognize and remember that this may not always be comfortable for others around you.
- Try to think 'off-the page', but be aware that this is not everyone's cup of tea.

Two of the processes in *Demystifying Strategy* that help where buy-in is crucial (over and above stakeholder analysis) are the buying and influencing. These deal with the agenda adjustment process and the process of strategic influencing; see Figures 4.1 and 4.2.

FIGURE 4.1 The buying cycle – the stakeholders (1 of 2)

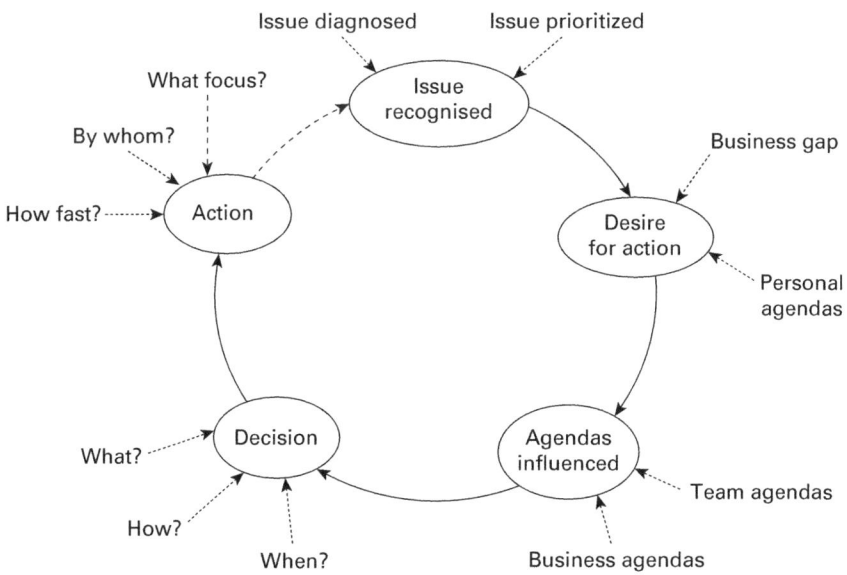

FIGURE 4.2 The influencing cycle – the advisers (2 of 2)

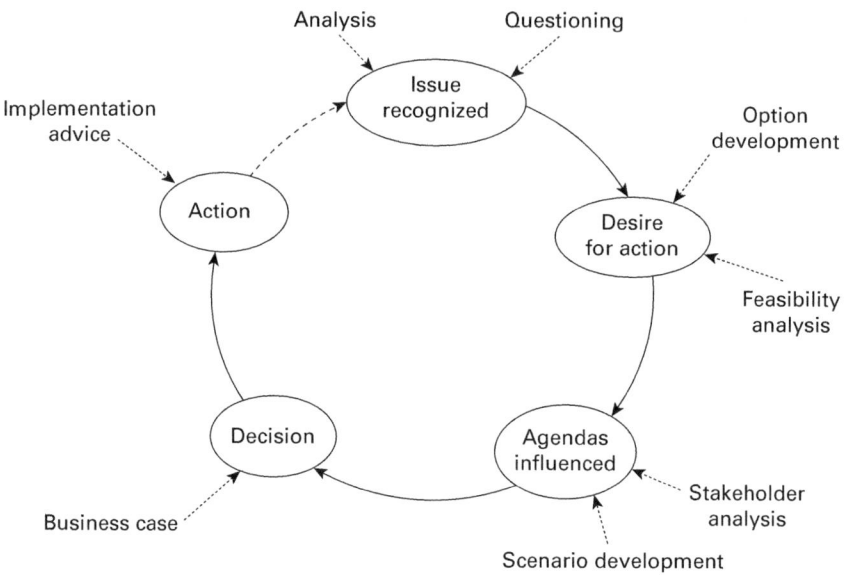

Virgin Galactic   05

Introduction

Virgin Galactic is a very special business. It will be the first 'budget' space flight vehicle with a number of co-passengers. It was inspired by the British entrepreneur Sir Richard Branson who has been responsible for a number of very successful businesses including Virgin Music, Virgin Megastores, Virgin Atlantic (Airline), Virgin Media and Virgin Money. Common themes are that Virgin brought excitement to what were businesses lacking that spark and often not giving customers much of a great deal – and poor service. They were also ones populated by what I might characterize as dead or nearly dead ('zombie') brands.

Branson brought a very fresh brand to these markets, which probably goes back to his cheekiness in the earlier days. About 15 years ago I used to show a really amusing and stimulating video of Branson's early start-ups and deal making – it was called 'The Music Business'. At one point he is interviewed and asked to recall how he broke into the music business. He remembered going to a club over a bar in London. At one point there was a sudden eruption of very heavy music. Branson jumped up and said to his music agent: 'That's amazing – we must sign them – go up there now and get them!' His agent went upstairs and discovered that they were called the Sex Pistols and they had been singing a song with the lyrics 'We are so pretty!' when they were anything but! Unfortunately they were already signed to EMI. Branson rang up the chairman of EMI and said he wanted to buy them: he wasn't successful. Branson closed by saying that if they ever wanted to get rid of that act he would buy them – if they were too crazy for EMI to handle.

A few weeks later (they were beginning to be known by then) they appeared on the 'Bill Grundy Show' (thanks Bill for making my surname a bit famous in the 1970s!). Bill made a lewd comment about how a girl in the band looked. Big mistake! The lead singer of the Sex Pistols led the attack, saying: 'You dirty old ba**ard, you dirty old ba**ard...' and the show ended in chaos. I think that that was its last time on air.

Branson allegedly got a phone call from the chairman of EMI the next morning to say, 'You can have the lot of them.' Branson, in a TV interview, went on to say that while the Sex Pistols didn't go on to sell an awful lot of records, other really good up and coming artists wanted to sign for Virgin as a result of this, rather than his more staid competitors. So that's how Virgin Music got off the ground.

Branson's corporate journey of discovery was very interesting as he was clearly a diversifier – not to spread risks but rather by identifying really great targets to deploy his particular competences on. He has always been very choosy and thus by and large avoids the failures of many diversifiers. He was also prepared to move on when the time was right, always aware of the optimal time cycle over which a business had a great competitive advantage curve and associated with that a positive and strong 'economic value added curve' (see Figure 5.2 later in this chapter). If he could see that these curves were on the wane and/or that he could get a shedload of cash from selling (especially if the buyers didn't quite see those downsides) then he would exit. The music business sold for £1 billion at the peak of its value: Branson was offered $1 billion; he said 'Make it pounds and you have deal'!

Branson, as we will see later, is an instinctive strategic thinker, but he is also one who is supposed to have a team of business analysts with MBAs or accountants to challenge his thinking. In theoretical terms he would have a quite simple vision that would be shaped as an 'emergent strategy' (Grundy, 2012) until it finally became a 'deliberate' one.

As a Virgin business, Virgin Galactic on the surface is a significantly new departure for Branson and Virgin Group as it is really quite high technology (much more than his airline or the trains business) and it carries more risk – safety-wise and commercially – than most if not all of his other operations, although it could be contended that Virgin Rail had some characteristics in common. It shares some of his own passions; indeed Branson is a keen flier: witness his much publicized long-range balloon flight many years ago that ended in the balloon crashing. Will he go up on one of the first space flights? I would think so.

The idea for the space ship came as a result of a competition called the 'X Prize': a pot of money was set up to see who might be able to come up with a potentially viable model for sub-orbital space flight. When the particular technology that won the prize was announced, Branson was captivated by the idea and decided to back it. Virgin Galactic was thus set up in autumn 2004 to achieve that goal.

Virgin Galactic first came to my attention around 2007 when I saw a documentary on it on the BBC's 'Money Programme'. On that programme it was clear that the price, to be paid in advance, would be $200,000. I decided to use the Optopus (see Figure 1.4) to develop new strategic lines of enquiry based on different markets, different customer segments, different ways of adding value to customers, etc. I came up with around 80 options all told – see later. I managed to have a quick meeting with Susan Newsom at Virgin Galactic's then head office in Leicester Square, London. Susan was very interested in the richness of the ideas that this had generated, but at that time the main focus was the technical feasibility, so my timing was slightly out.

Fast forward five years: I had updated myself with the progress of the venture and not only had many test flights worked well but also there were a large number of the deposits for future paying flights already taken. A very strong and impressive management team with glowing credentials had been assembled. I contacted Galactic CEO's PA and very quickly an interview over the telephone was set for 9 am. The 'one big thing that I forgot' was that she meant UK time: as it turned out I called George Whitesides eight hours early (it was 1 am): no wonder he didn't get straight away who I was. We did make the real call at 5 pm our time that day as he was driving – home, I think. The phone signal broke at one point but he got back to me as I was doing the dinner and we finished off. So here we go...

In this chapter we see the evolution of that part of the business model that is at the core of the business. We see that it made a big leap from the tiny model of a single pilot with one passenger to a small group of people who have enough room to float in space. But that model is still a fairly basic experience in terms of going up and down into space and floating weightlessly for a relatively short period of time; so we need to be aware that this is very much a special case of strategic thinking in an emergent and immature market. There ought to be more potential for doing that in a very imaginative way as the whole business model design is up for grabs, unlike in a more mature business. On the other hand, because there is a vacuum of competition and the price can more or less be set, and scale imposed, the pressure to actually think strategically might be less.

We go through a number of themes:

- strategy development;
- interdependencies;
- the business model;
- strategic decisions;
- 'light bulb' moments;
- criteria for strategic decisions;
- strategic assumptions;
- bottom-up versus top-down strategic thinking;
- strategic workshops;
- futures.

Strategy development

Tony:

Thanks for being able to talk to me. I have had a long-standing interest in Virgin Galactic and it is great that you have been able to talk to me about strategic thinking.

George:

Well, for a start I would say that strategic thinking is absolutely essential and sometimes hard to prioritize as sometimes you get caught up in the tactical. In the space world and in the aerospace world I would connect it with the most basic hardware decisions as a sub-set of strategic decisions. What I mean by that is that in the aerospace world 90 per cent of the project's cost is committed in the first 10 per cent of the project, because you make decisions at the front end that set your long-term cost trajectory and in the operational trajectory of the project.

It is really important to get those decisions right at the front end. So to draw an analogy to other spheres of thinking it is like aerospace. Once you have made those decisions then you have set on a particular course for the cost trajectory, both the capex and opex. It is very hard to change at a later stage, to try to change the capex or opex. Once you are three-quarters of the way through the project you are where you are.

In some ways in aerospace the number one aspect of strategic thinking is making the right technical choices and you know, we think that we have made a good set of choices. Are you familiar with the X Prize?

Tony:

Yes, I am (mentioning the visit in 2007 to meet Susan Newsom). There are perhaps two strands, there's the technical strategy and there is also the more commercial strategy which is equally interesting, but let's stay with the technological strategy first.

George:

The point that I was about to make was that we made a number of decisions at the front end of the business that in some ways were leap-frogged by a generation in technology development. So Spaceship 1 was very much designed to be a very fast prototype. It was designed to be possible for a small group of people to build a re-useable sub-orbital spaceship – you know – brilliantly; it only ever carried one person into space at a time, although it did have the capacity to take two people – two small people. Then the cabin was small and there were various compromises to achieve the goal in the time allotted.

So when Galactic sat down with deposits after the X prize, it made a series of technical decisions and I think the foremost ones were space and payload capacity and passenger capacity – enter an operational model. What I mean when I say that is that it was built as an eight-person vehicle with two pilots, and the passengers would be able to get out of their seats.

Interdependencies

George:
That was really a series of business decisions driving technical decisions. That was all before my time but the managers of the company believed that at a business level they needed to have several people per flight to have a good business so that they moved from essentially two passengers to six passengers and they also felt that passengers would want to be able to get out of their seats and move around, which then dictated a bigger cabin.

These were basically strategic decisions, you know, in terms of revenue per flight, net profit per flight, but they drove strategic hardware choices that have certainly shaped how this project has gone. I think that it is fair to say that in many respects by making those choices at the front end it was almost like we said that, 'to make a good business we almost needed to skip a generation of technological development'. By that I mean that you could have just built a sort of a spaceship, one that was basically a smaller size that did not allow people to get out of their seats, you know, and did not permit more than one or two people to ride along with the pilot. We could have done that. And that was arguably what a Spaceship 2 really might have looked like.

I always say when I speak to folk that what we are really doing is Spaceship 3 in a way, because we are a fairly big leap from Spaceship 1. I think that the reasons for making that choice are solid business decisions but it drove a sort of (set of) technical decisions that dictated the hardware trajectory in this company. That's the hardware side.

So at this point we are seeing the input that lifts up the nose, as it were, of the strategic thinking to a strategic vision, to a new level: as a special case of the strategic thinking process.

Tony:
What I am hearing is that you have got the different domains of strategic decisions: the technical, the business, and they work in their different ways: one will work back to the other and you follow it through like a bit of a zigzag in the way in which you make the strategic choices, and probably after the event it is all very logical and obvious but at the time it may not

have been obvious, because you are facing tough dilemmas about do I go this way or that way; which way should I go? In the sense that if we get it wrong it is not going to be a viable business model.

So here strategic thinking has to cope with the chicken-and-egg problems of managing interdependencies by positing assumptions in one domain, eg the market end of the business model, and then seeing what they do to another, eg the design, and doing a number of iterations.

George:
Yes, there are a lot of uncertainties behind aerospace projects: the development costs, the actual operational costs. We believe that we have those much better defined now, but those are hard things to nail down at the front end of the project so I think what the Galactic team did was to try to settle on a set of strategic business choices that they thought would generate a very healthy business. These drove an equally important set of technical choices.

I think that what's important in all fields and certainly in aerospace, is that linkage, back-and-forth (between the two). Anyway, on the business side, I think that what is really interesting is that we are kind of making things up as we go along, whether it is the hardware or the regulatory insurance or operations, all these different things, and we are doing it for the first time.

What is particularly interesting is the uncertainty, and that brings the business considerations in terms of things like competitive strategy or operational strategy, overlaid with the environment. We are not a company that has been around for a long time. We are a start-up, and certainly one of the more high visibility start-ups. So there is – I hesitate to use the word, on-the-fly strategic thinking as we try to work our way towards ...

One of the key techniques for dealing with uncertainty, as per Demystifying Strategy, *is to list the key assumptions about the future (based on 'the world going right') and to test these out in terms of, a) their importance, and b) their degree of uncertainty. The assumptions positioned in the bottom left-hand quadrant in Figure 5.1 (uncertainty-importance grid) are then used to do some scenario storytelling.*

Tony:
Well, there is the theory called 'emergent strategy', a term coined by Henry Mintzberg. An analyst once told me that, in an interview, Richard Branson said, 'You know me, sometimes we let the strategy just emerge, and then we make it a bit more deliberate', or something like that. So where there is an emergent strategy there is a lot of fluidity which you have to accept and tolerate at that point in time.

FIGURE 5.1 Uncertainty-importance grid

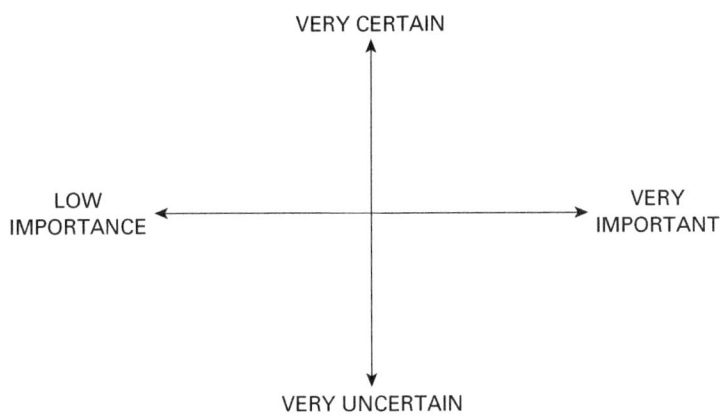

George:
Well, that is exactly right and Richard obviously has a lot good intuition (about the strategy) and the birth of Virgin Galactic, and he thinks that the detail can be worked out by itself. The basic idea was interesting. Why don't you ask another question?

The business model

Tony:
Well, what has fascinated me is – seeing it from the outside, going back five years – you might have seen this (the case on Virgin Galactic in *Demystifying Strategy*), there was an extract of the stuff that I brought down when I saw Susan five years ago. Basically, using a technique that I call 'the Optopus', it gives eight different lines of enquiry, and out of that came something like 80 opportunities, and Susan was thinking: 'Hard to handle, all of this stuff, we really need to get this off the ground, and the market potential is not our immediate priority.' But what I found fascinating was that if one time-travelled to the future then one could almost leap-frog into that uncertainty. One could have said, 'It has gone into space, it has done that job: what opportunities could one have?'

Working with groups (on strategy courses) I used this as a case study – there was vast potential in terms of sponsorship, media coverage, all kinds of stuff. So I wondered about that broader business model? When I was Googling I saw that you were involved in satellite launches.

George:

Yes, I think that there are a variety of things that we are involved in over a number of areas that will prove over time to be very good business and blossom, like sponsorship – that we will be looking at – due to the power of the brand, not just Virgin but Galactic, and the marriage of the two, and I do think that it is going to be a truly world-class brand, that you can leverage in different ways.

I do think that, you know, there all kinds of things that we are thinking about like small satellite launch vehicles that you might have seen we announced over summer and also future things like point-to-point high-speed transportation.

Tony:

Ah, yes!

At this point I was getting excited as parts of the potential business model mapped out independently some six years ago were being actively developed.

Tony:

Yes, that was one of the 'lines of enquiry': you don't need to just go up and down; we saw that in the business of the future there could be a whole network of flights, and one of the things that I used to do (when using the case study) was to ask: 'What would they (the aliens) do'? They could say: let's see where Virgin Atlantic goes: so this is what we could do with Virgin Galactic. So that's interesting.

George:

Yes, that is very interesting with the technology. I think that it is important to note that it is a big project with high development cost – very big. It is very do-able. There will be a high interest. When we have got operations running it will be a very profitable business, most certainly.

Here it might have been useful to map the economic value over time curve (see Figure 5.2) to see when the economic pay off actually happens and to optimize it, eg by bringing on stream sponsorship and media revenues, or replicating the flight routes.

Tony:

Is it still just 90 minutes in space or has it been extended? That was the original thing that I got from the 'Money Programme'.

George:

It is going to be two hours. You will be in space for less than that. You are only experiencing a few minutes of weightlessness, from wheels up to wheels down for two hours, and a week of training before that, four or five days.

FIGURE 5.2 Value over time curve

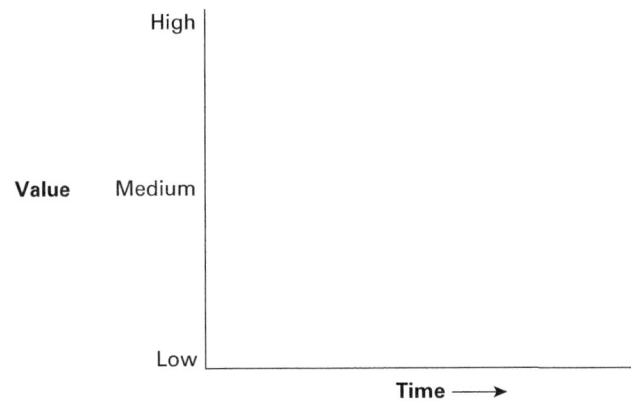

Tony:
I was going to ask you, you might have them being trained as astronauts, and the whole experience could be more than the $200,000 with the extras, but perhaps that's not something that you would be considering if you want that price ceiling?

George:
Yes, it is certainly something that we have thought about, to have…. It's interesting that all sorts of organic things come out of that. One of the biggest things that our customers like is a community of other astronauts, which is a thing that we really didn't expect. We have about a hundred people, that's not a trivial amount of people, who want to spend time in that community.

One of the things that I had wanted to probe was the whole variability of the price ceiling of $200,000. Now I don't want to end up being blamed for again suggesting to a company that it raise its charges (as is true for easyJet baggage charges around 12 years ago – that was me! I also suggested that Tesco Express prices could be a little higher than in the main store – a convenience premium.). But I had thought that the value to a wealthy customer could easily be more, especially taking into account a bigger package of 'experience', built around the core product.

This has always raised the issue for me of persuading Richard that 'budget' space flight is still 'budget' even at a higher price: I mean who is going to quibble at paying $250,000, say, for the ride of not just one, but many lifetimes? As long as the first one or two years were at that price, who is going to really care? After all, Virgin Atlantic has 'Upper Class' seats!

Another way of making this more implementable would be for some of that revenue, say, being used to give some disadvantaged child a ride to the stars, every five flights. Perhaps if one were to put this to Mr Branson that would be pushing on an open door? One of the really big points here is that one has always, in strategic thinking, – to be questioning one's assumptions – and that's difficult, especially if you are told 'you can't think that way', or you simply assume that to be the case.

One could envisage each flight being recorded on camera as 'reality TV', which could not only generate media revenue in its own right, but also make each seat more valuable as you get to be on TV. Maybe in the very long term it would be important as that is something that competitors might struggle to do.

Strategic decisions

Tony:

When I talked to Susan (years before), I played that to her. I imagined that I was the CEO of a football club; how would I run Virgin Galactic? And there were lots of lines of enquiry that came out of that… it was a fan thing, a social thing: groups were going up so you would go back on other trip and there is a season ticket. There is a community of astronauts.

So in terms of the strategic thinking that you have been doing, are you aware of when you are doing it? Or is it something that you can say for sure whether you were doing it or not? It's getting from the CEO as to whether you are doing it or not?

George:

Yes, I think at times you are conscious that you are not making larger strategic decisions. At other times you are making what is sometimes a tactical decision but, because of what you are or are not including in the decision-making process, it is actually a major strategic decision. And sometimes you recognize things post facto, the strategic importance of something, that wasn't evident the first time round. I think it is a mix.

In a start-up almost anything is a strategic decision as it has a wider relevance as you are constantly making choices about where you head and almost everything may have strategic implications. I don't know, what do you think?'

Tony:

Well, I find that when I am doing it, because I have a consulting business – I am not just an academic – that suddenly I get an idea, for example I got an idea when posting a letter that it is so antiquated in the UK, the Royal Mail, and by the time I had posted it I thought, 'This has to change. It is totally outdated, they will go bust, etc.' So I thought, 'I've got to do this: I have to write to the CEO to get them to time-travel into the future.' That's something that just happened in a sporadic way and sometimes you get those kind of idea. If I want to do more of this kind of consulting work then I could just pick up a (strategic) idea and run with it rather than wait for people to come to me.

So for me, I thought, 'I really should think about that.' Some of the people that I have talked to describe it as the 'light bulb' type of moment, which can happen at any time, and it is about being aware of it and recognizing the significance, like, 'I really need to think about that.'

'Light bulb' moments

George:
We all have a lot of 'light bulb' moments, because typically the really important ones are momentous decisions for the business and, to push really hard on one of these major directions, or a new angle or something, or partnerships or whatever, they are very big decisions so to some extent you need to think, carefully you know, whether they are sort of the right thing to do. I think that one of the things that Richard (Branson) is so good about is not over-thinking it. He has a good gut and he does it and that's really valuable to do that. Not everything works out but probably, as an entrepreneur, he is a lot about doing stuff, rather than over-analysing.

Now this is very interesting as to the influence of the intuitive versus the analytical in guiding strategic thinking. I have never met Sir Richard Branson (maybe we will try to catch him for my next book!) but I imagine that he is exceedingly shrewd in sniffing whether there is something to be made out of something or not, and what constitutes a sufficiently superior and defendable business model to create real economic value. Above all he is acutely conscious – and here he is outstanding – in terms of his sense of timing and the need for dynamic advantage: speed, mobility and adaptability (see Chapter 5 of Demystifying Strategy*). So if you have all those kinds of things going for you, you aren't in need of an extremely well-articulated 'deliberate strategy'.*

But that doesn't mean that he isn't familiar with all the main strategy models – I am sure that he is. In the same way as I don't need to spend half an hour judging the strategic attractiveness of a business idea – a minute or two will do, he will operate on a very intuitive, Pareto-like principal of 'get 20 per cent of things right that are 80 per cent of the really important stuff'.

Tony:

Well, it is an interesting point because in the kind of career that I have had, as a business school academic, I have gone around creating techniques and propagating them through big companies like Tesco, HP and Microsoft, and they are analytical techniques for evaluating options: the option grid, the Optopus, and I have observed people finding these really helpful, but aside of that it seems that people are not using formal techniques and gut feel or they are using it in a slavish way. I am interested to see whether you use any formal techniques or whether it is all the talk, and then making the gut-feel decisions?

George:

I think that the primary two techniques that I use are bouncing the ideas off other senior managers and also trying to get some idea of magnitude out of any sort of analysis for a set of scenarios which give you a sense of you know... that just helps this to crystallize, to put it into some sort of quantitative analysis. I have noticed that that's a thing that Richard does, to try to sketch it out to quickly, get a sense of the numbers. Obviously some of these numbers are not well defined, that's where the gut instinct comes in. That's where talking to other people comes in. But I think that between those two techniques....

Here George is referring to more strategy processes than strategy tools as such. A quick observation here is that many if not most CEOs still don't have at their fingertips many of the most useful strategic techniques that are tried and tested and available on the market – that is not a criticism, just a fact.

Tony:

One of the things that interests me is how people use numbers – I am guilty of being an ex-accountant myself, my research has been about linking finance with the strategy both ways, and when you say the word 'numbers' it feels, perhaps wrongly, that that is profit or return on capital. What numbers were you thinking of here?

Strategic assumptions

George:

Well I think that it varies a lot depending on the kind of thing that you are looking at. You know, we think about development costs, we think about time to complete the project, we think about how certain technologies will affect operational costs, the basic parameters of the business. In many other ways they are just like any other aerospace business, you have a development cost and an opex cost, and you know perming those variables is the primary way of improving the business, and so I think that it is a combination of what we do. What we do is probably not that exciting. We do scenarios of our base-line business model, and as I say, there are unknowns but that is just that part of the game.

Tony:
Well, in terms of a lot of the sources of uncertainty, those are all about the business in terms of its high technology, but equally, there's the revenue side, there are assumptions and they don't so often get modelled and tested quite as well. Six years ago when I saw Susan (Newsom) your Strategy Director, she only had 25 minutes or so, and I should have asked her these questions: number one, about competition; number two, about the fact that some people might not regard this as terribly 'green' as clearly you would be using a lot more fuel, etc. So in the longer term would those not impact on the assumptions about full capacity and stuff like that?

George:
On the green side, I think at one level the amount that we will be flying is trivial compared to global air transportation and so it is not of any importance on the global scene. You know there are forms of rocket propulsion that are the cleanest form of energy generation that humankind can use – liquid oxygen and liquid hydrogen as you know just creates energy and water, so longer term those forms of propulsion are... (available) and there's also other forms of propulsion technology that are even more creative along the spectrum than that. The thing at the moment is the air launch and the light, low mass of our vehicle. But there is a time in any business and particularly in a Virgin business that it has to address that point and it becomes critical and pretty fundamental... (signal getting cut off).

Tony:
(Resuming later on) Are there any other insights into the strategic thinking process that you could give to the readers, things that really work well, how you take people with you, anything that you can mention by way of giving tips to people.

Bottom-up versus top-down assumptions

George:
You know, I think that taking people with you is a really important thing. I think that you have to bring your folks on board where there is a big strategic decision, that's something that we work on, we work hard on. Sometimes you just have to do it but all things being equal, but if you can build that momentum around that choice then people will embrace it that

much more easily, rather than the 'top-down' thing where, you know, there is only one person in the organization that believes it and that makes it so much harder to make it work.

This is a common theme across APIL, the Samaritans and Simplyhealth, which is positive – that strategic thinking doesn't just happen in one or a couple of heads and is then just passed down through decisions, plans and very broad objectives and goals. The latter goals often predominate in the official 'strategy' and are often positioned as if these were the actual core of the strategies – of which they form merely a part.

Tony:
So, you will involve other people in that process?

George:
Yes, I think that you have got to have some sort of critical mass inside the organization for some of these things to take hold and be embraced; you know you have a series of events where you make that choice – I think that's just common sense.

Strategic workshops

Tony:
Do you invest much time to take a day out – you know we mentioned when we started that there is a risk of getting too tactical and too operational?

George:
Well, what we are trying to do is to take some time out once or twice a year to spend a couple of days with each other and think about where we are, and where we are heading, and I think that that is really valuable. We need to sit in front of each other and make the time that's structured and almost ample enough that you can cover the topics, and it is getting harder and harder to do that, but I think that it is really important.

Tony:
So do you go away to do that or do you sit in your offices?

George:
Well, we are based all over the world so what we often do is just do that in one of our offices; we have done it outside as well but I think usually we just pick one of our offices in the world and spend a few days out.

Tony:
I was visualizing, George. Where do you launch from? You could do it in the desert: the Negev desert?

George:
The Antelope Valley.

Tony:
There would be a premium on time because if we don't have a very strategic idea then we don't get out of here. That's fun.

George:
Exactly, exactly.

Futures

Tony:
Perhaps the last thing: storytelling is quite helpful for time-travelling into the future rather than just projecting oneself from sort of, time zero, which is a lot of what planning does. It looks forward from where you are now rather than imagining that you are literally telling stories about the future and how it would develop. So I wonder whether it would be really interesting to think about Virgin Galactic in 20 years' time. What would the market be then and would there be other competition then because I think that from what I picked up, and this is where the phone went dead – was it Ariadne, the French thing?

George:
Sort of, but not really. It is something that much quicker, and going orbital – there are some smaller companies that are trying to do a similar thing and I think that that is not a particular model. It is actually quite interesting, the idea of starting to tell stories....

Tony:
I played this case study (Galactic) with a number of Eastern European bankers and they were going: 'Ah, the Russians would love this, they will do it – they want to go on it, and then they would try to do it themselves, Russian billionaires.'

George:
I get that.
I didn't probe more on that – but I would have loved to.

This was five years ago, so we might have another chat, some other time, about scenario processes; that is interesting. I was thinking here about a whole range of things: from scenario development to the business value system and also some of the dynamic models, like the competitive pressure over time curve (Figure 2.3), the value over time curve (Figure 5.2), and a further model, the difficulty over time curve (see Figure 5.3), which can be used alongside the value over time curve.

FIGURE 5.3 Difficulty over time curve

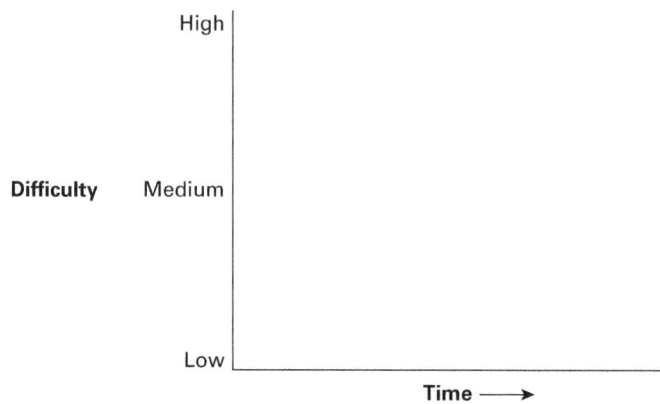

Virgin Galactic is a strategic thinker's dream as it is an opportunity to bring together emotional value, a multi-dimensional business model (that has only just been begun to be explored), a very big and global market, a unique and dynamic set of competitive advantages, and an awesome brand. This can be and most surely will be multimedia, and must leverage itself through alliances and sponsors. While much strategic thinking has been done to date, there are further opportunities to do a lot more of that going forward, and in particular, some scenario storytelling involving telling the story backwards.

Another model I felt might be useful to Virgin Galactic was the 'strategy onion' for gaining an overview of the various business models that might evolve over time, coupled with some scenario storytelling; see Figure 5.4. This model would also be an important backdrop against which the many different options that are available to Galactic as it evolves could be evaluated systematically, using the strategic option grid (see Figure 1.2).

The day after recording this interview, I was still very excited. At the ripe age of 58 I have been busily ticking off some of the more adventurous and exotic things that one can get to do on this planet before the end game. So, that evening, I said to my wife, Carolina, over dinner: 'Darling, this Virgin Galactic is so exciting; I wondered whether at a pinch I could barter some strategic help – lots – for a free or cheaper ride. What do you think? I believe that it is very safe. Would you mind me away for a week – I might be on TV?'

She took one look at me and, knowing how accident prone I am, jokingly said: 'Well, I'm sure that it is absolutely safe and your heart could stand it, but there's just one thing that concerns me: it would be very safe without you, but with you – you are bound to have an accident!'

So I had better pass. I will save that for my next life.

FIGURE 5.4 The strategy onion

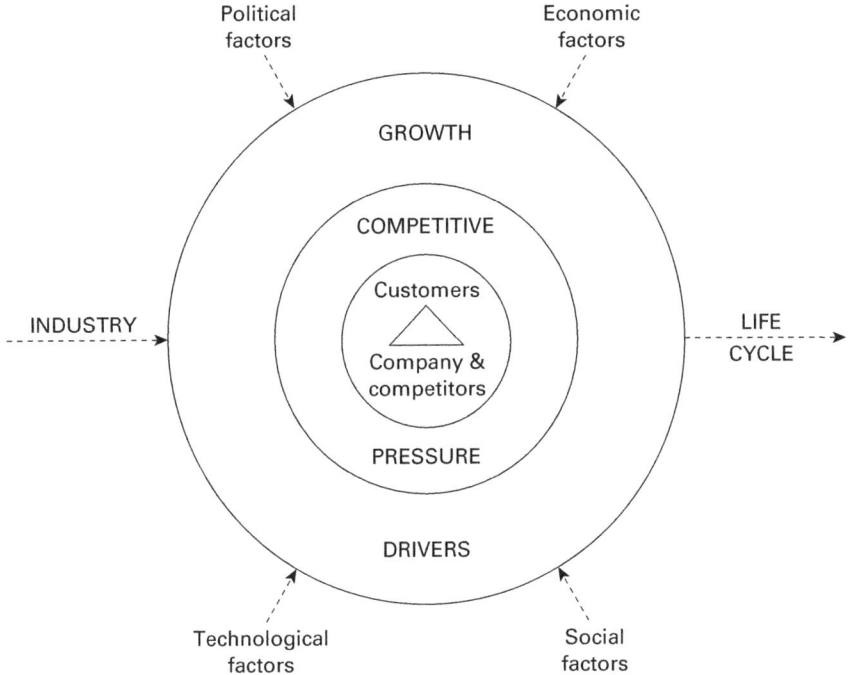

CONCLUSIONS

- Strategic thinking is very much essential to design, adapt or change any business model.
- That means understanding the interdependencies between the value and cost drivers of any business, and to look at configuration options.
- That in turn means bringing the ingredients from a diversity of sources to build a novel value system.
- This is often crystallized in 'light bulb' moments.
- Gut feel is an essential ingredient in effective strategies.
- The strategy process needs to be conducive to strategic thinking – and that needs a relaxed environment, ideally separate in time and space from the normal workplace.

06 Simplyhealth

Introduction

Simplyhealth is a fast growing health insurance business in the United Kingdom. It has evolved considerably over the past 15 years and now employs 1,700 people across an increasing range of activities that are about 'Inspiring people to better health'. I first experienced the business in 2001 when I was asked to do a number of workshops on strategic thinking for its middle management population as part of a wider attempt to build a creative and visionary organization. I found these managers a joy to work with – just very, very nice people who genuinely cared about their customers.

In early 2013 I made contact with its CEO, Des Benjamin, who I had met briefly in 2001 to explore with him his take on strategic thinking. The day we met in 2013 for the interview didn't start well. I had received a report from a social worker investigating the child family contact case I had been fighting and found its content and conclusions to be biased. I had been very displeased as a result, and getting off the train at London Bridge I was going through so many things in my head that I managed to leave my phone on the train. If it had been someone else I was seeing I might have not found the meeting easy at all, but Des's calm manner – quite unusual for a CEO I would say – not to mention his sympathy for my loss made it a welcome break from all the anxiety. For once my reminder to myself, 'What's the one big thing that I have forgotten?' didn't kick in. Miraculously luck and kindness intervened and by the time I got home the next day my wife presented me with the phone which she had got back from someone who had found it!

After introducing the interview and saying a little about who I had talked to so far, we got down to business over tea at the Institute of Directors, Piccadilly. There were a large number of themes picked up in the conversation:

- vision;
- leadership and beliefs;
- the role of strategic planning;
- strategic vision and operations;
- behaviour, emotions and service strategy;
- formalization of strategy;
- strategy and teams;
- hiring people – and the CEO;
- culture;
- strategic mindfulness;
- strategy development and diversification;
- futures;
- what businesses can we be in;
- strategy and honesty;
- facilitation;
- acquisitions.

In the rich conversation that followed, Des interweaves in a very fluid way some content-related strategic issues, as well as talking about the strategic thinking processes, and indeed more general leadership processes. In terms of Mintzberg et al's (2008) different schools of strategy I felt that he was very much in the 'visionary school'. We started on the topic of the pervasive role that strategic vision has in the strategic thinking process.

Vision

Des:
Let's start with perhaps a slightly different view (of what is strategic). I am not sure that the highest level of what we do is strategic. I think the implementation of what we are trying to achieve, and certainly the destination markers on a journey, can both be made strategic. I am not sure if the journey itself, it needs another word, is actually 'strategic', and the reason why I say that is that I think, I don't like the word 'mission', it is very tactical. It is a rather task-focused type of a word. I am more drawn instead to the idea of a 'descriptive vision'. This is the over-arching drive for an organization which involves implementing a number of strategies underneath it – which keep that vision in focus. They keep the movement of the organization going towards the realization of that vision.

When we sit down and we do our strategy days – and we do it as a kind of a formal, board-scheduled 'We must have a strategy, we must have a five year view' – for me, we tend to become two things. Firstly, we are a little bit delusional that there won't be so much change that we really can think that far ahead, but equally, and secondly, we are a bit too much in a process and planning-orientated mode, rather than in a vision/journey-clarifying mode. It is the latter that I would actually call 'strategic work', if not actually creating a strategy.

This then leads Des naturally into the adjacent role of leadership and also of beliefs.

Leadership and beliefs

Des:
And the reason that I say that is that sometimes we forget that we are in a leadership role, and in my personal view, the only thing that you can really lead is the people, and people don't follow benchmarks and they don't follow an individual target, they follow on the basis of belief systems.

And I think that a lot of human interaction in the workplace is dressed up as motivation; it all becomes about targets, it is so focused on deliverables and objectives, and actually the reason that people engage is at a different level – and that of course is their belief system. One part of their belief system concerns the fact that they have responsibilities. They need to have an income, they need to take care of their family and they need to look after their own hierarchy of needs. On top of that people also then need to feel the worth of what they are doing, so that they can feel as though, as human beings, they are making some form of contribution to their immediate environment, or to society, to the planet or to a cause, or to something else.

In trying to mobilize a team of people forward, that team of people is essentially the real business enterprise, which doesn't exist in its own right – it is really the people. And one has to lead these people on the basis of something of substance that affects them from the inside out. Therefore what you have to do alongside just having a vision to get real engagement is you ask the question of people within the organization: 'Could you commit one day of your life, one valuable day that you will never be given back, to doing this vision?'

Des is clearly driven by a strong passion for organizational purpose. For him, 'purpose' is not merely a collective thing that the organization strives to work towards, but also has to be taken on the context of individuals shaping their own purpose.

With Simplyhealth we are very clear what our job is, and what our goal is. But actually, in terms of our end point, we don't really have one, as our goal is to inspire people towards better health, and that is ongoing. So the question that I ask, obsessively, of both my employees and myself, every single day, is 'Have I got the energy, and have I got the sense of purpose, the drive, the thinking energy, and the time, to want to help to inspire people to better health?' That for me then creates an environment from which strategies for achieving that vision can emerge.

But I think that the idea of implementing things short term (and by 'short term' I mean five years or less), without that fundamental purpose is not appropriate. This fundamental purpose is as much a fundamental Maslow need as is food or drink. By focusing both on the more basic needs, as we have said, and this higher purpose – and all at the same time – this means that you don't have a vacuum of why the strategy is important to them. And then you can underpin it with things like how you would deliver it, what shortcuts you can and can't take, what principles you stick to, and what others you might develop if those don't work, what values you need to bring through the strategies so the outputs deliver to the end-vision, and so on and so forth.

The role of strategic planning

He then distinguishes, in a very marked way, strategic thinking from strategic planning.

Des:
And I think that we spend an inordinate amount of time on these plans, these goals, these system migrations and process improvements, and then forget to go back to the 'Why are we doing this?' Would you develop a system in that way? Or would you stop and think: now hang on a minute, how is it serving the goal of 'inspiring people to better health?' How could we in fact write a system or process that would help this?

An example that he picks out of a product of strategic thought is that of Simplyhealth's policy of having a person to answer all incoming calls rather than a semi-automated answering system. So strategic thinking is something that we should see manifest at an operational level.

By way of example, one of the things that I have done in Simplyhealth, is to develop a system that starts with the goal of making people feel better right from the minute that they start contacting me, because they are contacting me at the moment of illness. Therefore the last thing that I will do to them is to ask them to press 1 for this and 2 for that, 3 for this and 4 for that.

I answer every single phone call with, 'Good morning, my name is Des, may I ask who I am speaking to?', because that's courteous and polite, it means that someone doesn't feel as if they are going to be cornered and stressed into a place where they can't get the answer that they want, they can't speak to the person that they want to.

Tony:
Metrobank is one of the few examples where the people there seem really happy, they seem to be on a drug: they are all naturally warm and welcoming.

Des:

But thinking about inspiring people towards better health doesn't mean stressing them with inappropriate technology, we have got all that technology because we take several million calls a year. But actually the point is that if you are thinking strategically, long term towards a vision, you create technologies that support the human interaction and you don't process people, you don't process humans down technological paths.

I now pick up the more 'human' aspects of thinking strategically (as opposed to the process aspects), through looking at the more behavioural and emotional sides of strategy.

Behaviour, emotions and service strategy

Tony:

The thing that it sparks in my mind is that strategic thinking is often very much related to behavioural stuff, you know, about yourself, about the environment, how things might behave, and behave quite differently, and I know that behaviour is underemphasized in the strategy theory. I did some research some years ago into strategic behaviour, and no one has actually followed that up. But it is fascinating in terms of behaviour. You can gain real competitive advantage by behavioural advantage, by emotional advantage or value. Right across all kinds of industries you will see that that is there.

Tomorrow I am working in one of my favourite industries ever, the funeral industry, and what is fascinating there is that is extremely emotional, it is very behavioural stuff; get it wrong and you really screw it up but there's still a lot more value to be had out of doing things at even a higher level; there is 'grief work' and stuff like that.

Des:

Des continues with that theme, with an everyday example of John Lewis as an organization that has clearly thought strategically about customer feelings and customer value in determining its service strategy, contrasting that with one that has apparently not: the electronic retailer Comet.

Let me suggest to you where an area of strategy in John Lewis has played through, and the behaviours that went into that. This is based on impressions from my own experience, so it is probably not valid from an external point of view, except that every time I say things like this it seems to be valid. So when I say I think that people don't like pushing buttons, everyone sticks their hands up and says, 'I don't like pushing buttons'; what I say I feel often resonates with other people.

Standing in Comet (it was very close to its demise) I said to a chap, 'Could you tell me about that telly?' He started reading the label to me and I said, 'I could have done that. Can you tell me anything else?' – and he couldn't. Not daunted, I said 'Very good' and he asked, 'Would you like the guarantee?' I said, 'I think that next door that they give either a two-year or a five-year guarantee on tellies, anyway.' And he said, 'Ah ha, I will show you now why Comet's guarantee is better than John Lewis', and he read that it lasts a bit longer and it covers a bit of this and a bit of that, and all I heard was what Kaplan and Child call 'corporate duck': quack, quack, quack, quack, quack....

While he was doing that what my mind was doing emotionally was (thinking) 'This is a 10-year investment – if I have to phone him he is going to get me to bring it in; he is going to try and to refute that lovely guarantee. He is going to get me to collect it and he is going to insist, through his eyes, that it was my fault and that I broke it. If I go next door I will pay a few pounds more, and when I phone them they will say: 'I am so sorry that you have been inconvenienced – let's see how we can get this fixed in the most beneficial way for you.' And what that means is that it didn't matter what that price was, going one way I was going to have a war with a retailer who was trying to sell me the lowest (priced) box and the highest priced insurance commission, and the going the other way I was having a relationship where I fundamentally felt that I could trust the intentions of the company to look after me if something went wrong. I went with John Lewis. There is no proof in any of that, however the strategy of John Lewis can build trust as a fundamental in the organization and has played itself out in a single, retail transaction, absolutely to the benefit (of John Lewis).

Now, are they measuring 'trust' in the boardroom in any phenomenally exacting way? I doubt it. Do they believe, and this is back to belief systems, do they believe that this is the right way to a long-term relationship? I think that they do, and it works. And it is, for me, a single example of why strategically you don't build primarily around markets, economics or competitive landscape; you build around where can you take your value system and apply it in a way where people will value what you are doing for them.

Tony:

I teach at Henley these days, and they have a whole load of theories, like with strategy and with Porter, and it is all about the Five Forces and this kind of stuff, and there is all the stuff on resource-based theory of competitive advantage that says that Porter is all wrong, because it is all about your resources and products and maybe some competences. But actually neither picks up on the 'emotional advantage', which could be an alternative theory.

Des then identifies thinking about the 'emotional advantage' – as I have characterized that as a route towards achieving the elusive 'sustainable competitive advantage' which is the Holy Grail of many strategy theories, like resource-based theory.

Des:

Hundreds of people can do what you do to add value. Businesses add value in other ways that appeal to us emotionally, and appeal to our desire for convenience and to the way that we live our lives. Comet was very much about knocking a price down in the window and knocking up some high commission guarantee, and then serving me as little as possible at my moment of need. That is not how you really add value, that's yesterday's game when we thought that the cheapest is the best. Well, we have all moved on and learnt that lesson, so much so that the most popular position on price comparison sites I think has been about sixth.

Tony:

When you buy wines from a restaurant the second from the cheapest is the worst as that's the one they want to get rid of.

Des:

And you have got to work out how you engineer value to the customer: the product itself will be the commodity; the way that we serve will be increasingly our point of differential. So, in thinking strategically, yes, you have got to understand what your capabilities are, your core assets, what markets you are going to apply them in.

Now he takes us back to strategic thinking process which he, like me, very much distinguishes from the more formal, strategic planning processes.

Formalization of strategy

Des:

I think that to the extent that we can encourage boards and management teams to have those conversations, strategy is alive and well. To the extent that we feel that we have to have a business planning process and a strategy paper or set of papers, and deliver five years of spreadsheet numbers which of course only go from bottom left to top right, we are deluding ourselves. And perhaps the most important aspect I would want to deal with would be sustainability because, short term anything is possible – you can run some numbers in any direction. Given that the average tenure of a CEO in a large organization is something like three years it is probably better to do it that way.

Tony:

Do you think that that matters? In terms of strategic thinking, if that is true?

Des:

What I know, as much as they like to delude themselves, is that a CEO can't really achieve anything in three years.

I then introduced the theme of systems thinking, ie sensing how the different elements of a system come together and interact with one another, as a part of strategic thinking, with an example from the football industry. I sensed that this would lead our conversation down some interesting paths.

Strategy and teams

Tony:

Another industry that I am fascinated in is football: at Chelsea they seem to have new managers every five minutes, it is unreal. How would they do if they had more continuity, like Man United or even Arsenal?

Des:

I think it shows you that all the money in the world cannot buy you a team, and a team in our complex world, a team is infinitely more valuable than an individual; there is no question in my mind of that.

Tony:

In football, we have Robin van Persie who is too good for words – in the Manchester United team apart from Wayne Rooney the rest of them are not very special, but God do they play well as a team. Do Manchester City play so well (normally) as a team? Well no, definitely not (generally). So they are many points behind: it is the behavioural alignment that makes the difference.

Des then explores the consequences of what happens where there is tension and conflict within the system that is the business model.

Des:

Well, the business goal is assembled for the short term and then you crack a winner, and then you end up disappearing unless that is sustainable; that's one thing. But actually, that is not what business is about. Sustainability, again, is the issue that's important. Creating sustainability means that you can have strategies that are about these numbers. Your margins can be widened in the short term, but those strategies will make you recruit people who are good at cost-cutting, and good at margin manipulation. So you get good at shaving the edge off guarantees so that there are fewer claims, and at shaving the edges off products so that there is a bit more failure in them, and more repeat (replacement) purchases are necessary, and there has been shaving off service so that it is more difficult for the customer to get through to the organization.

And you can buy that kind of (margin-stretching) expertise, and in tough markets when you see your margins shrinking, what you really need isn't that, No – that is exactly wrong. What you actually want in is the engineers who can innovate to put something valuable into the product, so that the consumer sees the benefit and appreciates the difference in the product.

Hiring people – and the CEO

Tony:
In terms of setting the design for the strategy, some of it is about who you hire in and how they think and behave.

Which leads us once again inevitably back to the behavioural aspects of the strategic thinking process.

Des:
That's absolutely core.

Tony
The biggest strategic investment decision of the lot is appointing a chief executive.

Des:
The chief executive's appointment, yes, what follows from that are decisions on and what kind of people you want in, how you want them thinking, and also how you set the framework for thinking in the organization. But do we believe that we should set a framework for thinking or do we default to thinking that we can compete by making it cheaper?

Tony:
Since I last met you, Des, many things have happened in my life. My new wife happens to be a clinical psychologist, and she has introduced me to a thing called 'cognitive behavioural therapy' and the importance of belief systems, which I always felt were important, but if you look at that – they are actually crucial in determining the ways in which people think about strategy or strategic thinking. So by setting these almost general things like 'purpose', and 'vision', I have the thought that: 'Is it almost just a set of strategic principles'? Like rules of thumb, that we people will achieve this sort of thing. Whatever those things are, they need to be conditioned by, or play off the belief systems....

Des:
I think that it is fundamental and vital to have clearly defined principles in an organization of the things that you will do and that you won't do and that's

the nice thing about principles and values. If you are to write down values, it is legitimate, they should not change. And if they change they are not principles – they are just bit of paper with words on them. The most dangerous thing that you can do, as a chief executive, is to have bits of paper with words on them, because your credibility goes through the floor if you say one thing and do another; you will be regarded as rubbish by the population of workers who look at you and say: 'I hear what you saying, and I see what you are doing.' And you should set your business to live or die by those principles. Otherwise the message you give to people is that they (the principles) are great, but you break them when you need to.

Culture

Tony:
When I did a few workshops with you some years ago, when you were called 'HSA', I found a very different organization from many others, a nice one.

Des:
It is still there.

Tony:
Can you think of any other organizations that are like that? I struggle with that.

Des:
I do admire what John Lewis has achieved. I think that they have a culture that is rich and deep. You may remember from all those years ago (it may have developed after your time) that we have only two rules: one is that the job description for everybody is two words long: 'help people'. The fact that you are finance director means that you have got these duties and in the post room you have got those duties, but your job is helping people. The second thing is that there is only one way to help me and that is to be yourself: there is no place for fraud, or for any impersonation of being a professional man or woman, that's it.

We haven't come up with any other rules in 13 years but they are based on getting the innate best out of everyone, because if you are going to serve, and by serve I mean to help somebody else, then you have got to be in the best condition, have the best training, the best skills, the best equipment, and be mentally in a place where you can help somebody sort out their issues. So my job as a manager is to organize all of that.

We return again to Des' deep, underlying interest in visionary thinking as a part of strategic thinking.

Strategic mindfulness

Tony:
So, in terms of the actual processes of strategic thinking, would you say that the planning tends to drive that out? When do you think that it tends to happen in your experience?

Des:
Oh, for me strategic thinking is an everyday event. I look at, for example, the Health Service and try to conclude where that is going at the moment, and it is not possible. I know where I would like to take it, I know what I would like to do with it, but I have to watch for things that are emerging in terms of attitudes to change from the public, legislative change from NHS commissioning boards and NHS trusts. Marrying those two together leads me to questions of where I think that I can incisively apply myself, for the long term, in an area that is sustainable whereby principles and assets work, and therefore make a difference. That is all strategic thinking, but it must all cue into the vision of how can I inspire people towards better health?

I then asked about when strategic thinking is 'switched on' – and sometimes 'switched off' – in a CEO's everyday life, which is about identifying how pervasive it can and should be.

Tony:
That's the content, but in terms of the process, is it something that you might do at any time, for example when you are having a shower, or is it sporadic?

Des:
No, for me it's 24 hours a day. It is every time that I walk into a building I am thinking in the context of 'What do I make of this environment? What possibilities open up?'

Tony:
Sometimes, strategic thinking seems a bit like putting up a Christmas tree: you put it up over Christmas and then you put it away for another year.

Des:
I don't understand that (kind of behaviour). I don't understand that – ever. As a CEO, you work a seven day week in your head. Don't mistake that for 'My God he must be shattered' – I'm not shattered. However, the subject matter that I love, it never leaves my mind, and I always think with anything I am involved in, from classical music to a rugby game, for example, about how I can apply that to the organization I am in, and how I might use some

of the professionalism of Clive Woodward's rugby team to inspire my own managers.

This gave me the thought that being strategically mindful is something that maybe more people might practise. ('Mindfulness' is something that is often practised within Buddhist meditation and is about enhancing what one observes in the 'now', thus greatly focusing the concentration.) I know that I do practise that a lot, although even then you can suddenly be faced with business disappointments that you really don't want to know about, and that shuts the mindfulness down. But for someone who is not officially a career strategist but a director or manager of some operation, that must be so much harder to sustain. I turned to the dissemination of strategic thinking throughout the organization.

Tony:
So in terms of people around you, to what extent can they emulate that, or you encourage that, or how far does it spread in the organization?

Des:
I think that people have different predispositions. For example, in the senior team you don't need or want everybody to be a strategic thinker. So I have, for example, a couple of board colleagues who I would rate as, they are out there, they are really seeing and learning, and really thinking. Others not so, but on the board you need a blend of skills, which means that some are process driven and some are target driven, some are strategic thinkers and it is bringing that all together that is so important.

One of the mechanisms that we use is that once a month my executives and I go away for a couple of days; we call it a 'Strategic executive for the group'. The first day is very much the agenda stuff. The next day is no papers, there is no subject matter: you come into the room and we kick off a conversation on anything from women in the workplace, to global custodianship of water supplies or air quality – because the point is that, in starting to talk in the round, I believe you generate a strong view as a group about what 'good' looks like, and what is missing, and it really helps because, if we apply that to ourselves, what does that actually look like?

I found this a most interesting way of getting strategic vision to open up at board level – and actually a very surprising one: it is hard to interest many boards in thinking about the future beyond their most immediate environment, let alone wider, more global issues with no obvious relevance to immediate issues. It seems to be a novel process for other boards to follow.

Tony:

Well that's also being 'out there' in the world, and taking yourself out of your own perspective. I go to Hot Yoga once a week and a personal trainer too and if I didn't do that training I wouldn't be this fit – so one has to do things out of habit, like strategic thinking.

Des:

But I am much less concerned with what BUPA or Aviva are doing. I am sure that if they were doing something that was good then I would go: 'That's good', yes, but I am much more concerned about our purpose and how good we are at getting there and focusing our resources on being 'good'.

Changing the subject, he moved onto a personal concern and interest of his – mobility.

Strategy development and diversification

Des:

I want to talk to you about mobility. One of the things that we saw as a target, going forward, was that there is an increasing need in the elderly population for mobility aids for daily living…. You need to have special grips to pick up a kettle if you have arthritis, all that sort of stuff. So we entered that market three or four years ago, and we are finding that the principles of our brand – which are that you serve, you serve as many people as you can, the best you can at a fair price – are well applied to an environment where you are dealing with people in a vulnerable position who need a trusted agent to help them through to the resources that they need to prolong a better quality of life for as long as possible, and we fit into that market beautifully.

And so we have diversified. We have got seven or eight hubs across the UK and we are expanding each year in serving that growing population. What is fascinating is that most of our existing insurance customers have said: 'Yes, that's a natural territory for Simplyhealth to also help us in.' So you can look at it strategically but it is strategy built on: 'Are we helping people to get better health for longer, and are we able to apply our principles of caring and personal attention, serving the many and not the few, making things affordable and being able to communicate what "good" looks like to individual customers?' That's really where those principles and direction keep pervading in every investment decision that we make.

I now probe into the actual structure of the strategic thinking process to ascertain how that works in the screening, development and evaluation of new strategic ideas and opportunities.

Futures

Tony:

So basically you have got some very clear criteria for if a new opportunity comes up, for identifying that. Many years ago I did three workshops with your organization and we used one of my techniques called the strategic option grid, and we got people to evaluate the strategic attractiveness, the financial attractiveness, etc. Different kinds of principles but the idea behind that was that it is a systematic process that can become intuitive in time and judging things really quickly and prioritizing them and weighting them. So do you find that semi-structured process helpful?

Des:

We do; we would do that as the secondary process. The first process is (to ask): 'Can we apply ourselves, our skills and our values?' If we can, then, is the market big enough, what are the competitors, what is the structure of the market, what are the margins, where are the hurdles, what are the barriers to entry?

What businesses can we be in?

Tony:

So you take really very specific criteria for this thing and add in later the more general (criteria)?

I found this most interesting in terms of the way my own process of the strategic option grid might well be operationalized in different ways. For instance, I generally advocate using five criteria for evaluating strategic options, including: strategic attractiveness, financial attractiveness and implementation difficulty (Grundy, 2012). In the past I have also encouraged managers to tailor some much more decision-specific criteria to the evaluation. For example at Tesco when we were evaluating 'services' we set some criteria like: fit with the brand, quality assurance and space utilization. Then separately we would apply the strategic option criteria; that is precisely how Des is defining his process.

Des:

And do you know why? Because if you can't take your culture into a new market, then it is wrong for you as a business and the fundamental culture of the organization. You should not try to crash cultures together in a single organization, to my mind.

And no matter how far you have diversified – and I think that the Japanese are brilliant at this: Yamaha doesn't mind if it makes electronic organs or ships, or motorcycles – but my understanding is that if it is actually made by Yamaha then there are some principles that are applied to it, no matter what it is.

Tony:

It's funny because I was writing the start of the Virgin Galactic case and talking generally about Virgin. I have been interested in Virgin for many years and it can diversify because of the idea of rescuing those who have been ripped off, and of giving them superior service, excitement as well, and even something that is a bit cheeky. If you list the combination of (present and past) Virgin businesses, some of them have gone, but there is quite a lot of commonality.

Thinking about this afterwards triggered the thought that in an ideal world, strategic thinking ought to bring together (as personified by Des) the business mind and the business heart, as it were, with both thought and passion. Interestingly the 'heart' metaphor comes up again in the chapter on the Paralympics.

Tony:

Also Virgin Galactic sits like that but it is a bit of a step out actually; it is an intensive technology, it is proper diversification because you are into that. They seem to have brought it off really well.

Des:

That's really interesting. Also, I was trying to think the other day, because I am doing a couple of talks of my own in the next few days, I was trying to think of anyone who is good who has gone bust in the last 10 years and I was struggling.

There is a lot of rubbish that has left the system, or back to this theory of what value were they actually adding in the end? So with MFI, it got to the point where you couldn't take it home with you there and then, there were still bits missing when it did arrive, so what was the point of going through all that hassle? They might have sorted out a better process, from the customer's point of view, but it just didn't work – they had become irrelevant. I think that there are a lot of businesses that have disappeared like that. Rover was the same thing of course: you can be as British as you like and your styling can be a little innovative, but in the end wanting to get from A to B reliably won, didn't it?

Tony:

Rover is an interesting case; I have been running it as a case study for 23 years now. In 2000 they were given £1 billion and they went on doing the same thing. They just built the same models and didn't really think about how many cars they could afford to make. For example, they could have just produced 10,000 (special ones), so that everyone would be gagging to get them, and at a high price. And if you thought it through, using a thing

I call the 'Optopus' (see Figure 1.4) going back in time (to 2000), Rover Group was, potentially, saveable. That is the irony: if you started up and came in with a different mindset, a different belief system, then there was an opportunity still (with a re-shaped Rover Group), but not with how they actually did it.

Des:

Well, we had too much management (in the UK) which hasn't been skilled enough, it hasn't been inventive enough, and we have had a number of labour relations problems in a number of industries which were intractable.

That comment sparks Des to turn to the NHS, which he clearly thinks has lost its sense of vision.

Des:

Now, interestingly, I think that that is exactly where we are with the NHS at the moment. We are in real trouble, with management, with the workforce, with motivation: pushing that back into 'good' mode has got nothing to do with structure or money flows at all. It is about how you engage people with the mission that it was set up to do, and how you make that work with the 1.4 million people that are in there, so that they can make it work for the 60 or so million people that they support from a health point of view. That's where you need to re-engage that industry – it's about a fundamental call to mission, it is not anything to do with structure, nor is it anything to do with funding – there is plenty of money in the system.

Tony:

My wife works in the NHS as a clinical psychologist. Ever since I met her nearly five years ago they have a long waiting list to be assessed. They still have a long waiting list if you have a serious psychological problem.

Des:

I think that, to go back to this theme of strategy, it is very hard to predict the way the world is going, but actually we are in very predictable times: we know what is coming with technology, it is just getting faster and better and easier.

We know where age is going, we know the challenges to the food supply. I really do wonder if a big recession is a thing that is really not going to surface for a very long time, because with a middle income market growing every 10 years by about the size of Europe, with a population that will continue on an upward trend to around the 10 billion mark, the fundamentals of economics (are strong): we will need replacement power stations, motorways and bridges in the world, schools and everything else; it is so huge that demand is actually never going to go away. It is only a question of where the money rests, and therefore, the 'supplemental economics', the enterprise on top of infrastructure, is actually more marginal to an economic system than perhaps it has ever been. You know cities are going to need so much maintenance for the future, that that is going to absorb a lot of economic activity.

Tony:

You sound as if you have quite an insight into and in-depth knowledge of economics – is that's something that chief execs should have?'

Des:

I think that you have got to be exploring with your mind every market, every pressure; why, for example, has food gone wrong, why in governance terms did Murdoch ignore one of the centrepieces of his business, why did hubris take over in the financial system, and why were the children allowed to play with the banks when everyone knows that parental control is required? What you do as a CEO is to assess and mitigate any risks like these (in your own organization). You need to ask yourself: 'If it has gone wrong for them, could it have gone wrong for me?' And ask: 'What are we doing in my culture that says we won't be surfacing complaints from customers until you get what is going on with some NHS establishments at the present. Am I doing that in my own business and if I am, is that truly sustainable?'

Strategy and honesty

Tony:

I imagine that in your world it would be fascinating to go forward and look at some stories about the sort of, the radical, maybe not quite the collapse of the NHS but a huge crisis of confidence so that people pour into wanting your help, and you might be overwhelmed by demand.

Des:

Yes, we do have those imaginings; we even have an idea of what that timetable might be, we can't precipitate it, and we do know that if we go back 70 years, half the population had private insurance, and that's how things functioned, and we also know, without question, that every country in the world can't afford the health care that its population demands. The population won't pay enough in taxation to support the health care that it wants. Therefore, something has got to give.

We also have a view of what other countries are doing and I think that CEOs have to keep alert to other models in other countries, because some of them are way ahead of us, quite frankly, and therefore we play scenarios back to say: 'What would we invent?' And then we come back again to principles. One of my principles is, from the NHS point of view, no matter what change came, I would never want to deny universal access to health care in the UK. So I don't care what future system comes as long as everybody is included, and that's the 'live-or-die-by' principle. There is a second one: that as a tax-based system is an efficient way to collect the money for it, why not continue that.

Furthermore, the NHS does not have to be the provider; you can allow a plethora of capable organizations to try to drive standards up in the system by allowing what they would call 'competition'. However, it relies on another principle: that the government should provide oversight for commissioning and quality control, and they are not so very good at those sorts of things. But they need to become good at them, because this is a social imperative; it is a vital piece of social infrastructure. But these principles would then say that if that scenario came about, how would we plan to participate in those sorts of markets, and what would we do? You should be doing that all the time.

I was wondering at this point whether many CEOs could think in as wide-ranging a way about society, the economy, and different industry models as Des obviously could, on the bigger canvas of strategic thinking.

Tony:
So you could be looking at markets that aren't completely obvious then?

Des:
Absolutely.

Tony:
So, I you would ask yourself: 'We have got this thing called Simplyhealth – and these are the principles. What markets do we think that we can actually add value to?'

I was wondering whether Des has done this as an exercise. Probably Virgin has done that, and I know I once did it with Tesco, but it would be very interesting to test the brand stretch as a strategic exercise.

Des:
Too often in life those markets are determined by what is going on with the structure of your society. We have said it is called 'Simplyhealth' because we want to be in health care, and the reason that we want to be in it is that it is a big enough subject, and if someone has got to know what they are doing in it then it is going to take years to become an expert in it. And let's be one, because that is what is needed.

The second thing is that you now have a market that is defined by government regulation and stewardship of society: how do you participate in that? And there you have got to watch for how societies change over time, and take your markers from that. Strategically, there is nothing to stop us from running hospitals to GP practices to anything else – just like Virgin are.

Tony:
And there is the preventive stuff that might be interesting, like health clubs.

Des:
Whatever we felt what was appropriate – none of these might be, some of those might be – the point is that we would run them in a way which was absolutely in line with the culture of the organization and the principles, the operating practices and the destination. Could you run a hospital to inspire people to get to better health? Is a hospital the thing to run, or is it not? And if you can't answer that question then don't do it. So it's where are the opportunities, can you apply your principles, your vision, your culture?

What Des said resonated with me when I visited University College Hospital for a knee examination and waited two hours. I took a picture of the seven leadership tenets that were on the consultant's PC as I was kept waiting in his room for a further 15 minutes: Tenet number 2: Focus on outcomes – it is all about quality health care and tangible better results for patients.

Tony:
So if we did a lot of those things and integrated them into a mind map we would have a lot of things going on. And a lot of those things would be psychological – and psychologically understanding the markets in another sense because it is a human market that we are dealing with. And it is about understanding that human psychology has a history and a future, and it is also about trying to understand the shape of that future, and what the shape of that future psychology will be, what that future behaviour will look like. That's what you have to do when you design scenarios.

Des now uncovers another major plank of the framework that underpins his strategic thinking – the intent to build Simplyhealth into a trusted institution.

Des:
I have often talked about institutions of the 20th century that were trusted by the British people, and creating Simplyhealth as an institution of the 21st century that can be trusted by the British people, and part of the 20th century psyche and part of how we live our life. In the 20th century the BBC was a fundamental, trusted, structural piece of our society. You basically believed that the BBC weren't lying to you and that you got a reasonably balanced view of world events. And if you couldn't trust those institutions your life would be stressful, you wouldn't know where to turn. My own view

is that in strategic terms one of the drivers is to build an organization that can be trusted at that level – that it will do what it says on the tin – and that it will be there when you need it, and that what you will get from it is what you would expect.

Tony:
So, there is an element of honesty about that too isn't there? I have noticed an increasing dishonesty in tricky deals. I bought a Canon printer for around £80 and I thought, 'Why is this nice printer – colour – sold for that price?' But it wasn't £80 as I was paying £10 a week for ink cartridges.

Des:
And then, 50 pence for a plane seat and £1 to use the toilet... all of this is demeaning to the human condition. Just sell your product for a price that people will understand and it will make a better organization. Because, actually, we are all tired of the hidden cost stuff.

Tony:
If I wanted to start a movement – suddenly, a fad – it might be 'ethical pricing'; I think one could make a big thing of it. Like Henley has a 'Centre for reputation'.

Des:
Iceland does it. They price at £1, £2, not 99 pence. I admire that.

Tony:
Just going back to the evolution of HSA (as it was) through to Simplyhealth, I was just trying to get a sense of the history of the organization, what its origins were.

Des:
HSA was a mutual and is about 80 years old. We have now merged or acquired about a dozen companies to form Simplyhealth. That was a strategic decision: if we were going to help many people, then we were going to need some scale and operating as we were didn't allow us to invest the tens of millions in systems for the future in new developmental technologies, it didn't allow us the scale in the 21st century in health system versus health service. And so I had to gather some critical mass to broaden the product base across a wider range of offerings and allow us to become a significant player. We have gone from around 1 million people to 4 million, from about 500 staff to around 1,700. There are about a dozen companies in total.

So we now go from Cashplan for private health insurance, we own Denplan, we have the mobility company and a number of other products. So we are getting there, but there is a long, long way to go because the job of inspiring people towards better health is not going to end. So you kind of lock in for your part of the journey and keep it going there, and hand it over to others who can take it further.

Tony:
So is there anything in areas like terminal care, etc, even funerals like grief care, and all that kind of stuff?

Des:
There is a lot around that and there's a lot in the psychology of things. There is also a lot of need at the moment: you are in markets that are dysfunctional, where quality is too variable, where all sorts of other governance issues are rife, and one of the issues not being brought to bear, particularly about caring for the elderly population – that is something that needs strengthening dramatically in the next few years because that part of the population is growing.

Acquisitions

Tony:
Last question, I think: 'What is the one big thing that we forgot?'

Des:
Out of the 11 or 12 acquisitions there was only one that failed, and it failed because we thought that we could shift a culture, and I think that the lesson learnt was that pulling machines and buildings and policies together is one thing, but putting cultures together is not only not easy but I am not sure that it is ever possible, other than over a generation and I mean by that 20 years of working. Therefore be careful when you think that you have got a target market and you have a target enterprise and its behaviours are fundamentally different – you will not shift it, and you will consume your own energy, and you will bring your own reputation down as a consequence of trying that.

Tony:
One of my areas of interest is acquisitions. I tracked the acquisition of Rover by BMW; once BMW had acquired it, it fell into the trap of increased, escalated commitment. People think that they can get through the problem of controlling the escalation of commitment by the 'will to power', but that is really difficult. And, especially in terms of integration difficulty – you probably need a culture audit before you would ever consider such a thing.

Des:
It's a part of the due diligence.

Tony:
Yes, the organizational due diligence and that can be a stopper. The literature – it is all there – but people just ignore it.

Des:
They get the red mist, the deal is numbers, and the aftermath is huge, it is years long, and requires good managers.

I suppose the last couple of things to mention are strategy and the team. Nobody in this world is clever enough to have all the ideas. Your perspective, specifically your strategic perspective, is always enriched by people who are not like you. The ability of people in leadership positions to facilitate progress, as opposed to being the commander of progress, is very much the leadership style that I am absolutely sure is very much a part of getting through the complexity.

I was interested at this point in surfacing a little more of their strategic thinking process. We had already seen that Simplyhealth spent a lot of time at board level on strategic debate, used semi-formal screening processes for new strategies and also brought in the whole team. But how was that all steered?

Facilitation

Tony:
So when you have your strategy sessions, do you have a facilitator?

Des:
No, you sit there as the facilitator. You don't sit there as chief executive telling people how it is. You are getting out of them what they have got and that's all a part of how you get strategy to be quite strong.

Tony:
To be a facilitator is it sufficient just to have the skills of a strategic thinker? Or what else is needed?

Des:
You have got to be a listener, you have got to be an encourager, and you have got to have the attentive skills, which means that if you are sitting around a table and having a debate when you disagree or agree, it doesn't matter. You have to make people feel that they have a valuable contribution to make and not be dismissed by others, that the precious bits are absorbed. These leadership qualities are about knowing how to nurture culture, how to nurture the best out of your people. We are not going to have a compliant workforce in the future where they expect to be told what to do. I have got a brain and if you don't want me to use it in this place then I could

go elsewhere. You have got to hang onto the bright ones; they have got to participate actively and constructively in the most forward thinking, in the most strategic parts of your thinking.

Tony:
Thank you very much, Des, that's been fantastic!

Simplyhealth is becoming more and more prominent in our lives: I got a new Samsung phone this week and there was an App on it already from Simplyhealth – free! My wife is also working as a psychologist with one of its clients; we will see more and more of Simplyhealth.

> **CONCLUSIONS**
>
> The main points that impressed me from nearly an hour of conversation with Des were:
>
> - His genuine and totally authentic concern for the visionary: he was truly evangelical about the purpose of the organization.
> - The idea that strategic thinking should bring together the strategic mind and the strategic heart.
> - Strategic thinking should be practised as strategic mindfulness.
> - It needs to be fully shared within the board rather than individually driven.
> - Too much reliance on heavy formality and documentation can hamper strategic thinking.
> - To get real competitive advantage out of it, it needs to concern itself with the human, the psychological, the behavioural and the emotional.

Another thing that I took from this interview was that I re-evaluated the role of vision in strategy. Often managers think that once they have got a vision (or a mission), the strategies simply fit underneath that, without thinking these through in terms of whether they really are ones founded on competitive advantage, whether they genuinely add economic value, etc. Where the vision is not really specific or really special, a vision-driven strategy development process can be potentially dangerous: it is not competitively grounded and the strategies underneath it will not be very well thought through.

I would see the vision as naturally emerging after a set of strategies have been identified, refined, evaluated – and prioritized – in that order. So here the vision would definitely 'fit' the strategies very naturally and wouldn't be forced. But if we take a truly clear and special vision of the kind adopted by Simplyhealth, I can see how that would be extremely useful in the filtering process of strategic ideas as Des describes, particularly as that vision is embedded very clearly in the needs of the market.

In reality it should not be a question of which should always come first, the vision or the strategies, as one always needs to decide where to start in a flexible way, contingent on the circumstances. Using the vision as a strategy screening device may be a necessary condition of evaluating a strategy, but that is by no means a sufficient condition: there are always other considerations, like strategic attractiveness, financial attractiveness and the implementation difficulty of the strategic option grid (see Figure 1.2).

07 International Paralympic Committee

Introduction

The Paralympic Games were staged in conjunction with the Olympics in London in 2012. For several weeks there was a huge concentration of attention on these monumental events, not only from within the United Kingdom but also globally. According to Wikipedia, 4,302 athletes from 164 countries competed in the 2012 Paralympic Games (that is about 40 per cent of the numbers that participated in the 2012 Olympics).

Both the opening and closing sessions of the Games (the regular Olympics and the Paralympics) were staggeringly impressive. I remember thinking: 'It's an awfully long time since I remember anyone and certainly any institution doing anything this well.' The opening session had graphic celebrations of UK's industrial past, and of the industrial revolution in particular, which began around my home town of Bolton, in Lancashire.

If the success of Olympics Games was unprecedented, that of the Paralympic Games could in many ways seem even more notable. The professionalism and all the effort that had gone into them were remarkable. The Paralympic Games had truly arrived and were attracting equal interest from the media and the public.

It is not perhaps widely known that it was only in the very late 1990s that the Games had their very first professional employee. Only in this millennium did the current President and CEO establish what was to become its professional management team, working in unison with the volunteers and with input from a variety of non-executive board directors, from many parts of the globe. The President happens to be my cousin, Sir Philip Craven, who is a visionary but well-grounded leader, and who, in the opening ceremony, sat in his wheelchair with the Queen beside him (maybe fresh from that parachute jump), just couldn't help mentioning the virtues of his Bolton heritage. Boltonians are gritty, determined people who will fight against any odds. That mention was perfectly on cue!

Sir Philip had a climbing accident when he was 17 and would never walk again. I must have been around 13 at the time. I recall visiting him at Stoke Mandeville Hospital, expecting him to be down; I was amazed to find him as if nothing had ever happened! When I saw him at a family event in 2012 he gave me a lift to the station: he has no problem storing his own wheelchair and getting into his car and driving – cool to see that.

After convalescence he went to university and had a management career with the Coal Board. He went on to be an athlete in the Games and to become involved in the paralympic organization; he was finally elected its President. He was knighted for his services to the Paralympic Games, run by the International Paralympic Committee, or IPC.

The IPC is still a young organization and is in a stage of growth and quite rapid development: maybe a little beyond Virgin Galactic, but nevertheless still in an emergent mode. Yet is still had the vision, capability and the infrastructure to make the Paralympic Games in London in 2012 rival the original Olympic Games for public interest and attention. Demand for tickets for the 2012 Games was extraordinary.

The IPC has a double-act leadership: Philip, as President, looking after what might be called the 'political' front, and Xavier Gonzalez, its CEO, running the management and the 'business' aspects. Like Philip, Xavier has been with the organization for more than a decade. They developed the IPC's strategy together and have pulled off – with their team – what we saw in the 2012 Games.

I flew to Bonn to meet Xavier in May 2013. This interview is very interesting in the particular respect that Xavier, when we met, initially suggested that strategic thinking wasn't something he knew, in theoretical terms, much about, but actually, at a tactical and pragmatic level, he truly did, as we will see. I suspect that many CEOs are in this category. It is hoped that this book – and *Demystifying Strategy* that went before it – will reassure those CEOs and encourage them to dip a bit more into recipes for thinking strategically, to extend and deepen their current, intuitive powers.

This case covered an extensive range of topics:

- what is strategic thinking;
- use of jargon;
- the thinking process;
- vision;
- lead times;
- business scope;

- linking things;
- mindsets;
- non-linearity of thinking;
- strategic decisions;
- strategic conversations;
- multi-dimensionality;
- translation into action;
- openness to making mistakes;
- formalization and measurement;
- strategic thinking and flow;
- strategic model;
- strategic heart;
- strategic identity and engagement.

What is strategic thinking?

Xavier:

When I saw the questions, I thought that I would go and look at what some of these things were, because I do not come from studying management. I come from an event organization background. I run a sports organization, but when I said (to people) that we are a business, we are like a corporation, Philip dislikes it when I use these words. But we are a sport, a federation, so that means I am not one of your typical CEOs in that sense. I don't come from a theoretical background, so I had to check the idea of strategic thinking (from your questions).

Tony:

People use that phrase, and I am not sure that they always know what it means.

Xavier:

I don't use it (laughing), because I didn't know what it (precisely) means. We do a lot of strategic planning and a lot of strategy work: it is something that we do, and I have not said that we do not talk about this thing 'strategic thinking' – 'thinking strategically' is probably better, to be honest. I Googled it and I found what it was and I thought, 'We do not know what it is, but we do a little bit of that.'

Something that I had noticed in these interviews (that some readers might have observed too), was that although my questions had been very much about the cognitive side of the strategy development process – as thinking – a lot of the material that came up was more about either the content of the strategy or the more pure, process aspects. It seemed as if, at least some extent, these particular CEOs took the thinking bit for granted, and weren't always so aware of when and how they were doing strategic thinking and when they weren't. In other words, at a meta-thinking level, they were only fuzzily aware – to speak analogously, whether it was 'on' or 'off' – with exceptions.

Tony:
What fascinates me about this is the cognitive process that sits behind producing the plan: the journey and not the destination.... You are probably doing that without calling it that.

Xavier:
Exactly, that was what I was saying; we do 'strategic thinking' around here, but we don't theorize about it. Maybe we don't use it as a word to inflate what we do, you know what I mean?

Tony:
Symbolic?

Xavier:
We are not doing the things that are... cool... to talk about. You know what I mean?

Tony:
It is a buzz word.

Xavier:
Sometimes people use it because it is the trend, you know it is like you use words on Twitter, sometimes we say: 'We do it', because it is cool to say it.

Tony:
Maybe it is not helpful to have this buzz around it, it makes you think that you are not sure that you are doing it, or you are not sure that you are doing enough of it, or when someone says that they are doing some strategic thinking, they are getting, trendy.

It seems to me, from this, that while there is a genuine reluctance from CEOs to get distracted from the business realities by getting lost in jargon, this perception that strategic thinking is something 'designer-like', or cool, is unfortunate. It could so easily lead to a neglect of not just the strategy process, but to the psychological processes that both drive and shape it.

Xavier:
Well, I hope that I can talk a little about how we do it.

Tony:
Describe a bit of the background: the development of plans and planning and longer term – and then environmental thinking – and finally positioning within and shaping the environment, through visioning and through imagination.

Xavier:
It is very interesting because I would have thought that's how people should think. I always have a way to think first (about) the future: I imagine, I dream

it, I talk about it. Go to the bar with your mates, have a discussion, think in that (space)... think where you want to go, and how that reality will look like, then say how to get there.

The plan is only the steps to get there. Inevitably there's a lot of day-to-day work that needs to be done to. If you have not really thought about your journey, the plan doesn't tell you anything. I think that if you don't really have a clear understanding of where you want to go and how that reality will look like, it is a little curious that you say that this is something that is coming now. Is that not a logical thing to do?

He next describes another example of looking ahead in the sports industry and the need to look further ahead.

I also have a little difficulty coming from a different culture than the Anglo-Saxons – to try to summarize all in a vision. Even trying to do that, it puts certain limitations on (the thinking).

He now talks about the other five interviewees also being somewhat sceptical of 'vision' in some respects – and even more so of 'mission'.

Xavier:

If I could summarize, at the end of the day you do these things because we are in an era of slogans and you need tell the rest of the people something that they can put on T-shirts, or on a small piece of paper, that reminds them every day when they come to work what is the vision of the organization. Sir Philip, our President, uses the vision a lot – because I think that we have a good one, but I feel that not as a 'sentence' but in the real sense. The vision is also changing, it is not set in stone, but I feel that that is in particular in the environment that we live on today, you always are getting new feedback, new discussions, new topics, new opportunities in the organization.

What I found interesting in this part of the discussions, was the weight put on vision in the process at the IPC. More commonly 'vision' is something that, although a part of the overall architecture of a strategy, is not the most important part. I picture it as like the chimney of a house: it finishes it off, but it is the strategy itself that is the main part of the solid structure (with things like culture and core competences as the foundation).

At the IPC, perhaps because of the particular nature of the organization, it is far more central because of three things: it is about inspiring athletes and all others involved in the games (spectators and so on), etc, this uplift is a central output of the strategy; money is not the central point of the exercise, it is an enabler; and there is a high degree of discretion in defining what the strategy is, relative to say, a more pure business organization constrained with the need to compete in a given market place. Because of this, if there is a very clear guiding vision, the individual strategies/opportunities that come up can be thought through strategically by simply testing them against that vision.

Vision

Xavier:
We have a growing organization. That means that 20 years ago our world was small, and our thinking was also. Thinking what we cannot do today, what you can pay and what you cannot pay. Of course you need to do that. But as CEO I don't do this thinking alone. It is a collective discussion with people here.

But we had this broader vision, this more forward vision, but today we have more opportunities. There is more interest in us, there are more resources available to us, there are also new ideas, new opportunities that we didn't think about it then. Even if we were more visionary, because we didn't have the information we didn't really understand the possibilities.

Tony:
Some people call this 'emergent strategy', which forms itself through you doing things. I imagine that as you go through these four-year cycles the splash that has made will generate a change, a shift.

Xavier:
If it were 10 years ago when Sir Philip and I moved here, he took the political leadership and I took the management of the organization, I think that what you saw in London was the vision that we had. It was what we wanted, to see at least (that), and we wanted to see the people engaging in that, and we wanted to see the Games having been recognized – you know that's why we put the vision together but at the time we had been a little too cautious to share that vision too much with the outside world, because we worried about being called too visionary and consequently not too practical and unrealistic.

And I think that is because at the end of the day, this is a movement and we need to bring our mix of stakeholders and our members to support us together, to feel like... you also need to play the game a little in terms of what they could accept at that time versus engaging the people internally in particular in this office, with that vision, because otherwise it becomes very frustrating in particular and you don't have an large number of resources.

I ask to go back to the vision.

'To enable paralympic athletes to achieve sporting excellence and to inspire and excite the world.' This is one that we created in 2003. Previously we had rules that told us who we were. At a Strategic Planning Conference in

2001 there were a lot of ideas but nothing happened until Sir Philip was elected in late 2001 and he said 'We need to do something with this.' We hired Mckinsey; we called it a 'Strategic outlook'. We were not prepared at that time to do it, to go into the level of detail like a proper strategic plan, like the one that we have got now. We were not there as an organization, nor did we have the structure.

But we did two things: one thing was that we created the vision, and two, we had the strategic outlook. What we did then was we conducted a series of interviews and we developed a strategic outlook and the structure of the organization couldn't deliver the strategic plan.

Mckinsey put together a 'magazine' on the IPC, dated some time in 2014, when the organization would have achieved the strategic outlook. It was a nice magazine. It cost a lot of money – they wanted to play with us. I would love to see that as it is 2013 now!

Tony:
Couldn't you get that back from them?

Xavier:
No they move around so much... you know these (laughing) consultants. But one thing that we did do internally – we didn't use Mckinsey, which was mainly about the process to get there and our organization didn't have a lot of staff at the time – was the vision And if you go back to the vision that you saw in London, the images, it was about the athletes, enabling the athletes, producing sporting excellence, that's what we do. Now that was for us about the athletes performing to their best of their ability and inspiring and exciting people, because we want to produce an effect on the people who watch the event, and who interact with it. When you put that in front of the London images you can say: '100 per cent'.

There was one piece that we didn't add: 'And change the world'. That was the one that we didn't feel in 2002 (that we could add).

Tony:
You could do that now.

Xavier:
Exactly.

Independently, I felt that this was exactly what the IPC had begun to do through the Games: to change attitudes on what was possible in achievement both physical and non-physical, to be able to turn some disadvantage into an opportunity – and as a positive challenge, mind over matter, not moping about something that was not quite perfect.

I told someone I know very well about the experience of my visit and of the positive inspiration that radiated from the IPC. She had been telling me about some two-monthly meetings she has to attend in her job with lot of other psychologists and psychotherapists – they are called 'reflective meetings'. In reality they involve people off-loading their frustrations about resources, pressures, waiting lists and so on. In short they are mainly about moaning, which does have a therapeutic role. But as a naturally positive person I question some of that: negativity multiplies and depletes energy. I suggested that they can only moan if they suggest something positive: otherwise they get a referee's yellow card. Repeated offenders would get a red one, and have to leave the meeting. I also suggested that she takes my DVD of the Paralympic Games 2012, to show them next time! We both agreed that the UK seemed to be full of depressive people (or at least Croydon is!) and often without true reason. Those paralympic athletes seem to be anything but depressed. (Sorry, readers, for the digression, and to the IPC guys too.)

Xavier:
But again, we had that vision, strategically we didn't want to do it only for us, we wanted to do it in the world: it is changing and we want it to change. But to change in the right way.

We didn't know what that meant. We didn't even have the intellectual knowledge to articulate it. Sir Philip and I talked and imagined, to try to put it into words. To try to have a common vision between him and I, not on the details, not on the journey, not on the steps, not on 'we'll do that tomorrow'. There were 10 years, overall, to when this movement needed to go.

When reflecting on this some days later it made me wonder about the optimal time horizon for planning: how many cycles the Games might one be able to envisage realistically – two, three, or even more? Logically one might take that as a parameter and then add the number of years to arrive at the next Games: so if one were to look at that in the summer of 2013, one year after the last Games we have, with three Games cycles: three years, plus three years (to the second Games), and another four years to the third – that's 3+4+4 = 11 years. With four cycles that would be 14 years. Or am I splitting hairs?

Lead times

Tony:
Do they call that the 'event horizon' in modern physics?

Xavier:

And from then, it was a little bit of a job having that on its own, a vision, and at the same time to make it happen in the short term. Our first strategic plan was not done until 2006 – it took us three years to be able to be in that position, to transform our vision to the strategic goals, it didn't really change the big picture, but articulated it. And it took another four years to get to the one that we have now, to drill it down to more steps.

During that period there was a lot of pressure to have a strategic plan right away, and my view was always as an organization we are not ready, we needed less purely performance metrics. Things need to be a little more flexible for people to fit in and to get together. There were too many (internal) environmental issues, and we were a start-up organization, and we needed to bring a few things together. We still needed to meet the budget, and we still had to deliver certain things at a certain time, but we didn't want to tie us into too much checking, and more doing.

Listening to this put me in several minds: for instance I have witnessed events that have crystallized a strategy, for instance Tesco Non-Food was three days – with four different sub-businesses and sub-teams: so why was the gestation period for the Games so long? Well, strategy development has to fit with the culture, structure and skills and the mindset of an organization. Over and above this we also have stakeholder management – which is far more complex in a not-for-profit organization. At the IPC there were a hundred stakeholders at that time!

We found similar issues of getting all on board at both the Samaritans and the Association of Personal Injury Lawyers. At the Samaritans the gestation period of a strategic plan was also three years. So the 'limiting constraint in this situation was the culture and mindset and also, perhaps to a lesser extent, the skills. What would have been the point of developing a strategy that had to be left on the shelf? All that having been said, it shouldn't take an awfully long time to further develop/update the present strategy, if appropriate.

Tony:

Was that (earlier approach) a bit of an inappropriate planning model for you?

Xavier:

Well, that's what I thought. I don't know. Today as an organization that has grown, we went from 10 employees in 2002 to now when we are 60. We have had significant growth, in budget, and from 100 to 200 stakeholders in terms of a membership structure. The organization has grown exponentially. Now in particular we need a lot more processes in place. I now spend a lot more time talking about strategy, about 'big picture issues'.

Tony:
Can you put a percentage of your time on that?

Xavier:
Seventy per cent.

Tony:
Wow!

Xavier:
Sometimes I am acting as a (kind of) consultant. For me it is important to continue thinking where we are going, particularly because this is a new organization and it needs the commitment of people, that balance that we continue to have between 'professional' and 'volunteer'. It is an organization that has gone from being totally volunteer-based to a strong core of professional people. If you don't have a continuous feeling that there is a dialogue about where you want to go, to keep this spirit going – if it is only about tomorrow and what my performance is going to be in the next year, you become very much a 'perfect' organization. Sir Philip calls the spirit 'volunteering spirit'. To keep the people engaged, judge them not only on what they do.

Tony:
Well the Samaritans in the case study would be very similar to you in that respect.

It is in this kind of area that there is often vast potential to develop and I just look at the sort of activities that you could get into – like halo activities: sponsoring artificial limbs, for instance. What sorts of things could the organization do? When you look at the football industry 25 years or so ago when the Premier League was just about to start, the face of football was entirely different from what it is today. In a similar way you have the Paralympic Games but there are all kinds of things that could be built around that.

Non-linearity of thinking

Xavier:
Absolutely – and I totally agree. One of the challenges that we have is not to lose focus. In the end we are about sport and if we maintain the values of sport and we focus on that to ensure that even if we look into all the opportunities that surround sport we must not lose focus because we don't want to compromise so that sport just becomes entertainment. When we want to have an impact we want to resonate with people. We want people to leave at the end our events thinking: 'Wow' and looking at things differently.

There is no question that we are looking to (consider) things – I mean I don't know a lot about the new media (social networking), but we are willing to embrace technology and to take risks. We try to take opportunities; do we know what to do? Sometimes I say 'Let's get into it', we don't have the full plan, we could wait a long time to have it – and the opportunity will have passed. It's not that we jump at things without thinking, but we are also not trying to analyse everything to the last detail before saying that's where we want to go.

I also like (in strategic thinking) linking things. I spend a lot of time with my colleagues linking things and helping them not to work in a silo. I look at the overall picture of what the organization is doing. When opportunities come past – in Spain we say that they are like buses – the same bus never passes by again. Sometimes we say that we are going to develop something that we didn't have before.

Talks about how their Communications Director left for a dream move.

We hired somebody from a totally different background, (the world of) rugby. (He) didn't know us but brought a new dimension, new concepts, new ideas, things that we didn't know. We were at the time, not afraid, but not confident enough. But we started to invest, and put resources into something that wasn't even planned for. We moved quickly.

I talk about the fact that appointing someone or bringing on some new source of fresh thinking acts as a very strong catalyst for mew ideas, developments and change.

Tony:
It is about seeing things from many perspectives at the same time. It is like thinking on multiple dimensions. That's what strategic thinking is. I saw 'Iron Man 3' at the weekend and in it the superhero has some amazing computer graphics in three dimensions. It is all non-linear too, and it is great fun.

Xavier:
You are absolutely right. I always found that strategic planning is too linear. There is not enough about the other perspective that could affect things. And that is what I think a part of my job is: to help my senior management. They will normally work within what the strategic plans say, and where we are. And we are still not there. I help them to look across and to think – and I know that one of your questions is how do we do it (laughing) – On the plane I have a strategic conversation with my senior managers. We spend five hours on the plane.

I talk about easyJet and the journey over and how I was thinking about easyJet and some new value-added ideas. These included a group discount card, the 'Easycard', offering discounts from retailers and websites; a joint venture with Metrobank to launch 'Easybank' and a loyalty card with cumulative discounts and packages around Europe: not bad for five minutes of thinking.

Tony:
So I am on this plane, a captive audience: what could they do to sell stuff to me that would save me money, so that I am not bored and not wasting my time, or at least, to amuse me in some way. Then it turns out that they do have a loyalty card: it costs £100 a year to get a few extras, some of which I might have hoped to have got anyway. And that's a strategic idea that you could have anywhere.

Xavier:
Exactly. These things come up from conversations – you know when you have the time to talk about the strategy. In my weekly (activities) – because Sir Philip wants to travel less I am taking a little bit of the load that he had – we spend a lot of time talking about the big picture, and what we are trying to achieve. I also get involved in the detail: that's the part that I came from. I know more about the Games and understanding the complexities and the details that that requires.

But I know what you said about the movie: I try to design in my head a three-dimensional plan. And I think I cannot do it: I don't have the technology to do it. I don't know that it exists – that is why I do it in my head. I always try to bring things together in my head. And this is not thinking outside the box.

Here it emerges quite strongly that strategic thinking is very much curved-non-linear – if there was a physical visualization to it. An analogy would be having soldiers equipped with curved rifle barrels and mirrored sight so that they can see and shoot around corners in urban fighting.

Multi-dimensionality

Tony:
There are multiple variables that you are operating with; it is not three-dimensional reality, it is maybe 10-dimensional.

Xavier:
I also have another part of my personality, I am very pragmatic sometimes. Let's do this. Because if not, the strategic thinking is not supported by actions. And you know, the two things go together. You need to (actually) take decisions.

Tony:

I was at British Telecom once and we were talking about the word 'strategic' and someone said: 'When we call something strategic, it means that it is never going to happen.' Which is very sad.

Xavier:

I think you could do both, you need to be strategically thinking, but action-oriented. You need to be able to think forward, to be open, to get feedback from different people, to catch information, try to filter it, and you also have to deliver the stuff.

Xavier might not be widely read in the strategy literature but if he were to spend time there he would find lots on environmental scanning and on picking up weak signals.

Tony:

What you are doing there is, you are operating with pictures and you are operating in multi-dimensional reality. I find that if you start to use the two dimensions that you display things in, you start to get your head around that. Take strategic options: there are strategic options for *what* you do, for *how* you do them, and for *when* you do them. All those things form a huge amount of complexity, and you have got to find intuitively which 'cell' of those combinations is exciting – and it is not always easy to know. And this is not what they teach you on MBAs – they just ask you to get to the options and you might get lucky in what particular things you pick (from this menu).

So my take on this section is that strategic thinking can be about a variety of things: imagining the future; creating a vision within that future; seeing organizations and their environments from a variety of perspectives; issues, options and decisions across multiple variables and also in terms of their dynamics and their interdependences; coming up with creative options that may lead to a solution and absorbing uncertainties and risks – to the extent that actually making a decision is still possible.

Xavier:

Absolutely, and you have not to be afraid of making errors. It is not perfection, what we are aiming for: you need to be able to assume that in some of the decisions you will take you will not get it totally right, that's part of life.

From time to time all CEOs have touched on uncertainty and use a variety of analytical (and evidence-based) thinking, intuition, and cross-checking and comparing views from different directions (like the idea of 'triangulation' in research) as a key part of the strategic thinking process. Xavier very much follows this pattern.

Tony:
Well, you don't need measures, you need indicators. I do think that some of modern management is full of garbage of (inappropriately detailed) measures.

Xavier:
I do agree with that. It is very interesting that I have a board that is elected, it is not, shall we say, a business board. That means that we are really a corporately-run business: we need to deliver the things that we produce, but our board is more an association board. But it is very international.

And it is very interesting how the different board members look at things in different ways, like the strategy, or measurement. It is very interesting because you have people from one side of the world who all want to focus on the strategy. And we have others who want everything documented: charts and files. It is very interesting, as I understand that we need to do both. In an (international) organization like us we have to do something that works for us. Yes, we need to major on the monies, we need to have solid reporting mechanisms and make sure things are clear and know where you are, but you also need to ensure that you don't overdo it.

We have both a front and a back of the house organization – all together, and I can't have too much resource in the back of the house. So everyone needs to make sure that have an understanding of the 'big picture' of what we are doing. And I like to walk around the office when I am here. I am Spanish, I chat to people. I try to get the sense and to give people a sense that we are doing this for a purpose.

Strategic thinking and flow

Tony:
You are acting as a conductor of the organization and that means that you are contrasting the different perspectives of the board members and also the internal perspective – and it's that internal picture and the looking ahead picture. How would you describe how you do it?

Xavier:
Yes, we have formal processes. If we elect a new board, we would dedicate time early in the new year not only to develop them in the ways we work, but also to spend some time talking about the strategy. I normally do that once a year with the senior management team; that is for two days. We go outside the office and try to do it in a very open environment. Not too much about presentations but talking about topics. Now we have a strategic plan and we talk about that – new ideas, new concepts; how we can, together,

make it happen. It is at a very strategic level with the management, sometimes we get into the practicalities.

I also have a one-to-one once a year with the staff, talking about the big picture. Individually you may get some feedback that you wouldn't get from a collective group. Sometimes in environments like a plane, or waiting in an airport, with a blank piece of paper – let's see what can come out.

We have formal processes that we follow – it is part of the structure that we have – but also with Philip having a glass of wine when we travel together. We both like wine and can be together for a week, him and I, and our wives of course.

Tony:
Do you think that there are any differences in the effects of red wine versus white wine on strategic thinking?

Xavier:
(Laughing) I don't know, I am for the red wine! Sometimes, it (discussions) needs to be free, it needs to be 'continuous'.

Tony:
But sometimes it is about doing something out of the ordinary.

Xavier:
And again, sometimes it needs to come (out), when it needs to… when people collide. You get three people around a table and you start a discussion, and you start to exchange ideas, and you go away from the office and you know they are thinking: 'I am here in my eight hours (of work)', and you get into environments where you relax, and where people can have a conversation and share their visions, because everybody has a vision, everybody has ideas, everybody can contribute to building that reality that I was talking about.

When we started out on this there was just the two (of us), and Sir Philip is always the first to take the step, as you have to start from somewhere, and two is the next step after one. And afterwards you can engage the others, but it is amazing, you read something that is in a book, or a magazine, or you have some thoughts, or you talk to somebody outside, or go to a presentation, or someone throws up some ideas. I am not a big reader but I listen. I have a good memory for things I hear. I interlink things and I say, 'I heard these things'. And I incentivize those who talk about the bigger picture rather than say: 'Tomorrow, I need to do this, or I need to do that.'

So strategic thinking here is like anything else that happens in organizations: not only have the conditions for it to happen got to encouraged, eg away days, permission given to think that way, but also it helps if it is positively incentivized.

Tony:
Tacitly, I think that what we are saying is that a really good CEO should know what his or her cognitive capabilities and preferences are, and where these are conducive to strategic thinking, and to put themselves in situations where that is going to come out. Clearly, for you, you don't like too much formality but when you are in a relaxed state it actually starts to flow, and especially of you have got a double act with Philip. Whereabouts in Spain are you from?

Xavier:
Barcelona.

Tony:
Because, like Barcelona (there are two Barcelona football teams): in one there is this amazingly fluid team of which Messi is the centrepiece, and sometimes he is like a god. He knows he can do stuff, but in a situation where you are confronted with a Germanic team (ie Bayern Munich) which is very different, very strong, and you are in that situation, and Messi is not quite on form and he's under pressure, and then they can't do it, that fluidity goes.

And I am wondering whether, using that analogy, the best strategic thinking is where people aren't under terrible pressure to come up with an idea (like a 'goal') but where they have got enough time and space to play a bit, then get their skill level up. Training in this area can help people know what they are doing. I have found that in companies where people have been trained in strategic thinking, they go for it. And then they start to move around – more like Messi?

One of the things that has come through as a result of this study is the idea of 'strategic mindfulness' – mindfulness is about being somewhere, and being very, very aware of what's actually there and going on, like being in a park and the movement of the trees. In strategy it is similar – for a while nothing moves and then, there, something did move. So it is a non-busy state of mind.

Xavier:
Exactly. I think that you describe it very well. I think that how new ideas happen, the way you describe it is a mixture of fluidity and one needs to have a sense of urgency. There needs to be some need to drive the thinking for a new idea, even if it is not an immediate need. It doesn't mean that you need to get it by tomorrow. There is a sense of dynamic in the organization.

Tony:
Maybe it is an appetite.

Xavier:
The use of the English I will leave it to you.

Tony:
It is 'hunger', or 'appetite'.

This was another useful contribution from Xavier that I happened to find an informative, interpretative category for: 'strategic appetite'. I think this is a very useful idea as I have found that organizations vary enormously in the extent to which they have a strong drive to think strategically and to carry out strategic decisions. Of course that applies at the level of the individual CEO, too.

Xavier:
I think that it is also a goal of the organization. If we go back to Barcelona FC, and one of the continued debates is about them having the hunger to win, and consequently to find new ideas, to find new ways, introducing new elements, without changing the model, because the model is the culture, is the vision of the organization.

Without fully putting it into words Xavier is clearly operating with the concept of the strategic model of an organization; we might define this as: 'the scope of value-adding activities, the way in which they are interdependent with each other, and their overall purpose'.

Strategic identity and engagement

Xavier:
And it is a little bit like here. We have the vision and the culture and, with the team, we can tweak the environment, the way that we do things, the way that we create things, the way that we can resolve new challenges, the way that we can address the situation. We can generate new concepts or new ideas coming in that will allow us to move to where we want to be without changing our values.

Tony:
It is very much a kind of evolutionary model, isn't it?

Xavier:
There are components of learning, there is the environment, there are the people, you need to have people that are willing and able to participate in the generation of new ideas. And I think that it needs to be flexible, and there needs to be – you say – hunger; if not we will continue looking at the trees, and, yes there needs to be some sense of purpose.

Tony:
And if you don't get that from somewhere, some leadership, all of this isn't going to happen.

Xavier:
And there is something that may have nothing to do with what we are talking about and it is related to our organization because we are proud that we are very democratic, very participative, we are aiming at that. At the same time you need to balance that and link that with leadership. We need to have strong leadership not in the sense of the personalities but in the sense that you need to be going somewhere. We may vary the rhythm, the speed, the emphasis, but ultimately we have a clear vision of what we want to achieve. That's what I think: for us to have consensus in the organization even if there is a debate, a consensus in the organization of our ultimate aim to enable the athletes to perform. Many organizations don't have a 'centre' that is recognized by all as the centre of the organization, do you know what I mean?

Tony:
A heart?

Xavier:
A heart, or a soul.

Tony:
A 'strategic heart'.

Xavier:
A strategic heart – I don't know.

I have long been interested in the more emotional dimension of strategy, believing that often the cognitive side is over-emphasized to the point of it seeming to be the only dimension. An organization's 'strategic heart' can thus be given a working definition as: 'the common feelings across the organization about its strategic past, present and its future, and about its ambitions and options going forward'.

Xavier:
For us a person is not seen as an object, but as a human being.

Tony:
Yes, there is too much 'machine-speak' in organizations. In terms of fast-forwarding to visioning, a technique that I have learnt to use is storytelling.

Xavier:
It is very interesting because I am more a talker than a writer. In many meetings I will say: 'I am going to talk aloud. I am going to tell my story of the issue,

and you can intervene and tell me that I have got it wrong. I need to put in my own words what is discussed. And don't think that I am telling you what to do; I am talking about it and then you can contribute to build on it.'

I don't use the word 'story', but I say I need to put it into my own words. If I am able to articulate it, if I can talk about it, and then you can build (on that), and you can contribute, then we can make the full picture. I have the sense that talking is a more three-dimensional thing.

This is the most powerful thing, talking. I see people living in different realities through computers and I think (though) that since I was young I talk aloud and I tell my stories, I talk stories: I did movies in my head talking aloud. My parents said that I was bananas, it was not normal, because I walked around the table creating my own stories. I like to talk, to talk, to talk the things – not to write it on paper.

Yes, when you have the story clear you transfer it to a paper to a document, or to a chart. For me, talking is one of the things that we are losing.

Tony:

Maybe the generations coming up behind us won't be able to do some of this because they won't be able to talk!

Xavier:

Well, that's a difficulty. For me, even if you don't talk (on your own), it is when you do it with others that you construct the full picture.

Tony:

So is there 'one big thing' that we forgot to mention?

Xavier:

One big thing: for me it is people – it is engaging people, getting people to the front of the thinking. I think that there are too many processes, and I think that we all, as human beings, are able to participate and to contribute to the long-term thinking. And for me the big thing is allowing people to participate, allow the conditions to contribute, to be a part of that. We need to think where do we want the organization to go but everyone needs to do it, everybody needs to be part of it.

I had a conversation with our receptionist and we talked about the Games: 'Oh', she said, 'the Games! – and I really liked this part – and this is an area that I really, really, like.'

Well, you extract one idea from that. You know, what people like, what they don't like, that they engage with, and you work on it. And sometimes you get little pieces of information that you can work on.

Either as a part of strategic thinking or at least as a feed into it, is the process of strategic listening.

Tony:

Like clues? Strategic thinking is for me very much like detective work – like Lieutenant Colombo in the films – I have saved people many millions through saying, 'It is very, very strange...'.

Xavier:

You find clues, when you engage. When we do one-to-ones we also talk about where we think that the organization is going, what do they feel about it? Maybe we don't call it the 'strategy', but how they, in their position, see the organization.

Tony:

You know, if there is 'one big thing that we might have missed' in our interviews is that strategic thinking inevitably gives you a sense of organizational identity: so if you are involved (in the strategy), then it 'ups' that identity.

Xavier that was all fantastic! Very many thanks, for my last interview, and in Bonn.

CONCLUSIONS

In summary we see from this that:

- Strategic thinking is a very intuitive process, and deals with hard and soft data from a multitude of sources and directions.

- Because of uncertainty and the need to rely on a lot of intuitive thinking there are likely to be some mistakes.

- Doing this demands great skills in strategic listening.

- Where there is a very clear and specific guiding vision, it acts in part as a filter for what to think about and to prioritize in terms of a possible agenda for decisions and resource allocation.

- At IPC, this vision is also closely linked to the strategic model of the business, and also what we have tentatively called its 'strategic heart', or the common feelings that exist in the organization about the strategy. Where this is strong, as a spin-off it will help to encourage identification and engagement with the organization; while at the same time being flexible to take on new ideas from unexpected directions: it can be very spontaneous.

- It is processed through conversations – both the formally planned and those which simply emerge and, linked to that, to the process of storytelling (not necessarily linked to scenario development).

- It demands thinking in many dimensions, drawing together interconnections between different things, and on occasion, creating quite new ideas. This demands a lot of skill in cognitive modelling.

- It definitely shouldn't exist for its own sake: there needs to be a simultaneous sense that we are talking about things that we might actually make happen, and we need to have at least some degree of strategic appetite, both generally and specifically, to make this a reality.

My sense was that on account of the very considerable degree of freedom that the IPC has and the complexity of variables and thus options for development, some pictures like the strategic option grid and 'Optopus' (see Figures 1.2 and 1.4) might well be of great help. This would help to place less onerous demands on getting more pure intuition right.

Integrating important strategic thinking themes

08

Introduction

In this chapter we pull out some key themes from the case studies and compare what the CEOs said about them, albeit selectively. We then draw out any important insights that come up as we go through the material. After spending a little time on 'What is the nature of strategic thinking', we then look at the key research questions we posed in Chapter 1 – and try to answer them.

These Key Research Questions were:

1 Are they always aware of when they are doing it, or when they aren't doing they are doing it?

2 When they are doing it, what is it that they feel, how do they do it: what sort or recipes do they employ?

3 To what extent does the particular business and organizational context influence what they think about? (ie strategically)

4 Do they ever use any particular tools or concepts?

5 Do they typically do it on their own, or do they do it with others?

6 How much time do they spend doing it?

7 What does it actually feel like: does it have any distinctive sensation?

8 When they are doing it, what feelings are sometimes experienced, before, during and afterwards?

9 How do they keep track of, or even record their ideas and insights?

10 What value has come out of strategic thinking that they have done either solo or with others, in the past?

At the end of this chapter we conclude that, while a lot of illuminating insight came out of the CEO dialogues, this particular sample of CEOs had to talk a lot to make sense of their experience of strategic thinking: it was very much a tacit competence as one would expect, but this did mean that it was something very much driven by habit and by seizing the opportunities as they came up. But as far as reflecting on the thinking process itself, this was very much something that by and large they seem to have had little time to do. (Cognitive psychologists would call this a meta-process, ie reflecting on reflection.)

So our ending point is very much a beginning for us – in Chapter 9 trying to piece together some of the practical steps that can be taken not just by CEOs and directors but also other senior executives to mix what seems mainly an emergent cognitive strategy with more deliberate elements. In doing so, besides looking to vary interventions, such as more explicit use of strategic tools, etc, we pick up on the idea of strategic mindfulness as practised in Zen, and getting a better balance between more left-brain skills such as analysis and programming (the paradigm of traditional planning) and the more creative and intuitive in the cognitive mix.

The key themes of strategic thinking

The key themes we have chosen to concentrate on are:

- the nature and the centrality of strategic thinking;
- hierarchy of strategic questions;
- the value of strategic thinking;
- mission and vision;
- economic value;
- time spent on strategic thinking and the challenges of this;
- creative process;
- strategic conversations;
- inspirational light bulb moments;
- sharing and ownership;
- communication;

- intuitive economic analysis;
- helicopter thinking;
- concentration of focus;
- strategic processes and techniques;
- cutting strategy down to size;
- evidence-based strategic thinking;
- jargon;
- implementation.

These themes were arrived at through qualitative analysis of all the data across the six case studies through what is called a grounded methodology. Each of the comments of the CEOs was grouped with others that seemed to fall into the similar category. We then round up with a more general discussion of our key findings in terms of understanding the nature of strategic thinking and its role and the implications for practice. My own comments are highlighted in italics to save confusion.

While there is obviously some repetition of earlier material, this is in a different order. It is also now put in a cross-company context and has additional commentary and interpretation. We see probably about a sixth of the material again. This step is needed to cross the bridge that will help us answer the key research questions, to arrive at conclusions and to draw out the implications.

The nature and the centrality of strategic thinking

All the CEOs saw strategic thinking as being a vital and central part of their jobs, and not just within more set-piece planning sessions. We begin with Nick of Moonpig:

I think that it (strategic thinking) is absolutely essential. It is absolutely the foundation on which your business is based.

I don't see how you can do without it. It is so central, it is about ensuring that you are pointing in the right direction. It is absolutely critical to any business as opposed to people who say, we make these things, how do we sell them? I would always start one stage back and say 'What should we be producing?'

Nick thus sees strategic thinking as being just an extension of the more normal parts of thinking about an issue:

I don't think (that it is different from thinking generally). It is good to write it down, and it is a constant process. I tend to try to keep strategy separate from tactics.

Xavier (IPC) sees it as just a natural way of thinking about the future, and about the change and development that we encounter on the road there:

It is very interesting because I would have thought that's how people should think. In my way I always had a way to think first (about) the future – I imagine, I dream it, I talk about it. Go to the bar with your mates, have a free discussion, think in that (space) about where you want to go, and how that reality will look like.

One of the questions that I asked was about whether CEOs are aware of the fact that they are indeed doing it. This is how Catherine responded:

How do you know when you are doing it? Well, in an organization the size of Samaritans, you are never in any doubt (laughing). Samaritans is a very operational frontline service charity and I think that it is easier to put that delineation between when you are doing operational and strategic, because we are doing operational all the time.

Deborah (APIL) suggests that it is not something that is necessarily a long-winded process, but can be done fairly quickly – if one breaks down the topic of strategy into its constituent parts:

Well, it is quite quick as well; you don't have to do your entire strategy for your whole business in one go, you can do it in chunks.

What we see here is that it is a natural part of the day-to-day work of a CEO, and not really an add-on that necessarily requires some special procedures or set-up. We saw too in the earlier chapters that a key ingredient of strategic thinking is the ability to ask the right questions, and not just a deductive or inductive process.

Hierarchy of strategic questions

Nick of Moonpig now suggests that these chunks can be arrived at through having a clear view of the hierarchy of strategic questions that might be posed:

It did seem to me a rather long-winded way of expressing common sense, really. And my impression was that it was always best to stand back and to look at the bigger picture and the context and then work from there, working out a hierarchy of decisions that may need to be taken, because otherwise you can end up fluffing around sorting out all kinds of detail, when the reality is that you are doing that with detail that you shouldn't be involved in at all. That's one of the issues that I had when running Ark (a charity): you can look at it and spend a lot of time working out what kind of people we need to do what we are doing at the moment, when the big question should be 'Should we be doing this at all? And you might as well ask that question first, before you get into the detail.

It is a 'hierarchy of questions': if you don't answer the questions in the right order then it makes life complicated. So that's my approach.

So a characteristic of strategic thinking is that it has some sort of structure or implicit design or architecture where issues and areas for investigation are interrelated and interdependent. Nick again:

For me strategy is levels one, two and three, and tactics is levels four, five and six.

That comes back to my 'big picture' principle which is: the more that you think about the high level decisions the better the chance you have got (of getting them right). If you ignore the higher level decisions and start going down the wrong route, then you have got a handful of decisions at this level and this will be limited by your poor decision making at the top level.

George of Virgin Galactic divides up his strategy between the technical and the commercial – as a way of looking at this hierarchy of questions – at the very highest level:

Well, for a start I would say that strategic thinking is absolutely essential and sometimes hard to prioritize as sometimes you get caught up in the tactical. In the aerospace world I would connect it with the most basic hardware decisions as a sub-set of strategic decisions. What I mean by that is that in the aerospace world 90 per cent of the project's costs are committed in the first 10 per cent of the project, because you make decisions at the front end that set your long-term cost trajectory and in the operational trajectory of the project.

It is really important to get those decisions right at the front end. So to draw an analogy to other spheres of thinking it is like aerospace. Once you have made those decisions then you have set on a particular course for the cost trajectory, both the capex and opex. It is very hard to change at a later stage, to try to change the capex or opex. Once you are three-quarters of the way through the project you are where you are.

George describes how the level that you are at in the strategic hierarchy can be ambiguous at the time that opportunities and needs are emerging, so that in an emergent strategy context, the decision structure and possibly also the hierarchy of strategic questions may be murky:

Yes, I think at times you are conscious that you are not making larger strategic decisions. At other times you are making what is sometimes a tactical decision but because of what you are or are not including in the decision-making process, it is actually a major strategic decision. And sometimes you recognize things post facto, the strategic importance of something, that wasn't evident the first time round. I think it is a mix.

According to Des of Simplyhealth:

The first process is to ask: can we apply ourselves, our skills and our values? Then, is the market big enough, what are the competitors, what is the structure of the markets, what are the margins, where are the hurdles, what are the barriers to entry?

A domain of strategic thinking separate from the business world that Nick finds it useful to think about, is that of strategic thinking as applied to one's own career and life:

Well, I do a lot of personal strategic thinking (about) what kind of a life I want to live. Where do I ultimately get satisfaction from? And am I as good now compared to 10 years ago?

What comes out of this is that where you have only partially mapped out your hierarchy of strategic questions, you might be less able to realize whether something is clearly a strategic issue or not: and thus that might not automatically turn on strategic thinking as a process.

The value of strategic thinking

Deborah clearly believes that strategic thinking really does add value, and relates that back to why you are doing it anyway:

Well, part of strategic thinking is not just to think about it. What you are going to do but also why you are doing it. Why you are making those choices. It means that you start developing the messages in your head about why you are doing it so that you can communicate this to your staff and to the external world.

So for her strategic thinking is very much a deliberate process that one does precisely for the same reason as one might follow any other process: to add tangible value.

Moving on from strategy, mission occupies the interest of at least some of the CEOs but we see this met with a more mixed reception.

Mission and vision

Des is a visionary leader by nature, but it is clear that he shares my scepticism (see Demystifying Strategy*) on the role that mission is sometimes seen as having in strategic management:*

I don't like the word 'mission', it is very tactical. It is a very task-like word; I am more drawn to the idea of descriptive vision as being the over-arching drive for an organization through which implementing a number of strategies keep that vision in focus and keep the movement towards the realization of that vision.

Descriptive vision is also not a vague concept for Des; it is very much a concrete part of the strategic architecture of the business, and one very much at the heart of sustainability:

I have often talked about institutions of the 20th century that were trusted by the British people, and creating Simplyhealth as an institution of the 21st century that can be trusted by the British people, and part of the 20th century psyche and part of how we live our life. In the 20th century the BBC was a fundamental, trusted, structural piece of our society. You basically believed that the BBC weren't lying to you and that you got a reasonably balanced view of world events. And if you couldn't trust those institutions your life would be stressful, you wouldn't know where to turn. My own view is that in strategic terms one of the drivers is to build an organization that can be trusted at that level – that it will do what it says on the tin – and that it will be there when you need it, and that what you will get from it is what you would expect.

At Simplyhealth that vision is encapsulated in a very clear purpose, which one can see as acting as a continual guide to thought and action – both at strategic and tactical levels. (Normally vision is associated with the strategic but one can see it much more at a day-to-day level: for example, in that meeting we just had, what did we do to inspire anyone to better health, directly or indirectly)?

With Simplyhealth we are very clear what our job is, and what our goal is. But actually, in terms of our end point, we don't really have one, as our goal is to inspire people towards better health, and that is ongoing. So the question that I ask of both my employees and myself, every single day, is 'Have I got the energy, and have I got the sense of purpose, the drive, the thinking energy, and the time, to want to help to inspire people to better health?' That for me then creates an environment from which strategies for achieving that vision can emerge.

This piece of research has elevated the importance which vision, clearly developed and grounded in organizational reality, should have, alongside strategic option evaluation. Vision certainly features most in the thinking of the International Paralympic Games; here it is not a fixed organizational artefact, but something that that shifts, According to Xavier:

If I could summarize, at the end of the day you do these things because we are in an era of slogans and you need tell the rest of the people something that they can put it on their T-shirts, or on a small piece of paper, that reminds them every day when they come to work what is the vision of the organization. Sir Philip, our President, uses the vision a lot – because I think that we have a good one, but I feel that not as a 'sentence' but in the real sense. The vision is also changing, it is not set in stone: in the environment that we live on today, you always are getting new feedback, new discussions, new topics, new opportunities in the organization.

There was an issue at IPC as to what parts of the vision to show to the different stakeholders, and indeed how stretching to make that vision. Xavier (continuing):

Ten years ago when Sir Philip and I moved here, he took the political leadership and I took the management of the organization, I think that what you saw in London was the vision that we had. It was what we wanted to see at least, and we wanted to see the people engaging in that, and we wanted to see the Games having been recognized – you know that's why we put the vision together but at the time we had been a little too cautious to share that vision much with the outside world, because we worried about being called too visionary and consequently not too practical – and unrealistic.

The vision that was defined then was as follows: 'To enable paralympic athletes to achieve sporting excellence and to inspire and excite the world'. Xavier was clearly (and rightly) very pleased that this vision had actually been delivered:

And if you go back to the vision that you saw in London, the images, it was about the athletes, enabling the athletes, producing sporting excellence, that's what we do. Now that was for us about the athletes performing to the best of their ability, and inspiring and exciting people, because we want to produce an effect on the people who watch the event, and who interact with it. When you put that in front of the London images you can say: '100 per cent'.

This suggests, very strongly, that you must apply the 'did we deliver the vision' test. So while the concept of mission is seen by some to be too particular and too tactical, vision is very much seen as an active ingredient in strategic thinking, not just because it is forward looking, but also because it is integrates the overall picture.

The more specific issue of the economic value of a strategy only comes up explicitly in the context of the private sector companies.

Economic value

We can see Des working through his own hierarchy of questions or issues, as we now turn to the even more concrete challenge of competitive sustainability. This can be threatened by financial short-termism, and its consequences felt through value-destroying customer service:

Well, the business goal is assembled for the short term and then you crack a winner, and you disappear; that's one thing, but that is not what business is actually about. Sustainability is again the issue. Creating sustainability means that you have strategies that are about these numbers, and these margins that widen and whatever, but those strategies will make you recruit people who are good at cost-cutting and margin manipulation and good at shaving the edge off guarantees so that there are less claims, and shaving the edges off products so that they are less..., there has been shaving off service so that it is more difficult for the customer to get through to the organization.

And you have got to work out how you engineer value to the customer: the product itself will be the commodity; the way that we serve will increasingly be our point of differential. So, in thinking strategically yes, you have got to understand what your capabilities are, your core assets, what markets you are going to apply them in, and you have to work equally hard to apply those strategies to service: do they deliver the end-results?

In terms of how this particular CEO thinks, there is therefore a very clear pattern that revolves around guiding purpose and adding true and incremental value to society.

Catherine feels that creating both the qualitative and more quantitative outputs of strategic thinking sometimes requires different kinds of skills:

In terms of important insights, I always caveat these, well you have to create head-space, depending on what it is that you are doing, and you have to recognize that there are different types of skills needed for different kinds of strategy. I have got people who can produce a strategic budget but fall on their face in a strategy plan. It is fantastic: all the numbers add up and all the Is are dotted, but actually, does it relate to the strategy? You need to get the right people to do the right parts of that production, and you need your own head-space. If you don't think about it, it doesn't work. Therefore that strategic thinking thing is really important.

It isn't always easy to ensure that economic value is truly sustainable, as Nick highlights, and this is where these sometimes polar aspects of strategic thinking, the qualitative and the quantitative, need to be cross-checked:

I always thought: we are making amazing money here but that's not going to last. Also with the growth rates that we were getting, we were going to get a cracking multiple on the super-profit. So get out while you can. Otherwise you end up with so many other retailers and they turn over £200 million and they are making £3 million. That's not attractive at all. I don't look at that and think, I will put a lot of money into that kind of business....

Definitely, it's not sustainable. Somebody ultimately will take it off you. There just comes a point where you are making a 10 per cent net profit. It is acceptable, but any less than that and you wouldn't be doing it, and it keeps the competitors out. Everyone is always looking at you and saying: 'That looks fantastic, let's copy that.'

This cross-checking between the soft and the hard analysis may be thought of as rather difficult, but Deborah identifies one particular incident where there was a strategic thinking breakthrough, where the resulting value added was actually very concrete and measureable:

We started working on it on one of the days that we had with you, maybe half a day with you. Then I had to task my team to cost the options without me as I was out of the office and I think that they spent about another two hours on it, and interestingly it was the costing of the options that actually defined the strategy because when they thought it through there was one option that was going to deliver a much better reward and at less cost than the others. But having done the (strategic thinking) training they were able to do that on their own – and they just delivered me the result.

Time spent on strategic thinking and the challenges of this

Three out of our six CEOs explicitly volunteered that they spent a very large amount of time on strategic thinking. According to Deborah:

I would say that between a half a day and a day a week is going to be spent on strategic thinking. It will be pure thinking time: sensing the environment, talking to people, doing the influencing and negotiating and doing the messages – and all of that sort of thing. (How much is all that sort of thing, I asked.) At least another two days of the week.

Catherine says:

I would probably say on the combination of strategy development, implementation and thinking it is about 30 per cent of my time.

This is quite impressive and I doubt if most CEOs follow that pattern. Indeed we are obviously dealing here with a slightly biased sample of those CEOs who agreed to spend an hour being interviewed on the topic in the first place: those more tactically driven probably were among those who turned the invitation down.

This time seems to be spread around the week but is concentrated, particularly in quieter moments of a more mindful, meditative kind. Xavier, at IPC, went the furthest of all of the CEOs, based on the fact that he spent a lot of his time being effectively a consultant on different strategic issues and challenges, no less than 70 per cent of his time on strategic thinking.

I also like (in strategic thinking) linking things. I spend a lot of time with my colleagues linking things and helping them not to work in a silo. I look at the overall picture of what the organization is doing.

Catherine again:

I can think about multiple things but if I want to think about really important stuff like changes in direction, the future, potential challenges, issues, I have to have a quiet space. For instance on a Friday morning when I am working at home I will turn the phone off, and I will sit down with my pad of paper and ask why is this bothering me? I will draw visuals, because you can put as many things as you like in a picture.

Devoting such a high proportion of time to strategic thinking is clearly something of a challenge as there are always lots of issues competing with it, and a CEO's life may be anything other than ordinary. In Catherine's case at the Samaritans, for instance it is anything but a serene existence being a CEO.

If you are a chief executive, you are never not busy, so I work quite hard to reflect on how well we are doing, assimilating all the things that come across my desk, because I could be doing this interview with you now, and I have got a telecon at 4 o'clock with our biggest project provider, and then I have got to review the latest draft of the corporate plan that is going to the board on Friday, with all the associated budgets. And then I have got one at half past seven with a group of volunteers about an issue they have got. In any one day I have mixed up strategy, operational delivery, fire fighting, media, external engagements....

Des says that he just doesn't switch off: I myself operate in that mode – every shopping experience is an exercise in Strategic Thought (don't my local Tesco Extra know that – I have to allow 10–15 minutes for giving them feedback: invariably with some input of real strategic importance):

For me it is 24 hours a day. It is every time that I walk into a building I am thinking, 'What do I make of this environment? What opportunities open up?'

As a CEO, you work a seven-day week in your head. Don't mistake that for 'My God he must be shattered' – I'm not shattered. However, the subject matter, it never leaves my mind, and I always thinking, with anything I am involved in, from classical music to rugby, 'How can I apply that to the organization I am in and how might I use some of the professionalism of Clive Woodward in a rugby team to inspire my own managers?'

Such a mode isn't actually stressful because it is inherently stimulating to the mind. The high proportion of a good CEOs' time spent on strategic thinking also needs adequate shared thinking at board level and also, it would seem, where the issues and the decisions are quite complex, with the board, as Deborah now states:

I also take away the whole management team away for a day of strategic thinking where we concentrate on nothing else, outside the office, and everyone puts onto the table ideas or things they want to discuss.

According to Catherine:

It is easier to plan to do strategy and have a schedule. The board has a strategy awayday annually and we agree at the beginning of the year what that is going to focus on, the evidence base for the new strategy and it is for a full day and is externally facilitated.

George says:

I think one of the things that we try to do is to take some time out once or twice a year to spend a couple of days with each other and think about where we are, and where we are heading, and I think that that is really valuable. We sit in front of each other and make the time that's structured and ample enough that we can cover the topics; it is getting harder and harder to do that, but I think that it is really important.

So time is spent at the CEO level (solo), in one-to-one or larger groups and also in board level discussions, thus information is disseminated within and flowing around other echelons of the organization. Again, in terms of process, there can be interesting challenges if the board consists of a large variety of stakeholders, as at Samaritans and at IPC; in the latter case it is made more challenging because of cultural and mindset differences.

Creative process

One of the qualities distinctive to strategic thinking seems to be that it has a very strong creative element. Deborah describes this quality as follows:

It is quite a rush of thinking because lots of options start going out at once and it can all go off in different directions but it does get the adrenalin going, definitely, and it is that shift into being imaginative and creative, so it does feel different.

I spend a lot of time scribbling on pieces of paper, and I tend to draw a lot more pictures than words. So if I am thinking strategically it is always about drawing pictures, strategic thinking isn't just about writing lots of words on a piece of paper. Maybe the final business plan might look like that, but that doesn't aid the thought process. It feels a lot more creative. It is really creative and imaginative. It really stretches both sides of your brain, and I actually write with both hands at once when I really get into it, because your brain is completely engaged. It is very visual when you have finished it, but it is much easier to digest and understand it. You get far more on a piece of paper.

Catherine operates in a very similar way:

I use pictures, yes. And it might not be every Friday but I know, when I have got lots of things in my head, that I have got to do it.

This is helped along by scenario storytelling. Deborah says:

We do quite a lot of storytelling – if we do this, what impact will that have? What will they say, what impact will that have further down the line? And because there are so many interlocking changes going on, we need to sit and look forward at the sum total of how these things will impact. Actually storytelling when and how changes will impact on our members is a really good way of seeing it through, allowing you to travel with your vision, rather than just staying in one place.

At IPC, Xavier concurs that strategic thinking is a very fluid process, but as well as being guided by the vision it is also influenced by the need to actually drive the organization forward, so there is often strong drivers to strategic thinking:

I think that how new ideas happen… is a mixture of fluidity and one needs to have a sense of urgency. There needs to be some need to drive the thinking for a new idea, even if it is not an immediate need. It doesn't mean that you need to get it by tomorrow. There is a sense of dynamic in the organization.

Without a real hunger, or strategic appetite that drive to search for creative strategies might well be dampened. Xavier again:

I think that it is also a goal of the organization. If you can establish a goal… one of the continued debates is that having the hunger to win, and consequently to find new ideas, to find new ways, introducing new elements, without changing the model, because the model is the culture, is the vision of the organization.

This playful, exploratory environment was also mirrored at Simplyhealth. Says Des:

But one of the mechanisms that we use is that once a month, I and my executives are away for a couple of days, we call it a 'Strategic executive for the group'. The first day is very much the agenda stuff. The next day is no papers, there is no subject matter and you come into the room and kick off a conversation on anything from women in the workplace to global custodianship of water supplies or air quality – because the point is that, starting to talk in the round, what I do believe is that you generate a strong view about what 'good' looks like, and what is missing, and if we apply that to ourselves, what does that look like?

Catherine at Samaritans also emphasized the playfulness ingredient in strategic thinking, but it seems that she needs not to overdo it or do it in ways that stakeholders might find slightly too unsettling:

I think that the less tangible thing is where someone is confused in thinking that a strategic discussion is blue sky thinking or where they think that it is just Catherine thinking outside the box. You know (they are thinking) let her just play over there. Again you have to be quite mindful to make sure that you have the strategic conversations; you have to flag this is strategic: it is a strategic paper, there are implications therefore, for the organization, otherwise if you don't you will find that in six months' time people say, 'Oh, we thought that you were having a bit of an out-of-the box moment.' That's where it is less tangible.

Some of the end products of this more playful and creative style of thinking have come through to fruition at Virgin Galactic, and appear to be potentially a part of the strategy that is emerging there. Says George:

I think there are a variety of things that we are involved in over a number of areas that will prove over time to be very good business and blossom, like sponsorship – that we will be looking at – due to the power of the brand, not just Virgin but Galactic, and the marriage of the two, and I do think that it is going to be a truly world-class brand, that you can leverage in different ways. There all kinds of things that we are thinking about like small satellite launch vehicles that you might have seen we announced over summer and also future things like point-to-point high-speed transportation.

Strategic conversations

Xavier highlights the role of talking informally in generating strategic ideas:

Sometimes it needs to come (out), when it needs to… when people collide. You get three people around a table and you start a discussion, and you start to exchange ideas, and you go away from the office and you know they are thinking: I am here in my eight hours (of work), and you get into environments where you relax, and where people can have a conversation and share their visions, because everybody has a vision, everybody has ideas, everybody can contribute to building that reality that I was talking about.

This process occurs for Xavier through creative dialogue:

When we started out on this there was just the two (of us), and Sir Philip is always the first to take the step, as you have to start from somewhere, and two is the next step after one.

After you can engage the others, it is amazing: you read something that is in a book, or a magazine, or you have some thoughts, or you talk to somebody outside, or go to a presentation, or someone throws up some ideas. I am not a big reader, but I listen. I have a good memory for listening to things. I interlink things and I say 'I heard these things'. And I incentivize those who talk about the bigger picture in preference to people who say: 'Tomorrow, I need to do this, or I need to do that.'

Closely related to strategic conversations, is the concept of 'talking about the strategy', which only needs a willing audience for the speaker to be able to generate strategic ideas through a kind of thinking out loud. Xavier says:

I am more a talker than a writer. But I have always been a talker. In many meetings that I have I will say: 'I am going to talk aloud. I am going to tell my story of the issue and you can intervene and tell me that I have got it wrong. I need to put in my own words what is discussed. And don't think that I am telling you what to do, I am talking about it and then you can contribute to the build-up.' I don't use the word 'story', but I say I need to put it into my own words. If I am able to articulate it, if I can talk about it, then you can build (on that).

This is the most powerful thing, talking. I see people living in different realities through computers and I think (though) that since I was young I talk aloud and I tell my stories, I talk stories: I did movies in my head talking aloud. My parents said that I was bananas, it was not normal, because I walked around the table creating my own stories. I like to talk, to talk, to talk the things – not to write it on paper.

Inspirational light bulb moments

These highlight that strategic thinking is frequently characterized by rich insights, either into the significance of something or its linkage to other things. Catherine says:

It has got a light bulb with it: I think 'Oh!'

George says:

We all have a lot of light bulb moments because typically the really important ones are momentous decisions for the business, and to push really hard on one of these major new directions, or a new angle or something, or partnerships, or whatever, they are very big decisions so to some extent you need to think, carefully you know, whether they are the right thing to do. I think that one of the things that Richard (Branson) is so good at is not over-thinking it. He has a good gut and he does it and that's really valuable to do that. Not everything works out but, as an entrepreneur, he is a lot about doing stuff, rather than over-analysing.

These light bulb moments could be moments of either connecting different things, or simply recognizing that something is important, or that there is a big opportunity or need that was previously a blind spot. Such moments might come up through a random, everyday trigger (and thus be totally emergent), or might come up in a deliberate planning session when a new insight comes up unexpectedly. Generally, concluding this theme, strategic thinking does seem to be differentiated from purely analytical thinking through its inventiveness.

Sharing and ownership

Five out of six of the CEOs studied emphasized explicitly the value of sharing strategic thoughts with lower levels in the organization. This is clearly seen as being very important and helpful, particularly in testing ideas, in building commitment and in generating a feeling of togetherness and organizational unity, for instance. George says:

You know, I think that taking people with you is a really important thing. Often where there are strategic choices I think that you have to bring your folks on board where there is a big strategic decision, that's something that we work on, we work hard on. Sometimes you just have to do it, but if you can build that momentum around that choice then people will embrace it that much more easily, rather than the top-down thing where there is only one person in the organization that believes it and that makes it so much harder to make it work.

According to Des:

You have got to be a listener, you have got to be an encourager, you have got to have the attentive skills that means that if you are sitting around a table and having a debate you have to make people feel that they have a valuable contribution to make and not be dismissed by others; that the precious bits are absorbed. These leadership qualities are about knowing how to nurture, how to get the best out of your people. We are not going to have a workforce in the future that you will just tell what to do. 'I have got a brain and if you don't want me to use it in this place then I could go elsewhere.' The bright ones have got to be involved in the most forward thinking, the strategic part of the organization.

Deborah of APIL makes particular use of small group work, which she finds really helpful:

When I am making a decision, I would plan to sit down and think about it. I will invite two or three people to come and join me in that process. If I am on the train I will do it on my own, obviously. I do actually decide to do it – and I do start thinking differently. It is not something that I will just mix up in other work. You make choices all through the day and those are the little choices. For the big strategic decisions you must put time aside.

So while no one is saying here that strategic thinking is only something that the individual does, or that's where it predominantly occurs, it does seem to have a more social focus than perhaps more routine thinking does.

Deborah suggests that this social reflection and ideas-generation is particularly helpful in being creative and also, in effect, generating more angles on something that an individual would generate on his or her own:

Generally, get a group of people around you, and we'll sit and brain-storm, call it whatever you like, just basically throw as many ideas on the table, and we will look at it. I will be at a meeting or at an event and I will think: 'Oh, that's really interesting', or, 'I haven't thought about that strategically from that perspective.'

This in turn suggests that the notion of the CEO as the solo strategic thinker is maybe not a helpful one; rather they act as its centre of gravity and also as its orchestrator (even if Deborah doesn't quite use those words):

It helps enormously. Obviously it means that they get to input to the strategy as well. There's never, ever, been one occasion where they haven't come up with something different to what I thought about and that ends up in the final plan.

Des's view on encouraging participation echoes Deborah's take on it:

I suppose the last couple of things that I would like to mention are: strategy in the team. Nobody in this world is clever enough to have all the ideas. Your perspective, specifically your strategic perspective, your ideas, are always enriched by people who are not like you and you need the ability of people in leadership positions to facilitate progress; is very much the leadership style that I am sure is very much a part of getting through the complexity.

An adjacent sub-theme is getting buy-in. Thinking about getting buy-in is a crucial part of strategic thinking. Catherine, at Samaritans, underlines this quite graphically:

I say 'pick your battles carefully'. Just because an organization has the potential to do something really exciting, (that) doesn't mean it's right. If it is culturally abhorrent to the organization or it is generally going to be a real fight to get everyone to agree that it's a good idea it may be better to present a different option, to do some development work on it for a period of time to warm everybody up for later.

If you present that, none of the other stuff gets done because everyone gets so focused on the one thing that nobody wants to do. Everything around that gets rubbished. If you don't get the first page of the strategy right or the first picture on the front is wrong you have lost everyone before you start.

So strategic thinking is most sensitive to the political context. We see this echoed by the other CEOs. Somewhat less dramatically Deborah says more or less the same thing:

It helps a lot with relationships and certainly influencing.

Again, in terms of process, there can be interesting challenges if the board consists of a large variety of stakeholders – as at Samaritans and at IPC, and in the latter case that is made more challenging as a result of cultural, and mindset differences. Xavier says:

It is very interesting how the different board members... they look at things in different ways, like the strategy, and measurement. We have people from one side of the world who all want to focus on the strategy. And we have others who want everything documented: charts and files. It is very interesting, as I understand that we need to do both.

George of Virgin Galactic is also very mindful of bringing the organization together, and that means some systematic sharing of the strategic thinking:

Yes, I think that you have got to have some sort of critical mass inside the organization for some of these things to take hold and to be embraced. You know you have a series of events where you make that choice – I think that that's just common sense.

Xavier at IPC is a big believer in actively encouraging as many staff as is practicable to provide an input to the strategy:

One big thing for me is people – it is engaging people, getting people to the front of the thinking. I think that there are too many processes, and I think that we all are able to participate and to contribute to the long-term thinking. And for me the big thing is allowing people to participate, allow the conditions to contribute, to be a part of that. We need to think where do we want the organization to go, but everyone needs to do it. Everybody needs to be part of it.

Communication

Deborah interlinks strategic thinking with organizational communication:

Well, it is mainly one-sided communication where you put your thoughts down and you wait for someone to come back: whereas if you were talking to somebody it is far more intertwined. I do like the more old-fashioned ways of dealing with things, talking to staff at least once a month. Talking to the managers as a group at least every two weeks and also seeing individual managers independently; we do the same with groups of lawyers for our policies and strategies as well as using the experience of those at the coal face, and we would never deign to think or assume that we know what suits everyone until we have that input. A lot of strategy development is conversational.

Intuitive economic analysis

Another process is that of intuitive economic analysis where quantification through approximate modelling of some key variables (one might call it doing what-ifs) is done, to go beyond purely instinctive gut feel. George says:

I think that the primary two techniques that I use are bouncing ideas off other senior managers and also trying to get some idea of magnitude out of any sort of analysis for a set of scenarios which just helps this to crystallize, to put it into some sort of quantitative analysis. I have noticed that that's a thing that Richard does, to try to sketch it out to quickly to get a sense of the numbers. Obviously some of these numbers are not well defined, that's where the gut instinct comes in. That's where talking to other people comes in.

Interestingly we didn't get that echoed elsewhere in the other organizations but we need to remember that two were not-for-profit and APIL is similar in many respects: probably with a different sample or organizations we would find more prominence given to that theme.

Helicopter thinking

In Demystifying Strategy *I made much of the idea of visualizing with three-dimensional perspectives, as you would get in a helicopter, not to mention the mobility that that metaphor implies. Catherine says:*

That's why I have a helicopter on my desk. In my experience executives *hate* that helicopter. They come to me with all kinds of stuff and I will pick the helicopter up and I will stick it on the table and say, 'You tell me what your strategic issues are and I will go away and work on them.'

In a busy frontline charity such as Samaritans it is very easy to get sucked into operational delivery and finding time as an executive team to focus on the strategy can be very challenging. The idea of helicopter thinking in its simplest of formulation (see Demystifying Strategy *for more) is about lifting above the detail and (as a helicopter does), looking at things from different vantage points. So the top-down or bigger-picture view on issues, and seeing them from all kinds of different angles, seem to be qualitatively different from getting deep inside an issue such as a very self-contained problem. Catherine indicates here that she has found this as helpful a model as I have over the years.*

Strategic thinking can also be supported through more formal and analytical processes: there should be no real surprises there as strategic thinking not only applies to the more creative options-generation of strategy, but also to, a) the evaluation of those options, and b) the work to identify and diagnose the current position and the relevant issues surrounding it.

Concentration of focus

Xavier emphasizes the need to avoid stepping beyond the organizational scope in too many directions:

One of the challenges that we have is not to lose focus. In the end we are about sport and if we maintain the values of sport and focus on that to ensure that even if we look into all the opportunities that surround sport and to grow into other areas we don't want to compromise as others have so that sport just becomes entertainment.

At the same time he tends to prefer to rely largely on instinct to decide whether something quite new should be done or not:

We try to take opportunities, you know when things sometimes come to us. Sometimes I say: 'Let's get into it.' We don't have the full plan, we could wait a long time to have it – and the opportunity will have passed. It's not that we jump into anything without thinking. We are not trying to analyse everything to the last detail before saying that's where we want to go.

Des thinks that the formal processes are often taken too far:

I think that we spend an inordinate amount of time on these plans, these goals, these system migrations and processes, then forget to go back to the 'Why are we doing this?' Would you develop a system in that way? Or would you stop and think: hang on a minute, how is it serving the goal of inspiring people to better health? How could we in fact write a system or process that would help this?

Again this is a warning to those who think they are doing strategic thinking but really they are just doing routine planning, and that may well be not much more than summarizing what they were planning to do anyway and sticking some targets and measures on them. Such a process may be conducted with little insight, and even less fresh insight. Indeed one could say that it is precisely the element of freshness that we are seeking from strategic thinking: not just a repetitive review of what we have already thought about and rehearsed.

In footballing terms, planning is like a set piece move like a corner, a free kick or a throw-in. The options here are usually quite obvious and predictable. By contrast moves that come from open play, which is much more fluid and less predictable and often very surprising and skilful, are more akin to strategic thinking.

Strategic processes and techniques

Within this theme we see:

a writing a plan, or a paper (Nick);

b formal strategy tools (Nick);

c linearity (Xavier);

d matching the tools to the job (Deborah);

e evaluating strategic options (Deborah);

f imagining what other players in the game may do (Deborah).

We now take each in turn.

a. Writing a plan or a paper

Nick finds the process of writing helps to articulate the strategic thinking (just as talking out loud did for Xavier):

Whenever I write a document I write a skeleton plan and then I flesh that out. I think, if I am writing about the market, here is the overall market, the competition, then I will write about the UK, the US, then and hang on, should I write about the UK and then the US market, and the UK and the US competition? That's different... in merely putting that all together it makes you think about it fairly logically.

b. Formal strategy tools

Nick again:

Those (tools) make me laugh actually. I see them so many times from people who are looking to do an investment and they do them. The SWOT analysis, using Porter's Five Forces to do this (laughing a bit). It is the reference to it: (as if) it must make sense because we have used the name of the great Porter. I don't consciously use that framework. I try so hard not to use any kind of business jargon, but ultimately I am going through that framework, I am thinking, I don't tend to think of it as SWOT, strengths and weaknesses... I don't think of it as that, but I do have my own framework of thinking, and when someone comes to me with a business plan and they want investment I just think 1) how big is the opportunity, 2) why are you in a particularly good position to take part in it?

c. Linearity

Xavier sees much of strategic planning as being unhelpful for effective strategic thinking as it suffers from too much linear thinking. This is parallel to Des's views:

I have always found strategic planning is too linear. There is not enough about other perspectives that could affect things... I know I try to design in my head, not in my brain, a three-dimensional plan. And I think I cannot do it: I don't have the technology to do it. I don't know that it exists – that is I do that in my head. I always try to bring things together in my head. And this is not thinking outside the box.

(Extra commentary here: I had been talking just before this about having seen the Marvel movie 'Iron Man 3'. In it Iron Man is showing a girl his three-dimensional computer model of the workings of his own brain and you get a real sense of the multi-dimensional capability of the brain that can't possibly be captured in two dimensions: there are many. Even the relatively simple model of the strategic option grid (see Chapter 1) has eight: the five value dimensions of strategic attractiveness, financial attractiveness, difficulty, uncertainty and acceptability, and also the three dimensions of the what, how and when of the options themselves. So it is rather difficult not to use pictures

of some kind (or 'tools') to break that down: streams of words aren't really sufficient to allow codification and manipulation of the whole as a model).

d. Matching the tools to the job

Deborah says:

Beforehand you need to pick up a couple of models and decide when to use them. And you need to be careful that your team can keep up with you, so that you don't run at a million miles an hour, and make sure that everyone is on board, and then just see where it gets to, and there is not necessarily going to be any wrong answer but just seeing where the team takes that decision. You need to avoid anyone being overly dominant and you don't want any conflict in this, and just see what happens. I think that they will all be pleasantly surprised.

e. Evaluating strategic options

Deborah again:

It is particularly satisfying, yes, and it is pleasant even with a particularly difficult problem, because it is about finding ways forward. You do get a lot of job satisfaction from seeing that you have options. You are unlikely to hit conflict when you are doing strategic thinking because it is all options, so really nothing can be said that is wrong. When you are having a discussion with your managers it is about sharing ideas, it is not an argument at all.

Deborah here was the only one of our CEOs to have had experience of more advanced visual models as she had been using the strategic option grid for over five years and so it had become second nature to her, way past the pain barrier (which is very short anyway) and into pleasure and endorphin production.

f. Imagining what other players in the game may do

Deborah says:

Well it's like a football match, basically: you know what you are going to do but you don't know what the other side is going to do so you have to respond to moves by the other side. You are not the only person who is in control of this environment. As long as everyone appreciates that that's the way things are going to be and that when every decision is made you sit down and you review your strategy again, that's fine.

More specifically, she finds this incredibly useful for sharpening up the stakeholder analysis: APIL has a very large number and diversity of external stakeholders:

We do regularly try to see things from the other's point of view, as you can imagine. We have a lot of debates about the insurance sector from the personal injury lawyer perspective. They are the compensators – they pay these claims and they pursue these claims. We regularly try and see how an insurer would react to proposed changes and quite often it is the polar opposite of how we would react because they are trying to get their books to balance, trying to get their premiums down. So from their point of view, fewer claims and less value are very good things.

Cutting strategy down to size

Deborah also emphasizes the need to go local in determining what it is that you are going to think about: ie breaking down *the whole domain of the strategy into manageable chunks, otherwise it is likely to be far too overwhelming:*

Well, the best way to start is firstly to pick your topic: what is it that you need to think strategically about? And there is going to be a myriad of options, but just pick a topic, so it could be about getting a better relationship with other stakeholders. So, if you wanted to look at something like that then you would sit down and get everyone round the table, and if you were a new CEO you would get the benefit of their experience, they would have known those people longer and they would chip in and say what has happened in the past. Then you can start thinking about what has happened differently, and then you can get lots of options and then you analyse those options.

Evidence-based strategic thinking

In evidence-based strategic thinking we need to support judgements and decisions with factual, empirical support. Catherine is the strongest advocate of this:

In terms of process, I have tried doing it every which way, but the only way for me to do it properly and to have a proper evidence base it has got to be end-to-end, otherwise it is a waste of time. For instance, I start to present early concepts and ideas (warm-up) well in advance of strategic decisions being required.

While one might associate data collection with more conventional planning it is actually often very interpretative and that it is a reflective process. It might entail looking at data in new ways: not just thinking, it is actually both creative and strategic. Deborah also sees evidence-based thinking as very important in the process:

We do a lot of data collection. Firstly we do research and go around the country and talking to people. I will go to conferences and meetings, I talk to as many lawyers as I can and I will find out what they think and what the personal impact of these changes is, because our members have different business structures and they feel things in a different way.

Xavier echoes this concern with the tangible, taking it on to the practical and the action-oriented:

I think you could do both: you need to be strategically thinking, but also action-oriented. You need to be able to think forward, to be open, to get feedback from different people, to catch information, to filter it, and you also have to deliver stuff.... I had a conversation with our receptionist and we talked about the Games: 'Oh' she said, 'the Games! I really liked this part, and this is an area that I really, really, like.' Well, you extract one idea from that. You know, what people like, what they don't like, what they engage with, and you work on it. And sometimes you get little pieces of information that you can work on.

Jargon

None of the CEOs, predictably, had a great fondness for jargon – their stance was very practical; even Nick – with an MBA from Cranfield. In terms of culture fit, a lot of MBA language is opaque and of little use to non-MBA people. MBA language may have all of its special terms and ways of putting things, but it isn't usually mainstream. Management terms have to be taken on board by a whole team and all at once so no one feels left out, or like an idiot. Let's look at what Catharine says:

We had an example of someone who used (the term) 'boiler plate' in a technical project and we spent 40 minutes in this blessed steering group meeting before one of the volunteers asked, 'What does "boiler plate" mean?' Don't use it (jargon) because it slows things up, people feel inferior.

(Also) don't have multiple strategies and don't use terms like 'competitor analysis'; always use plain English and boil it down. I know what 'competitor analysis' means and half of my trustees would know what it means.... For example, in the initiative 'A call to action', we tried to imagine which of the charities would like to sit in the hot seat and coordinate it, so we said we needed to look at the 'competitive nature' within the charity sector. We needed to look at where the challenges will come from, from these agencies, so I want to do a little work on that, that's competitive analysis.... It is not rocket science. But then again, if I had gone in and said it was going to be competitor analysis, I would have lost everyone. I would call it 'competitive analysis' with my executives as they would know what I am talking about.

Implementation

Finally let's hear Deborah on that vexed topic of implementation – often dubbed the graveyard of strategy, again focusing on practicality:

It has never seemed to have been a big issue. We are always planning for something that is going to happen, so implementation hasn't been so much of a choice which, perhaps, puts us in a different environment to where you are maybe making proactive decisions to do something unusual like launching a new product.

This is a very interesting view as Deborah is saying, in effect, that of course she would think through implementation strategically, so it doesn't get to be a big problem.

Xavier also emphasizes the inseparability of strategic thinking from implementation:

I think that how new ideas happen, the way you describe it, is a mixture of fluidity and one needs to have a sense of urgency. There has to be some need to drive the thinking for a new idea, even if it is not an immediate need. It doesn't mean that you need to get it by tomorrow. There is a sense of dynamic in the organization.

A recap on the nature of strategic thinking

The evidence presented in this book so far shows that strategic thinking is qualitatively different from the thinking that you see in more everyday management:

- it is typically multi-dimensional in nature;
- it invariably involves asking some deeper strategic questions;
- it has a very distinctive creative element to it;
- while it is still grounded in the detail it is frequently characterized by deeper insights, beyond mere strategic analysis.

- it isn't particularly linear in nature;
- it is generally very creative.

The majority of the cognitive processes are actually right brain rather than the traditional left brain. It would also appear from all the interview material that this particular set of CEOs were not necessarily aware at the time whether they were doing strategic thinking or not. It appears therefore to be something much more of a tacit skill. Although I had very clear questions set beforehand and I repeated them at the start of the interview, it seemed to be somewhat unnatural for them to focus on strategic thinking as a process separate from the content of the strategy itself and from the planning process.

It would appear that for CEOs the words 'strategic thinking' conjure up, first and foremost, the strategy content itself. The process of thinking about these issues seems for some if not most of them to be secondary. Indeed, while this view varied somewhat, most of the CEOs did not seem to have done a lot of reflection prior to the interview about the nature of strategic thinking as a process, save for Deborah from APIL. That tends to suggest that while these CEOs spent a lot of the time actually doing strategic thinking they did not spend much time thinking about it as a thought process at a meta-level. They did, however, seem to have spent time reflecting on the planning process.

In interpreting these propositions we need to look at the nature of our sample and how it arose. We inevitably had a somewhat skewed sample here as there are many CEOs who declined to be interviewed: perhaps they were too busy or maybe they weren't as involved or as active. One would therefore imagine that the general population of CEOs might devote generally less time to strategic thinking.

An analogous top management process would be that of leadership. I guess that a rather higher percentage of CEOs see their role as being a leader than being a strategic thinker. But even then being a leader may be something that CEOs do not spend much time thinking about as a process, whether cognitively or behaviourally.

The key research questions

1. Are CEOs always aware of when they are or when they aren't doing it?

These CEOs do seem to be aware to some extent that they are doing it generally but vary in their conscious awareness of that blow-by-blow as they do that in their jobs: it seems to be a tacit activity. In some ways this could be likened to the act of driving. After making a journey by car you might be aware in a general sense that at the time you were having to do some things associated with navigation, but at the actual time it was something that you just were doing in parallel with other things. So you were possibly not conscious the of what you had been doing in terms of, eg its logical sequence and how it fitted in with other things such as manoeuvring the car and avoiding speed cameras, etc. Some of the CEOs had done some obvious reflection prior to the interview as they had some notes jotted down, but a good deal of material was more about strategic context and general content issues, and thoughts on the planning process rather than strategic thinking specifically.

2. When they are doing it, what is it that they feel; how do they do it; what sort of recipes do they employ?

I probably didn't always get very direct answers to this question, other than them mention an array of different if complementary activities. For example at Moonpig it was asking the right questions, while at APIL there was calling together a couple of people for a debate – and perhaps using the strategic option grid. At Simplyhealth it was having a strategy day out every month and getting inspiration from debates largely unrelated to the business.

This suggested that while all six CEOs were strong advocates of strategic thinking there was still scope for looking at an even more unified set of processes that would act as the infrastructure for strategic thinking. This might include, for instance, greater use and dissemination of strategic thinking techniques, and a culture of seeing all of the more complex management issues as the domain of strategic thinking. This could extend to all projects and initiatives, to all management reviews of performance as well as the more traditional strategic planning process.

All reports could be put together using a thorough process of strategic diagnosis, gap analysis, option generation, evaluation, implementation planning and testing, storytelling the possibilities and the consequences. Even at APIL, where the CEO has been implementing many if not most of these things, there was still further potential.

3. To what extent does the particular business and organizational context influence what they think about?

Organizational context was clearly crucially important for these CEOs. Stakeholders played an important role across all of the companies that were studied. The particular business model in place also had a role in shaping this and changes in the environment (eg at APIL and at the Samaritans). Defining a strategic vision for the organization was one way that they found helpful for filtering and examining issues in the context of the overall organization. Strategic vision thus was a way for CEOs to evaluate possible strategic options and to facilitate the cultural integration of the organization: the conventional functions it is there for. But it was also helpful for sense making of issues to see whether pursuing a certain path was in general alignment with the direction being taken, prior to any screening and evaluation of specific strategic options. These CEOs all seemed to be strong in this respect.

4. Do they use any particular tools or concepts?

Perhaps unsurprisingly there was very little use of strategic concepts and tools, with the exception of APIL. CEOs appear to prefer to operate largely intuitively which could be both a good and not so good thing. It's good in the sense that they are training their antennae to pick up strategic signals, and they have a tacit map of strategic issues in their head; it may not be so good in that, without using visual tools their cognitive maps might be incomplete, and the trade-offs they make not tested out as well as could be through explicit reasoning and decision criteria. Even if they have somehow overcome these challenges their strategic messages will have to be transmitted substantially through words alone, so their ideas and justifications may not always be fully understood. I am not saying that this is necessarily so, as I don't have concrete evidence from these particular interviews (I didn't interview the executive levels one and two strata below). However, it certainly is a possibility, if not in some of these organizations then certainly elsewhere.

If we go back to my previous book, *Demystifying Strategy*, there were a wealth of strategic tools and processes for visualizing strategy, which we will touch on in Chapter 9. Surely such techniques can only help make more effective the mapping, manipulation and communication of the strategic thought processes reported here.

5. Do they typically do it on their own or do they do it with others?

There seems to be a mixture of views on whether strategic thinking should be done solo or not, but with the majority tending to do it with other directors and managers. The one exception to this was Moonpig, but at the time it was a particularly entrepreneur-led organization. Even during the latter period before the business was sold, Nick Jenkins, its CEO, was spreading strategic discussions down the organization much more.

Obviously this is an area where one perhaps shouldn't make general prescriptions and where a contingency theory approach should apply: ie where one has to consider the context before making any kind of decision. However, it seemed clear that unless there are compelling reasons to the contrary, the CEO ought to use his or her directors, managers and staff as a sounding board and to get ideas from them about the future directions, the possible strategic options and how to tackle implementation. It would seem very old-fashioned and not very enlightened to keep all strategic conversations so hush-hush that field commanders and troops are unaware of the strategy!

6. How much time do they spend doing it?

They seemed to spend a lot of time on it, when one considers both formulation and implementation. Of course there may well be CEOs in certain types of organization who don't spend anything like 30 per cent of their time, and they self-selected themselves out of the study. That would be something for potential future research. From what the CEOs who did take part all said, the time they devoted to it seemed well spent, and Deborah of APIL went so far as to say that a lot can be accomplished in a very short time using strategic thinking.

7. What does it actually feel like: does it have any distinctive sensations?

We saw that it *did* feel quite a different process in the sense that it was more cognitively demanding, and it also had a very strong creative feel to it. The 'wow' or 'light bulb' moments seem to have a very distinctive quality, too. But what characterizes such a light bulb moment? From the way that the CEOs have illustrated this and, based on my own experience, it seems to come about in a variety of ways:

- seeing the interconnectivity of issues that hadn't been realized before;
- understanding the real significance of a problem or a puzzle for the first time (or reframing);
- identifying a new issue that is to do with future change, whether it is an opportunity or a challenge;
- surfacing a new business or organizational model that is in some way very clever, maybe even cunning;

- seeing that they have missed something fundamentally important;
- suddenly identifying a latent or underserved market need.

In Chapter 9 we look at how such intense insight experiences might be researched subsequently with some neurological study of the human brain when engaged in strategic thinking.

8. When they are doing it, what feelings are sometimes experienced before, during and afterwards?

This is pretty well answered in the answer 7: basically it is felt as a power-generator, and there are often feelings of exhilaration and of excitement. It can also be a great energizer. It would be fascinating to know what goes on in the human brain when that happens: is it the same as what normally occurs when people are generally creative or is it even more special?

9. How do they keep track of or record their ideas and insights?

Funnily enough, the respondents seemed to have glossed over this question. I suspect that a lot of their discussions didn't tend to be captured in detailed recording of their strategic ideas as they go.

There was obvious scope for CEOs to carry around some sort of strategic diary or log. One could visualize all the directors having similar diaries. Who knows, something like this might be one of those things like Facebook or Twitter: the only wonder being why they took so long to invent! (Now, there is a strategic thought.)

10. What value has come out of strategic thinking they have done in the past, either solo or with others?

Here, most of the CEOs pointed to the huge difficulty they would have in giving their organizations a direction and a focus without doing quite a lot of strategic thinking. In addition, there were clearly benefits from using strategic thinking to solve a real-life strategic problem, as Deborah indicated in the case of avoiding a regulatory fine.

It would be interesting to see if this could be pushed a lot further by doing a regular value audit of the potential economic value of the ideas that have come up, say in the last half year or year in a particular organization (see the chapter on the value of strategic thinking in Grundy, 2002).

CONCLUSIONS

We are very fortunate to find these enthusiasts for strategic thinking in such a set of fascinating organizations. I extend my greatest appreciation to all of them for spending their scarce time in reflecting and adding to our knowledge and insights. I am sorry that in some cases they needed to spend more time than expected on this work to turn the original transcripts into more presentable management material. I do appreciate that this has been a pain for some and wish I had been even more explicit in setting expectations. That said, as a researcher I could only transcribe what they said and not what they wished they had said.

I am aware that interviews often generate a lot of 'thinking in progress' material. The fact that there was rather a lot of this thinking out loud/thought stream material was actually of some significance as it suggested that strategic thinking, while being something that they did a lot of, was something that they reflected on only a little.

I believe that more conscious reflection on that by CEOs generally might lead them to realize that even if their organizations are doing generally well out of strategic thinking as and when it's used, a more integrated and deeper infusion of cognition along those lines throughout management processes would have even greater benefits. Just spending an hour with me taking about the topic has no doubt sharpened their awareness of what they have been doing, how effective it is and how it could be improved.

In the next chapter I reflect further on the implications of what has come out of this study and put the lessons into a very practical context. In particular I suggest that managers at all levels might cultivate a deeper, reflective state of strategic mindfulness.

09 Concluding lessons

> *A warrior never resorts to trickery but he knows how to distract an opponent. When he sees that his strength has almost gone he makes his enemy think that he is simply biding his time. When he needs to attack the right flank, he moves his troops to the left. If he intends beginning the battle at once, he pretends he is tired and prepares to sleep.*
> (PAULO COELHO, *MANUAL OF THE WARRIOR OF LIGHT*)

Introduction

In this book we set out initially by looking at what strategic thinking is. We then explored how six CEOs went about doing it, in a very diverse set of organizations. The core of this book was not only very practical in its focus, but has also been a piece of exploratory research. In thus penultimate chapter I will touch on a number of things including:

- reflections and lessons on methodology;
- an overview of what we know about strategic thinking;
- understanding your own strategic thinking capability;
- the enablers and constraints of strategic thinking;
- managing strategic projects;
- the role of toolkits in strategy cognition.

We also look at the value of the two Appendices for contingent strategy and Porter's Five Forces. The purpose of this final chapter is thus to look a bit deeper at the processes of strategic thinking, beyond the findings from the research on the CEOs.

Reflections and lessons on methodology

This section is a very brief note to future researchers so that the lessons from the study can be picked up. This study was not intended as a very structured and formalized piece of research designed to be utterly devoid of all conceivable potential bias, but it was nevertheless conducted according to fundamental research principles. For example, almost all of each interview was painfully transcribed. Research themes and categories were systematically abstracted from the data, letting the evidence speak for itself.

The interview process was generally very successful, although much of the discourse needed revisiting with a few of the CEOs to knock it into an acceptable shape. This process turned out to be more time-consuming that I envisaged, although I probably should have appreciated that CEOs are, after all, the prime representatives of their companies and therefore are very conscious of the way they come across. That certainly posed tensions with my concern as a researcher to preserve as much as possible the naturalistic feel of the data. While some of the English has been polished and most of the hesitations that occur in normal speech have been removed, nothing of meaning or sense has been changed.

I learnt that it is easier to get a CEO to agree to be interviewed about an issue like this, than to take time out to go through what they have said, to a timescale. Although I tried to set expectations that an hour's interview generates 10,000 words, and that I would have enough from that to fill an entire chapter of a book, there was still some perception that the end product wasn't going to be that long and that it would be heavily edited by a journalist, and that I would therefore not be trying to keep it as close as possible to the raw data.

Future researchers must work harder than I did to position what they are trying to do, and maybe be more flexible than I was at first draft stage where I stayed verbatim and didn't pre-edit and smooth the material to look better. This brings me to some possible areas for future research. Briefly these include:

- Naturalistic observation of board meetings and other less formal CEO–director encounters involving strategic thinking.
- Deploying some psychometrics in addition to surface CEOs' perceptions of their own skills.
- Using the case study method to home in on specific decisions: this would help add colour and context to the generalized thinking that sometimes flavoured the interview material.

- Conducting some action research to explore what happened when a strategic thinking process was orchestrated for a specific 'real time' decision.
- Possibly associated with that a 'kick-off' strategic workshop, and exploring if and why it made a difference.

There might also be interesting avenues to explore in neurology. For instance, what areas of the human brain are activated when someone does some strategic thinking? In a slightly parallel world there have been studies of the human brain where someone is gradually brought into an orgasmic state, if it's ok to mention that here. As that state approaches, many different areas of the brain light up and become much more charged. One wonders if the 'light bulb' moments that we have documented are characterized by some similar, if not quite as spectacular activity. I should ask my wife what institutions might be interested in collaborating in that kind of cognitive work (as you know she is a clinical psychologist). Maybe I could be a guinea pig? Can you imagine the potential in choosing future strategic leaders if we could test their brain patterns for innate or learnt competences like strategic thinking... hmm I sensed a cunning plan coming on....

And what is the quantity of endorphins that are released when there is a particularly deep moment of insight? It would be fascinating to find out. What brain waves are at work – alpha waves, or a mixture? My suspicion is that at some moments there are thought patterns at work that aren't that dissimilar to the states of mindfulness and meditation practices. (As a meditation practitioner for over 18 years I do sense considerable similarities.)

I leave these thoughts to ambitious PhD candidates or MBA students embarking on their final projects – or even those strategy academics who read my stuff and aren't 'not invented here' people. Who knows, someone might one day get some CEOs to try out some meditation techniques to see if that enhances their ability to 'up' their strategic thinking capability even more, and causes shifts in brain activity.

An overview of what we know about strategic thinking

Before this research the literature we already knew already prescribed that senior managers should be strategic thinkers. It was also suggested that CEOs should be doing even more of that; we found that from this sample they certainly were.

The literature emphasized that strategic thinking was differentiated not just by the need for complex analysis, but even more so by creative thinking. We found that the CEOs emphasized that too. This either just occurred spontaneously or through more set-piece planning sessions, but there seemed to be a variable emphasis on developing strategic thinking capability more deeply and broadly throughout the organizational levels such that those levels were able to model the issues visually, too.

Going back to the literature on strategic thinking there are numerous references that stress the more creative function of strategic thinking – 'thinking outside the box' or 'off the page'. Much of this points back to the psychologist Mihaly Csikszentmihali (1975) who used 'the flow' to characterize states of high challenge and high skill level, between 'control' and 'arousal' where the mind shifts to a new level of creative performance. This is called 'the zone' in sport. People more likely to reach 'flow' are ones who:

- are curious;
- are persistent;
- are not very self-centred;
- have high intrinsic interest.

I suspect that 'flow' is maximized when the degree of skill is just a little higher than the challenge level, and the inherent complexity and variety of the task are also high (as it is when dealing with strategic issues). The experience of 'flow' is also a characteristic of the martial arts, Zen Buddhism and Raja Yoga (meditation). In 'flow' we experience 'spontaneous joy' through deep focus on an activity (ie mindfulness).

In *Strategic Behaviour* (Grundy, 1997a) I found that normal management discourse alone was often inadequate for getting to grips with the multi-dimensionality and the non-linearity that Xavier of IPC highlighted. Visual tools also had the interesting side benefit of dissolving organizational politics. This suggested that there was still somewhere to go to fully exploit the potential value of strategic thinking.

CEOs may have a particular challenge in getting to and maintaining a state of 'flow' as much of their life is characterized by episodic meetings and this must mitigate against achieving a high degree of clarity – even if they are in effect circling issues, like birds in thermals, or aeroplanes in a 'hold' pattern. Equally, teams that maintain a very fluid cognitive agenda are likely to find maintaining a common focus as precondition of 'flow' an even bigger challenge. It is no wonder that the process school of strategy (Mintzberg *et al*, 1998) has thrived so much at an academic level.

From where strategy professors sit it must indeed seem that the management of strategy is largely disorganized and at best only logical in bits and pieces (Quinn, 1980). Senior executives would probably rather it not to be like that, and I sympathize with the latter view. At BT Group Technology Strategy, for example, the team really struggled with that until, that is, I gave them a couple of the strategy models to have a go with. This seemed to yield some surprising and magical results in what had previously been a climate with a somewhat confused dynamic. They not only became far more productive, quantitatively and qualitatively, but they also managed to spend over 15 minutes on a single strategic issue at a time. This gave them enough consistent cognitive dynamic to result in 'flow'. This was a good thing as they did – just – manage to capture the key insight from the 'uncertainty grid' (Grundy, 2012): 'The internet looks not only very important, but also very uncertain, so maybe we should think a lot more about its impact' (a 'light bulb' moment). The rest is history.

Just like yoga or meditation require consistent practice, so too I believe does strategic thinking. Over a period of 15 years or so I have been cultivating a much higher level of 'flow' and connectedness through advanced meditation and energy work so that one is operating at a deeply intuitive and sensing level (earlier work was published in Grundy and Brown, *Exploring the Inner Energies*, Minerva Press 2001 – sadly out of print). These possibilities are on the border of this present book so any readers interesting in exploring how to, for example, sense issues as energy (whether these are business or other), or to send positive energies to organizational and personal situations, then go to the end of Chapter 10 for contact details. I have used such techniques in the consulting process at BT, Direct Line, the Prudential and while teaching executives at Cranfield and in strategic coaching for many years. On one occasion at Cranfield I took a bunch of faculty and got them into a very high meditative space where they could focus on very singular thoughts in a space of clarity for 20 minutes when none of them had ever mediated at all. Strategic thinking, when you can access that space at will is almost a doddle as the whole of the mind can be mobilized in a thought mode of calm and complete concentration on the essentials. I would love to see what effect this might have on some CEOs (if only they had the time!)

So, beyond the three main levels of strategic thinking in *Demystifying Strategy* – the cognitive, the behavioural and the emotional – we now add a fourth: the energetic. An organization that is in a 'defender' situation typically is laden with a very heavy, negative energy: not only sometimes of a 'can't do' nature, but also of a 'can't decide' or a 'can't even think about' nature. In terms of the more practical findings and pointers that came specifically out of the chapters these are:

- creativity;
- strategic and economic modelling;
- strategy frameworks and tools;
- strategic thinking processes and structures; and
- strategic thinking recipes.

Creativity

Creativity is about the softer elements of the strategic thinking process that are less deductive and more inductive modes of arriving at and grasping strategic insights:

- Be alert for 'light bulb' moments.
- Make it playful and draw pictures: switch on the right brain.
- Try to think 'off the page' but be aware this is not everyone's cup of tea.
- It demands thinking in many dimensions, drawing together interconnections between different things, and on occasion creating quite new ideas.
- At the same time being flexible to take on new ideas from unexpected directions: it can be very spontaneous.
- Strategic thinking is a very intuitive process, drawing together data from a multitude of sources and directions.
- Gut feel is an essential ingredient in strategies.

Strategic and economic modelling

Strategic and economic modelling is the systemic exploration of the way in which an organization adds or *might* add value:

- To get real competitive advantage out of it (strategic thinking), it needs to concern itself with the human: the psychological, the behavioural and the emotional.
- Resource and organizational constraints are a strategic issue: there may well be options for challenging them.

- Within strategic thinking you need to assess the economic value of the strategy – explicitly.
- This entails understanding the interdependences between the value and the cost drivers of any business, and looking for different configuration options.
- This also means bringing together ingredients from a variety of sources to build a novel value system.
- Strategic thinking is very much essential to the design, adaptation or change of any business model.

Strategy frameworks and tools

- Strategy theory gives us useful frameworks to think strategically about complex business issues, but it shouldn't be worshipped for its own sake.
- Limit the jargon to what people know and can grasp.
- Do some training first (to maximize what people can use).
- Concentrate on a few tools that you find most useful.
- Use the strategic option grid – create options.
- Where there is a very clear and guiding strategic vision, it acts as a filter for what to think about and prioritize in terms of a possible agenda for decisions and resource allocation.
- Apply the idea of the 'uncertainty gap'.
- Storytell the future using scenarios to help to close that gap.
- Where there is a lot of residual uncertainty, use the idea of the 'contingent strategy'.
- Do a lot of stakeholder analysis, ongoing.

Strategic thinking processes and structures

This is about the more formal mechanisms that can be used to engage the CEO, directors and managers in their efforts to reflect strategically:

- Design your strategy process not just around the strategic agenda/issues but also for the organizational context – the strategy process needs to be conducive to strategic thinking – and that needs a relaxed environment, ideally separate in time and space from the normal workplace.

- Break down the strategy into chunks.
- Don't try to work on it all at once: make it issue-focused.
- Do enough preparation work on complex issues before starting to debate.
- Learn to do it yourself first before buying in planners or consultants.
- Too much reliance on heavy formality and documentation can seriously hamper strategic thinking.
- Do 'position papers' to prepare the thinking ground, the options and the supporting evidence base – they must be properly based on the evidence.
- Don't automatically make the time horizon three years: think about the range options you could go for and their pros and cons.
- Hold strategic events, have enough of them, and have them professionally facilitated.
- The vision can be closely linked to the 'strategic model' of the business, and also tentatively to its 'strategic heart': where this is strong, as a spin-off, this will help to encourage identification and 'engagement' with the organization.
- If there are long lags in the process to realize its value, why are these there, and how can they be reduced?
- Don't look for excuses in implementation.

Strategic thinking recipes

These are the miscellaneous prompts that can be used to steer strategic thinking:

- Use the analogy of helicopter thinking and any other mechanisms and signals to people to engage more in strategic thinking.
- Also use storytelling (not necessarily linked to scenario development).
- Strategic thinking definitely shouldn't exist for its own sake: there needs to be a simultaneous sense that we are talking about things that we might actually make happen, and we need to have at least some degree of strategic appetite to make this a reality.
- It needs to be shared with the board rather than individually driven.
- Don't do strategic thinking alone – do it as a group.

- Create a congenial climate and environment for it, attending to little things like laying on some tasty snacks.
- At strategic meetings, don't try to deal with more than three issues/decisions: keep a tight focus of attention and debate.
- It is often about formulating a 'hierarchy of questions'.
- Don't get too intoxicated with 'strategic excitement': ground it in practical activity and turn ideas into possibilities, prioritize these, and then plan.
- Strategic thinking should be practised as 'strategic mindfulness'.
- Because of uncertainty and the need to rely on a lot of intuitive thinking, there are likely to be some mistakes.
- Understand why you are doing things.
- Recognize that this (strategic thinking) is not always comfortable for people around you.
- It is processed through conversations, both ones formally planned and spontaneous; this requires great skills in strategic listening.
- There are huge differences between the different types of planning skills: remember that it takes all types and manage the mix of styles and skills. Some are very analytical or practical, some intuitive, and some creative and visionary.
- Even very long dilemmas and uncertainties can be resolved and at least partly solved.
- The end product is likely to be very valuable indeed – you are not wasting your time.
- It is appropriate and healthy for the CEO to spend 30 per cent of his or her time on it.
- At senior executive level a huge constraint is the fact that directors are torn between being dragged into operational day-to-day management, delivering the existing strategy and developing new strategies – a tricky juggling task.

Changing gear a little now to the more practical, we start with some individual-level strategic thinking psychometrics, which give you a health-check on your all-round capability to get into the 'flow'.

Understanding your own strategic thinking capability

Searching the internet draws a blank when it comes to finding tailored psychometrics that deal specifically with strategic thinking. That seems surprising when one considers the huge variety of questionnaires available for 'leadership', for example. I have used a relatively simple questionnaire as a device for self-diagnosis for executives coming on my strategic thinking courses and it has worked well, so I have now developed it further, based on some of the insights from this book; see Table 9.1.

Here's how I set up the reflective space to arrive at this list. Picture me in the garden in South London. I had a fire going nicely and the garden looked good as I had just cut the lawn. The sun was setting and I was drinking a nice glass of wine. I got through the first 13 questions quite quickly but by that time it was beginning to get really dark. The keyboard was getting harder and harder to see and I began to make more and more mistakes. The computer was beginning to get hot with the fire too, so I had to sit sideways-on – all very uncomfortable.

I began sneezing and this got worse and worse as I got to around question 17. I could hardly see a thing by the time I got to question 19. By that stage I was concentrating really, really hard. At last, I was finished and I came into the house, my eyes and nose streaming: the one very big thing that I forgot was my hay fever – tested to failure! So I got a great strategic result – but I am not sure how strategic the process actually was! Technically this is called the 'escalation of commitment' in strategy: the more time, effort and resources you put into implementing a strategy, the more difficult it becomes to reflect on whether what you are doing and how you are doing it really make strategic sense! You can easily overlook the most obvious problem – like being allergic to cut grass – especially if it just creeps up on you incrementally! Now have a try at the questions.

The first three questions are very much in the land of strategic analysis: looking at what is currently going on and understanding the causal forces at work and the patterns within those forces. While this requires some intuition and judgement these are areas that aren't that difficult.

Questions 4 to 8 are about strategic creativity, not just in terms of the basic ability to come up with and evaluate some options but also doing so in a genuinely innovative way. Question 9 on identifying the critical assumptions is about strategic reflection: while it isn't usually difficult to come up with a couple of assumptions it is a higher order skill to come up with all of

TABLE 9.1 Strategic thinking psychometrics

	Very strong 5	Fairly strong 4	Ave. 3	Fairly weak 2	Weak 1
1. Sensing signals from the external environment					
2. Understanding the dynamics of external and competitive change – and their knock-on effects					
3. Analysing and diagnosing a key strategic issue					
4. Identifying and evaluating strategic options for what to do					
5. Identifying and evaluating strategic options for how to do a strategy					
6. Being able to come up with a 'cunning plan' for both the 'what' and the 'how' of the strategy					
7. Stepping outside prevailing mindsets					
8. Being able to sense possible alternative business models to the prevailing one					
9. Defining and being able to challenge the critical strategic assumptions					
10. Storytelling the potential dynamics of the external or internal environment, or both, either publicly or in your head					
11. Asking the right strategic questions and just at the right time					
12. Being able to easily put yourself in the position of your customers and seeing the world through their eyes and understanding their industries and the pressures on them					
13. Being able to easily put yourself in the position of your competitors and imagine what they might do and how in the future					

TABLE 9.1 *Continued*

	Very strong 5	Fairly strong 4	Ave. 3	Fairly weak 2	Weak 1
14. Readily being able to make comparisons with models from other industries and being able to use these to suggest ideas and solutions					
15. Visualizing the migration path of changes and sensing the most critical blockages and constraints					
16. Being able to turn that into an intuitive, visual picture of how that difficulty will change over time					
17. Being able to put oneself in the position of other stakeholders and come up with inventive options for influencing them					
18. Imagining before one ever starts on a piece of strategic thinking where that might go and how the process might go before the event, yet not prejudging the outcome					
19. Being able to clearly express strategic thoughts/arguments orally					
20. Being able to clearly express strategic thoughts/arguments on paper, or on PowerPoint					
SCORE:					
TOTAL:					

RESULTS

Over 90: you are either a strategic genius or have delusions of grandeur!
80–90: become a strategy lecturer or consultant.
70–80: well done: identify the areas where could you work on and prioritize these.
60–70: a very good start; you have made an honest appraisal.
50–60: many if not most managers are likely to put themselves here or just slightly better.
30–50: probably you have had some exposure to planning but not truly to strategic thinking; as you are learning, this is a different animal.
20–30: are you sure about your scores or do you have a self-esteem problem? You may be very self-critical.

the really important ones. For a relatively complex strategic option this will usually be of the order of 5–10.

Question 10 is about being able to look forward in the external environment so that requires activating some imagination – besides being able to mentally model a number of interrelated variables like the state of the economy, market growth, competitive pressure and the moves of some of the key players in the game.

Question 11, about asking the right strategic questions, presupposes that some deeper reflection has been done and that this has teased out some particular lines of enquiry or areas of challenge which, if followed, could be deeply insightful. Questions 13 and 14 are about understanding the perspectives, the agendas and the intentions of the key players in the market place: the customers and the competitors. This skill we have called 'having an out-of-body experience'. It requires great mental agility and an ability to project oneself into someone else's situation – and not looking at what you think they are likely to do sat in one's own perspective.

Questions 15 and 16 apply strategic thinking to implementation. Conventionally taught strategy at business schools seems to almost exclusively focus on more external, competitive strategy, so that even well-trained strategic thinkers may not be skilled or practised in thinking about the dynamics of implementation and change strategically. Question 17 on understanding the key stakeholders logically follows on from this as this area straddles strategy formulation and implementation.

Question 18 got onto the agenda later on as it was nearly pitch black in the garden. As a facilitator it is necessary to imagine where the strategic debate might head. This is a necessary skill both for planning the strategy process and for steering the thinking itself: indeed this is strategic thinking ahead about the very process of strategic thinking itself.

Finally, questions 19 and 20 are about the skills of presenting strategic ideas and arguments through words, pictures and diagrams so that they are readily picked up and understood. There are many, many ways of presenting strategic data and the choices need to be carefully thought through.

The enablers and constraints of strategic thinking

We have seen in this book the value of strategic thinking to CEOs and also generally. So it may seem to be an odd thing that many senior executives struggle to focus sufficiently on it. Why is that the case?

There seem to be a number of reasons for this. First of all, managers often don't recognize the opportunities to use it as they associate it with lofty topics like corporate vision and corporate strategy. Operations management is seen as purely 'tactical' and yet even the most apparently tactical of issues can reveal some deeper strategic issues.

Another major factor inhibiting strategic thinking is the perceived shortage of time. Managers' default practice even at quite senior levels seems to be very much bound up with doing things. As the then CEO of Champneys Spas, Lord Thursoe, once said: 'Strategic thinking – well that would be a good thing. But sometimes it would be good if managers were to begin to think in the first place!'

The penalty for just getting things done is that you may be doing many of the wrong things or doing the right things in the wrong way. To understand how this can happen, take a look at Figure 9.1. Here we see the vicious cycle of tactical thinking, which doesn't resolve the fundamental strategic issues and performance deteriorates, putting greater pressure on resources which in turn leads to even more tactical activity.

Contrast that with the virtuous cycle of strategic thinking in Figure 9.2, which highlights the value of taking time out for strategic reflection: as much as 30 per cent at CEO level so that there are very effective strategies in place, which take the pressure off. This improves the strategic thought process further still and completes the cycle. Companies that get into this mode are really hard to catch.

FIGURE 9.1 Vicious cycle of strategic thinking

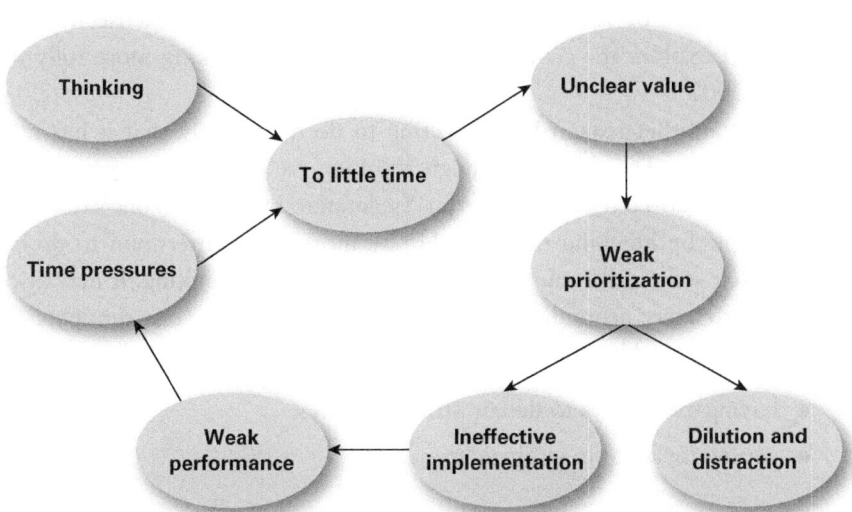

FIGURE 9.2 Virtuous cycle of strategic thinking

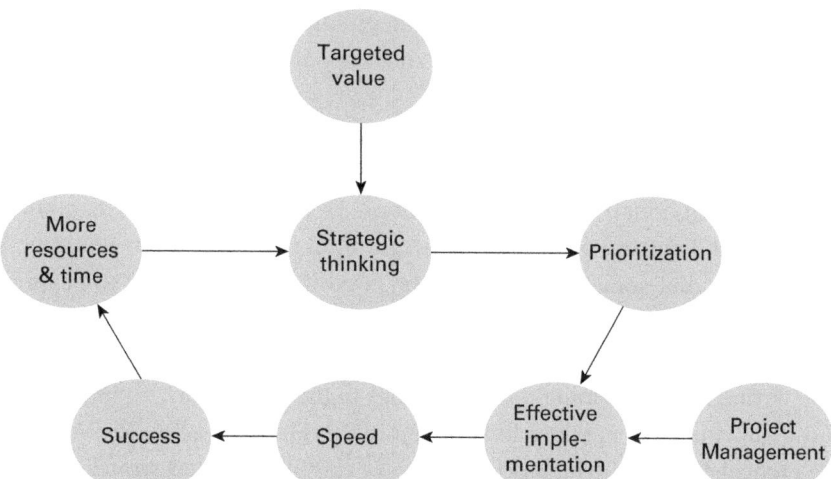

A third reason why strategic thinking is not often engaged in sufficiently is to do with the uncertainty of getting real value out of it. This is a very misplaced fear indeed. Strategic thinking, if it is properly done, almost inevitably yields a considerable multiple extra value relative to cost. An example of a strategic coaching session that I did with the Sales Director of Zurich Life's IFA Division, Chris Keogh, many years ago: we identified a number of changes to his working strategy and style which saved him six hours a week or 300 hours a year. He saved 1,000 hours before he moved on to another job, in time terms a value-to-cost ratio of 1,000! Uncertainty about the value of strategic thinking is just a convenient excuse for not doing it. (I explore the economic value of strategic thinking more fully in Grundy, 2002.)

Finally, another reason for neglecting to do it is simply that it has not become a habit. The skills of strategic thinking are just like any other: they need to be practised regularly. It is thus essential to build it into one's routine, for example by blocking off every Friday morning or afternoon to do it: create what some call some 'white space' for freed-up thinking. It may also be useful to carry around a special note book to record your thoughts as you go. Other enablers of strategic thinking are:

- having away-days to debate strategic issues;
- getting involved in strategic projects;

- writing strategic position papers;
- searching the internet and other sources;
- reading competitors' annual reports;
- visiting customers;
- studying other industries and interesting companies;
- practising strategic thinking techniques;
- having strategic coaching, for yourself or for others;
- being a strategic facilitator;
- applying strategic thinking to everyday issues including those in one's life outside work.

Another cut of it is found in Figure 9.3, which highlights the need to integrate a whole cluster of activities in order to get value out of it. Here we not only mention the more obvious things like strategy tools, but also asking the right questions, spending enough time on it and when working in groups to agree the 'P' behaviours that we really don't want (being personal, picky, political, pedantic, etc).

FIGURE 9.3   Successful strategic thinking: some inputs

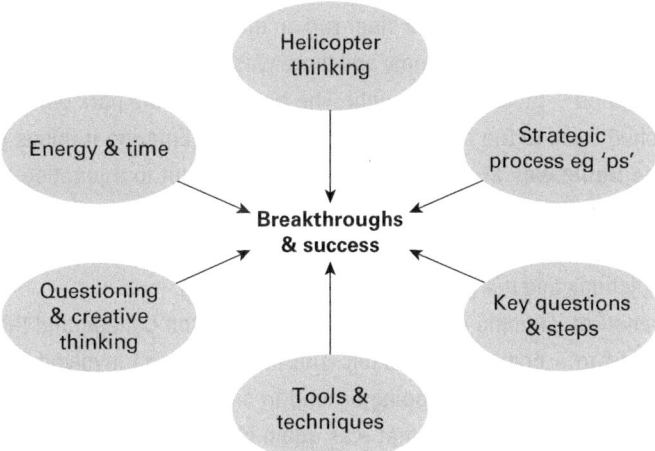

In the next section it is worth thinking a little more about a more structured process – which tools could be of help and how this maps onto the different cognitive styles of strategic thinking.

Managing strategic projects

Strategic projects are a major opportunity to practise strategic thinking. They go on all the time, all round the year: you don't have to wait for the annual planning cycle to come around.

The next case study is an example of where there was an attempt to manage a project strategically but in one respect this seemed not to have been successful. The cycling event itself was a huge success, but what happened afterwards less so.

CASE STUDY Prudential Ride London

In early August 2013 I was on a round tour in the South East, a trip which I did every three weeks, and it took me to Aylesbury. Normally I can get back from there to Croydon in around two and a half hours. I thought that I would out-guess the busy M25 traffic around London and go straight through London, saving me 25 miles and queuing.

I was in Richmond, South West London, in an hour. The traffic seemed to get slightly slower but nothing out of the normal. I thought as it was slowing up I would detour across Richmond Park – a clear run on the map – and then head east.

The side roads were really empty and there was evidence of some cycling event that had finished – 'lucky me' I thought. The entrance to the park was blocked so I was pushed back to the easterly road into London. Entering it things got much worse. The traffic was at a snail's pace and when I got to a junction the police had blocked the main road into central London. Was this a terrorist threat? A gas explosion? There were plenty of police dozing off in their vans oblivious to my gesticulations and the gridlock that was developing.

I took another 'cunning detour' towards Roehampton College and the A3. The traffic ground to a complete standstill. The police weren't involved in directing the traffic, so most cars were going around in circles. We were funnelled up to Richmond Park once more and that was again blocked. After about an hour and a half I eventually escaped by going all the way back I had come and eventually got to Croydon four hours after leaving Aylesbury. I was very tired and clipped a curb, twisting my steering wheel.

The next day I was drained by the experience. Probably tens of thousands of people had their Sundays ruined by gridlock in one of the greatest capital cities. After the huge success of the Olympic and the Paralympic Games in 2012 Games and the scores of visitors to the capital, with was no obvious major disruptions, this was very disappointing. Either the traffic management strategy in Richmond was flawed, or its implementation, or both.

The event was called the Prudential Ride and over the next few days I did a 'deep dive' into this issue ('strategic diagnosis'), and I uncovered a multitude of organizations involved in the event:

- the Met police;
- within that locally, Richmond police;
- Boris Johnson' office (Mayor);
- London and Surrey Cycling Partnership;
- the London Marathon Organization;
- Richmond Local Authority;
- Surrey County Council;
- Transport for London (TfL);
- the Prudential.

The Met Police, The Lord Mayor's office, Richmond borough and the Prudential 'passed the parcel' of responsibility – truly I was being sent around in circles. Only London and Surrey Cycling Partnership/the London Marathon were quick to take my observations both seriously and responsively.

Some fundamental strategic questions that should have been posed if this had been managed as a truly integrated, collective strategic project by these organizations were:

1 What are the key objectives of this event?

2 What value can it add and what value might it destroy and to whom, and how can the latter be minimized?

3 Who should project manage this and how and with what project management organization?

4 How do we work across the stakeholders to deliver it?

5 What are the key strategic options for what to do and how to do it – the ride itself, road closures, communication and warnings, traffic management, contingency plans, etc?

6 What are the likely enablers and constraints and how can we manage this (eg cultural differences and differences in agendas across organizations)?

7 What are the key uncertainties and what scenarios can we create for the project not going so well?

8 What in-built flexibility and contingency planning can we build in?

9   How do we maximize information flows and responsiveness of decision making on the day in real time?

10 How will we review it after the event?

(All these questions are from Grundy and Brown, 2002b.)

Between Monday 5 and Friday 9 August I made my investigations a strategic project, resulting in feedback to the Event Organizer and to Boris Johnson, Mayor of London.

To mayor@london.gov
9 August 2013
FAO Boris Johnson, Mayor of London

Dear Boris
Hope you are well and bouncy!
Following the Prudential cycling event last Sunday around Richmond there was terrible gridlock as a result of which I was stuck in traffic for one and half hours and late for a birthday celebration. I was so drained that I nicked a kerb in Streatham on the way home: the steering is bent and the repair bill is over £360.

Thousands of other Londoners were trapped in an endless attempt to find escape routes round side roads and in the zone of greatest congestion. There was no evidence of traffic management on the ground and the police were only sited in one spot blocking the A205 east from the junction with Priory Lane and were not actively managing traffic. They seemed to have set that up causing the congestion.

I am sure that many got a lot of pleasure out of this event – I know that you are a big fan of bikes and I applaud that. But why couldn't it have been organized to minimize the terrible congestion that was caused?

This event was a strategic project and had a big impact on Londoners, so it was worth managing as one. I happen to be writing a book on strategy so I made it my mission this week to see if I could get to the bottom of what went wrong. I hope to use this as a case study in my book on strategic projects and invite comments from you.

This week I have uncovered around 10 stakeholders with a finger in this pie: maybe that complexity alone and possibly diffuse responsibilities were instrumental in contributing to the problem.

So far I have talked to:

The Met Police: who referred it to Richmond Police; left a message saying that there hadn't been sufficient warning signs: I rang back but my message has been ignored.

Concluding Lessons

- The Met rang again and said that this wasn't their responsibility and it was that of the Mayor's office.
- Your office said that it wasn't its responsibility either, although it was admitted that as Mayor you had 'strategic control' over London and thus of the ride. It seemed that someone called John Paul had some role in project managing it but he has been unavailable and hasn't returned several messages.
- It was also suggested that Richmond council were involved but they deny any role.
- Your office referred me to the London and Surrey Cycling Partnership (LSCP) which led me to one of its partner organizations, the London Marathon and the event organizer, Hugh Brasher. We had a long chat and I e-mailed him a blow-by-blow account of my movements and observations of that day. He felt that there had been massive media coverage of the event and that it was very surprising that I hadn't heard about it or seen any signs. I had not and had been on holiday recently. That day I had travelled all round London and nowhere saw any warning signs, especially as I approached Richmond late in the afternoon.
- It seems that thousands of other Londoners either didn't know or had forgotten as there was a vast quantity of cars stuck. No one said 'Oh it's the cycle ride' when we got out to chat: many of us got out of our cars some looking for a toilet in suburbia (I found a spot near Richmond Park).
- I mentioned that the police at the road block on the A205, which seemed to be the root cause of the problem, were distinctively inactive. Some were lolling around in a van when they could have been informing us which way to go. Hugh's take on the police was that it wasn't their job legally to attempt to manage the traffic: I honestly think that if they are so hands-off like that then they don't do their brand and reputation any favours.
- Hugh also said that there was a central control room managing the traffic under the control of TfL. I rang TfL and the operator was unable to put me through to anyone who was involved and I would have to send a query to an anonymous e-mail address; I am still awaiting a reply to my e-mail. (They eventually replied three months later)

I was impressed by the steps that Hugh had tried to take to coordinate this vastly difficult project and his meticulous collection of data to do a post-project audit. But the fact remained that there was unacceptable gridlock in the capital and on the ground nothing seemed to be done to either mitigate it, to communicate with the drivers that were stuck or to prevent them from going round in pointless circles. Surely there should have been more contingency planning that could have been used to mitigate the problem that tiring afternoon: none of those trapped will forget it in a hurry.

In my last book I wrote a case study on the London riots; I do hope that this will be my last one of that ilk.

I also contacted the Prudential who were the sponsors: they promptly referred me back to LSCP! One of the most frustrating things has been that many of the stakeholders think that they can just 'pass the parcel': my (strong) hypothesis – unproven – is that there was something about the project organizational set-up that led to a fragmentation of responsibilities and project management of very specific and tightly defined outcomes. (I happen to be an expert in strategic projects – see my book *Strategic Project Management,* so I speak with some knowledge.)

I await your comments: does this problem concern you or not and what learnings have you taken from the first year of the event for the future?

Many thanks
Tony

Dr Tony Grundy

A 'project' is something that is complex and has its own distinctive environment, a multitude of choices and options; it exhibits uncertainty and often difficulty. It is invariably a mini-strategy, or in this case a bigger strategy. Where they are many and diffuse stakeholders it is even more imperative to treat them as a 'strategy'. So not only manage projects strategically *but also think strategically about them!*

The role of toolkits in strategy cognition

A classic model of a strategic thinking process is shown in Figure 9.4. This was developed in the 'Breakthrough strategic thinking' courses that I once ran at Cranfield School of Management, 1995–2008. I ran a number of these in Simplyhealth during which I first met Des, the CEO. Deborah has run these both at Legal Complaints Services and at APIL.

FIGURE 9.4 Strategic breakthrough process

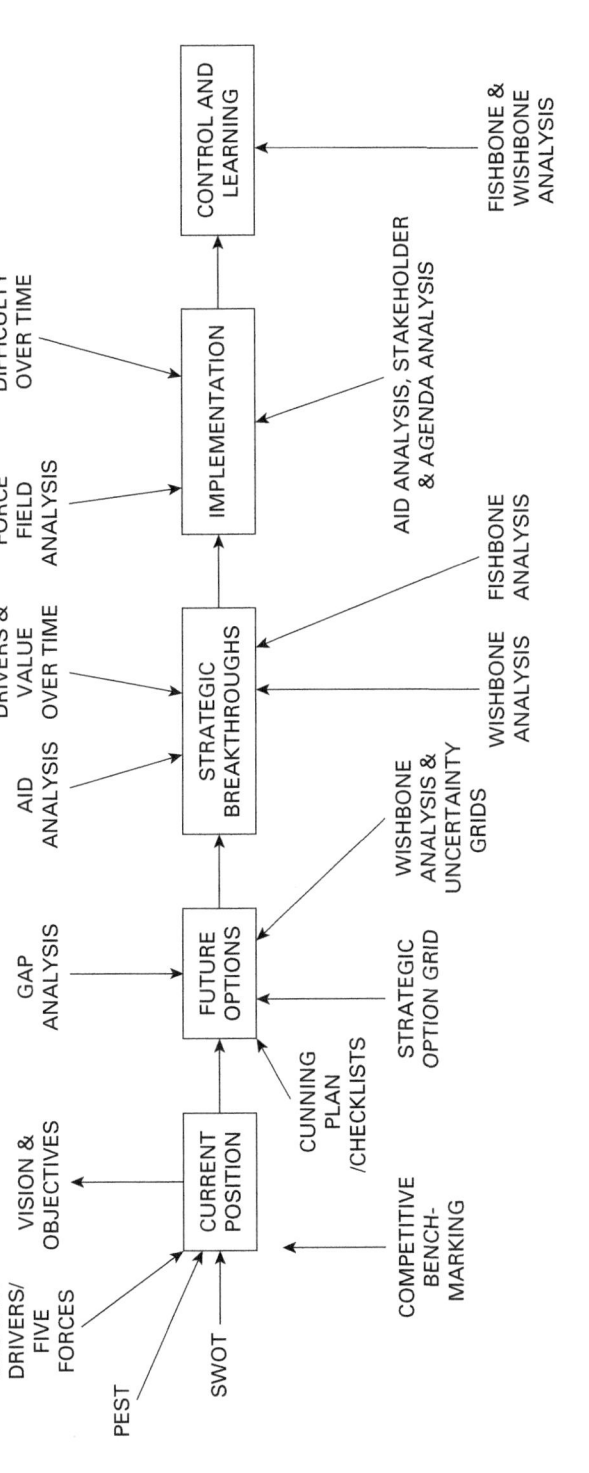

Demystifying Strategic Thinking

This process contains a set of eclectic techniques which formed part of a flexible menu of recipes that dealt with any kind of strategic issue and at any stage of the strategy cycle that takes an idea to full reality. My choices come from scanning possible techniques from a variety of sources, such as fishbone analysis, value drivers, cost drivers and the 'uncertainty grid' besides ones like the strategic option grid and the 'Optopus', and those invented by managers themselves like the difficulty over time curve. Some, like the attractiveness-implementation difficulty grid came from a client need that I was faced with, see Figure 9.5. (The 'AID' analysis has been widely plagiarized; I'm flattered!)

FIGURE 9.5 Attractiveness/implementation difficulty (AID) analysis

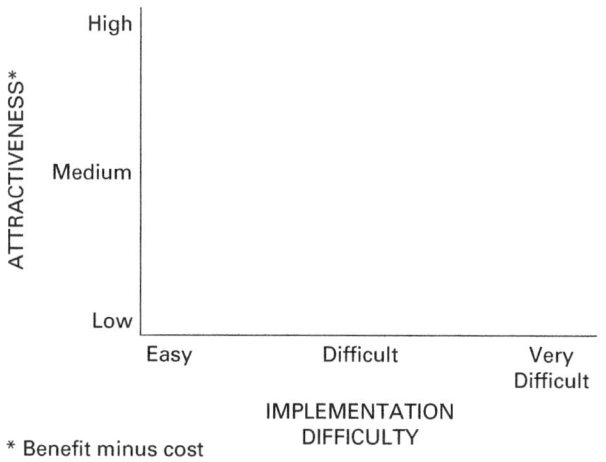

The AID analysis would be particularly useful for deciding which of your strategic skills you should try to improve, or the different options for shifting your capability (courses, mentoring, strategic projects, etc). The AID analysis is also useful to apply after the 'GE grid' shown in Figure 1.3 when screening new strategic projects and is an alternative to the strategic option grid in Figure 1.2.

These breakthrough strategic thinking courses were extremely popular particularly as they gave senior managers true helicopter thinking, rescuing them from the worst 'rabbit holes' of narrow, tactical management. Managers found it particularly helpful that they were structured in a two-plus-one-day series of workshops – the final day held three months later to allow interim work so that managers could use the tools day-to-day. Besides going through every stage and tool of the process and actually applying them, I taught them that strategic thinking was applicable to much smaller scale thinking – at the 'mini-strategy' and the 'micro-strategy' level, too.

Coming back to the process, this dealt with the array of issues at each stage. 'Current positioning' was an essentially analytical skill (Figure 9.4). 'Future options' is a phase where inventiveness is key, as is 're-framing' the situation. It also requires a degree of visualization of the shape of a future strategic option. In the 'testing' part of evaluating options one returns to the analytical once more. One needs imaginative skills to get a deeper insight of the likely outcomes, blending also the analytical with the intuitive. To achieve this requires simulating and modelling skills.

'Implementation' requires more of the programming thought processes which are driven by more sequential and analytical thinking. However, this phase needed to be coupled with the intuitive, the inventive, and the reflective. In 'control and learning', the mindset needs to shift towards reflective detachment. This maps onto analytical, creativity, visualization, imagination, simulating and modelling, intuition, programming and reflective detachment.

If we look at the skills mentioned by the CEOs, the areas stressed the most were: creativity, imagination, visualization and intuition, which is interesting. One suspects that these skills are rarer to find in the senior management domain than skills like 'analytical' and 'programming'. Even 'analytical skills' are often lacking, at a strategic level, which can't be helped by the fact that, drawn from the sample of probably 500 courses over the last 24 years, almost all senior managers have only used a 'SWOT' analysis and less than 5 per cent actually used Porter's Five Forces.

Senior managers do tend to try to speak using some strategic terms, principally 'vision' and 'strategic objectives', but this is a very limited vocabulary and one that they rarely define. Just like it is said that we probably only use 10 per cent of the brain's capability we probably only ever use about the same of the 'strategic mind'. Sadly even MBAs seem for the most part to have overdeveloped analytical skills, and underdeveloped creative, imagination and intuitive skills – with rare exceptions.

In Table 9.2 a few of the 20+ tools in *Demystifying Strategy* are mapped against these dimensions of strategic thinking and I have rated them according to the extent that they typically involve those particular cognitive processes. You will see that while some tools tend to have a slightly more analytical focus like Porter's, they can all be used in different cognitive ways, particularly the strategic option grid. Note that the 'cunning checklists' are non-visual and are simply a list of 55 recipes for being inventive strategically.

TABLE 9.2 Tools and cognitive processes

	Porter's forces	Optopus	Strategic option grid	Cunning checklists	Stakeholder analysis
Analytical	***	*	***	*	***
Creative	**	***	***	***	***
Visualization	**	***	***	*	***
Imagination	*	***	***	**	***
Intuition	*	***	***	***	***
Storytelling	**	*	**	***	
Programming	*	*	*	*	*
Reflective detachment	**	*	**	***	**

None of these particular tools majors on programming: that is the domain of project management, economic value management and implementation techniques. Some of these tools are more demanding to use than others, like the strategic option grid, which involves evaluating strategic options. In one case a High Street retailer's top team really struggled to fill in the scores and despite repeated encouragement and nudging they were never able to do that, preferring to fly in a circular path over their dilemmas rather than making some tentative choices. Underneath this was clearly a large amount of collective anxiety.

Another one that can be sensitive is stakeholder analysis, but generally managers warm to it as it is a relatively safe way of taking them into the 'zone of uncomfortable debate'. One of the most sensitive of the tools is the General Electric grid (see Figure 1.2) which plots a business portfolio against the inherent market attractiveness of the different strategic business units (or SBUs), and against their relative competitive strength. One would normally position these on Post-its. Moving them even slightly in line with the debate sometimes feels like doing open-heart without an anaesthetic! If you are acting as a strategic facilitator be aware of that.

While I have emphasized the use of strategy tools not only for analysis but also for creativity and in particular for visualization, there is a very important role for intuition, as many strategy writers emphasize. This involves much more use of the right hemisphere of the brain. Without shooting off at a long tangent, psychologically and energetically intuition is a very special quality. Perhaps one of the crispest ways of capturing this is from the eastern writer, Osho (1990: 1x):

> Intuition travels without any vehicle – that is why it is a jump: that is why it is a leap. It is a jump from one point to another point, with no interconnection between the two…. Only if I come to you without any steps is it a jump. And a real jump is even deeper. It means that something exists on one point A, and then it exists on point B, and between the two there is no existence. That is a real jump.

Certainly I experience intuition just that way as a strategy facilitator: obviously I work with many of the strategy tools that produce both data and insights, but I am also guided by hunches as to what is going on behind all of this. Sometimes I seem to get patterns or a specific hypothesis or insight emerges. One has to trust in that, and that instinct is usually about 98 per cent right. Probably at such 'peak' moments or experiences it is a matter of 50 per cent analysis and reasoned evaluation, and 50 per cent intuition, where one's mind just seems to 'leap across the gap'. I guess that is the kind of thought-space that a strategically minded CEO is in.

A useful model of the different ingredients of strategic thinking is shown in Figure 9.6, which shows eight of the nine cognitive processes as spokes of the wheel, those adjacent being more likely to be proximate in the process. There is also a natural progression clockwise around the wheel. The 'right brain' aspects are shown to the right and the 'left brain' to the left (except 'Imagination'). At the centre of the wheel is the process of 'reflective detachment' (one might know this as 'helicopter thinking'). All of these processes are grounded at some stage in one or more of the CEO case stories. Note that only two out of the nine are the kinds of processes more commonly taught on MBA courses: the analytical and the programming. Even 'reflective detachment' is something that MBA students are typically not strong at: only about 10 per cent seem to be able to couple strategic analysis with an automatic 'So what?' from this. Maybe that accounts for

Demystifying Strategic Thinking

FIGURE 9.6 The strategic thinking wheel

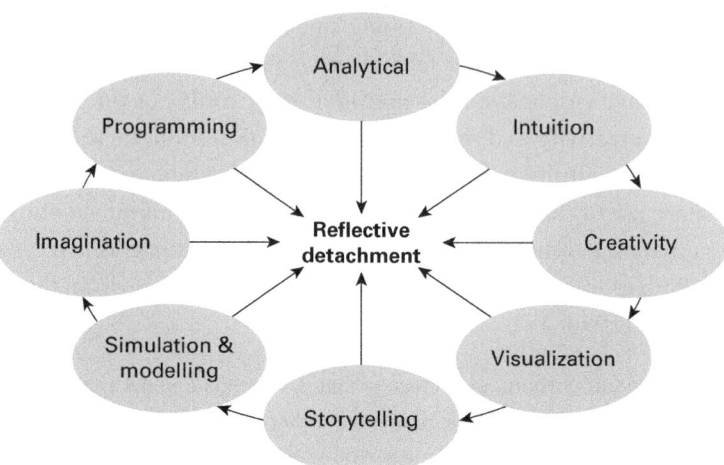

the old joke of 'MBA means More Boring Analysis' – and I say that as one who has one!

This 'Strategic thinking wheel' can be used not just during strategic thinking training but also in helping reflect on a strategic debate after the event, and thus as a tool in strategic team-building and in strategy facilitation generally. It can also be used for action planning to see how one might become an effective strategic thinker, and as a health-check as to what extent one's strategic thinking on a topic has been complete.

Coming back to the practicalities, once you have gone through the strategic thinking psychometrics in this chapter, if you haven't done so already you could study the techniques in *Demystifying Strategy*. If you are not sure whether to pursue this, what the one-time Strategy Director of Standard Life's IFA business said of the toolkit may help:

> Tony, I am so glad to meet you after so long – five years. I want to tell you that I was sceptical about the number of tools. I wanted to tell you that the time of the workshop five years ago I found it hard to take on board that you were suggesting that we might need so many tools to do strategic thinking. But over those five years I have used all the tools – every single one! I would just like to tell you that.

In my comments on the strategic thinking practices of the CEOs in this book, I marvelled at how much they have done without apparent reference to many strategic thinking tools (with the exception of Debora Evans of APIL). Leading CEOs seem to be able to develop these skills intuitively. But I imagine that there will have some trial and error in this process and we don't know how much was involved in getting there. Also, many other CEOs may not be quite as successful as our sample in doing this without the benefit of some tools.

Out of the 2,000 executives that I trained at Cranfield, only one I remember was a CEO. So once people have made CEO some may see it as too late to train (if only because it may be embarrassing). So, just in case you happen to get picked out as CEO material, and then whooshed up to that level, best probably to train properly. It is hoped that current CEOs, their HR directors and heads of leadership development take a regular look at the strategic thinking development needs: across the dimensions of the analytical, the creative and the intuitive.

The Appendices

In Appendix 1 we take a fresh view of Porter's Five Forces in a contemporary context. Almost without exception markets are tougher and more competitive (even for not-for-profit organizations) and CEOs would do well to use this kind of model, although this doesn't mean working through the diagrams slavishly. Readers other than CEOs should find the adaptations to the model very interesting, particularly if it was something once taught to them but never actually used.

The material on contingent strategy in Appendix 2 is also particularly helpful at CEO level as a way of dealing with uncertainty of such magnitude that a 'deliberate strategy' is not really appropriate. Yet there may be sufficient clarity about a number of possible futures that that it isn't quite appropriate to deal with this through a purely 'emergent strategy': ie waiting until some sort of successful pattern in the strategy materializes.

CONCLUSIONS

We saw in this chapter that by combining the insights from the study of CEOs with 25 years' experience of research, executive development and consulting, there are many ways of enhancing strategic thinking within complex organizations, namely:

- To understand more of one's own cognitive capability and the different types of cognitive processes that are involved across the whole range of activities.

- Practising what are relatively uncommon mental modes like 'strategic detachment and mindfulness' to achieve far greater states of calm and clarity, from which flashes of insight should come.

- Addressing the enablers and constraints, especially the simplest of things like actually devoting enough time to it.

- Rather than seeing strategy tools as somewhat cumbersome and unnecessary, and maybe a little embarrassing, instead using them sensibly to get more 'hands free' when manipulating complex data and thoughts.

- Being very clear in one's mind that there is a continuum of 'tactical' versus 'strategic' that one should play along, and that even where an issue isn't obviously hugely 'strategic', it may still be useful and necessary to think about it strategically.

- Recognizing that it is a great idea to apply strategic thinking to true 'strategic projects' and to get more practise in it that way.

In Chapter 10 we take a closer look at how everyday life can throw up opportunities and challenges for making strategic thinking something that rarely, if ever, is shut off.

Strategic thinking: visioning

10

Introduction

An emergent theme from this book has been the significance of visioning in strategic thinking. If one is mindful one can always look for situations and for opportunities in everyday life to do strategic thinking and to practise strategic visioning.

We change gear in this concluding chapter and look at visioning in a somewhat lighter mode. There is a case study on strategic influencing which goes beyond the zone of just 'cunning' into that of 'stunning': my step-daughter Frannie's case for a very big Halloween party. Frannie decided that what she really, really wanted was a party, and she set out very strategically to get it. There is also a lighter story from a business trip to Dubai, and from everyday life where strategic vision triumphs over constraints, which emphasizes that strategic vision can drive everyday experiences: never settle for 'average', and allow yourself to be playful and different. The message from this chapter is that one should be inspired to look at all things – including life's challenges – as opportunities to think strategically.

Strategic influencing: why not have a Halloween party?

The following case study is an entertaining and persuasive document written by a 16-year-old girl encouraged by her mother to provide a rationale for having a large party with her friends in our house, our garden, and in our summer house, which was to be a disco.

Teenagers of that age tend to lack sophisticated influencing skills. As is apparent from this book, where an issue is complex and sensitive, 'influencing' needs to move up a level to become 'strategic influencing', which takes in all of the issues, all of the stakeholders. It also requires recognizing the need to allow for the stakeholders to move through a process of becoming aware of an issue or opportunity, building an interest in it and for that interest to turn into a desire, and for that desire to solidify into a strong commitment.

In the following we see Frannie is exercising strategic influencing. She anchors her points skilfully in exactly those hot spots on her mother's agendas, particularly:

- wishing her daughter to develop her social confidence and her social network;
- wanting her to grow her organizational skills, eg project management;
- supporting her female assertiveness (as we see in the references to women's rights movements);
- making this a light process through the 'tongue in cheek humour', thus avoiding the pushiness often associated with teenagers wanting something from their parents.

While the case study is quite long it is never boring: with its twists and turns the reader is absorbed into Frannie's thinking journey. How many business cases and strategic plans are written in an engaging way? At the end it reaches such a natural conclusion that there seems no doubt in the readers' mind that they should trust that this party will be a success: in effect Frannie has brilliantly closed the sale when she says very simply: 'A party should take place' (I think that in the future Frannie might have an excellent career in sales and marketing). If a 16-year-old can do strategic influencing at this level then shouldn't we all be able to do that, whether we are a CEO or not?

CASE STUDY Strategic influencing: 'Why I should have a Halloween party', by Frannie, aged (then) 16

There are several reasons as to why I should have a Halloween party; one being that I have not had a party in a long time; secondly it expands my socializing skills and allows me to interact with people I wouldn't normally have a chance to interact with; and thirdly the actual organizing of the party will permit me to improve my organizational skills.

Another reason as to why I should have a party is that it will enforce the equality and the independence of women and display that the many feminist movements have made a difference.

By having a party at home there is no danger of me getting drunk as it is a controlled environment where you would be able to monitor what is going on. I have not had a party in a long time and I believe that parties are an enriching activity and allow us all to have fun with friends and family. I know that Tony, Basty and you enjoy parties *very, very much* and there have been very little negative consequences (aside from the cleaning the next day but that gives us an opportunity to have a nice tidy up – which Tony likes).

Secondly, as you know I find it difficult to socialize at times with certain people and a party provides a ground for me to talk to people. Plus it does make me *more popular*, and I am aware that this is not the strongest of reasons to you but it *really means something for me to be seen to be popular* among friends – even if it is only for a short period of time.

A party gives a base for conversation: I can talk to people I wouldn't normally engage in conversations with. This will sanction me to become *more socialized* and increase my confidence, which I know is very important in today's society, for example, in job interviews I must be confident but not arrogant and a party will let me do this.

Along with this a party gives me the opportunity to 'play the hostess', which may be beneficial for the future. On the subject of socializing, three of my closest friends have gone away to other schools and I miss them dearly. A way to remedy this is to have a party because this will bring us all together and give us a chance to catch up and interact.

Thirdly, the party will require organization and as I'm sure you know I really need to improve my organizational skills. I'm not necessarily extremely disorganized but I still lack in organization skills. Organizing a party will involve sending out invites, keeping an up-to-date list on who is coming, decorations and refreshments. On top of this, something I know you will be pleased to have done is, we will have to clean the house from top to bottom. I promise both me and Basty will help and do the majority of it since we are the ones who want the party. I understand that parties require a large amount of organization and I think it will be good practice for me for me to organize a fairly large event.

I think we can agree that there are several (if not many) reasons as to why we should have a Halloween party. Also I believe that it would be in our *best interest* to have a party as there are many benefits for all of us.

I almost forgot: in relation to the equality of women, feminism has made massive differences in today's society; women can now vote and are no longer obligated to stay at home and care for children. Now, I believe that having a party would be enforcing feminism because it shows that women (of which I am one) are capable of throwing parties and organizing them as well. Along with this it would display that women have friends that are not their husbands' and are allowed to interact with them in social situations without it seeming wrong or un-ladylike.

From my History classes I have been taught that before the suffragette movement, the expectation of women at parties was to be a good hostess by not interfering with the male conversations and looking desirable so that her husband or guardian could parade her around and show her off because that was what the expectation was. However, in today's day and age women have a higher position in society and are respected as individuals rather than as possessions to be bought and sold. Therefore if a Halloween party were to take place it would be promoting the independence of women.

Equality of the sexes and the furthering of women's rights are positive aspirations; yet people tend to describe feminism using negative terms, and feminism today has acquired a bad reputation. 'Radical' is an adjective commonly applied to feminism as a whole, when really feminism is about nothing more than wanting equality for women, and is that so much to ask? (And equally, having a party?)

Moreover, women have been victims of male supremacy for such a long time and a party hosted by our female-dominated household will discard this allowance of male supremacy in the 21st century. On top of this we could make the party a celebration of all our accomplishments this year such as Tony's advances in a certain challenging court case; you finally getting ahead in setting up your business; the fact that I have not *completely failed* in sixth form; Basty starting Year 7 successfully with only a few minor issues; and Milly's amazing accomplishment in learning to not only use the cat flap, but the litter box as well! As you can see we have all triumphed in our own little ways.

This would also enforce feminism because it would demonstrate (particularly your achievements in setting up your own business after working your way up in psychology) how women's achievements have come further than simply making an excellent meal, and so we need to celebrate the amazing advances of women in the world.

Furthermore, the fact that I am allowed to even have access to a higher education should be celebrated because it was and still is in some cultures thought as wrong for women to even have an education. There is a charity that is dedicated to helping girls throughout the world gain an education; the charity is called Plan UK. The fact that there are some places in the world that do not permit girls an education is obviously wrong and we should challenge that by rejoicing my higher education with a party.

Additionally, as mentioned prior, parties require organization and organizing a party will display women's ability to independently organize an event and that they are capable to take on responsibility.

This will discredit the gender stereotypes that women are incapable of retaining knowledge – as illustrated in Harry Enfield's parody about 'Women: Know your limits' (**http://www.youtube.com/watch?v=LS37SNYjg8w&safe=active**). In this sketch a dinner party setup is re-enacted in two different ways: one is that the men are talking about important national issues and when the woman gives her opinion, however valid it may be, the men disrespect it; in the second scenario the same situation ensues but instead the woman makes a remark about kittens and this is praised by all the men at the dinner table. This is then followed by an animation showing that knowledge can only stay at a certain level in a woman's brain whereas in a man's it can fill the brain completely.

Unfortunately, whilst this piece of evidence is only meant to be a parody it is also a sad reality, not so much now in many countries, but of course there are still some places in the world where this attitude toward women is still present. As a group we need to dispute this view by having a party and allowing a female-organized party to be thrown. However, I understand that we must not become radical feminists and of course the males in our household will have some involvement in the organization of the party, but the party will be a chance for us women to display that we are capable of taking on responsibility and not failing.

Furthermore, the party will also show our advantages above men – our ability to multi-task and our flexibility when it comes to tasks. Obviously there will be some problems that will arise throughout the duration of the party and as women have the amazing ability to quickly adapt to any last minute changes; this shows our slight advantage above men. Although as we are only feminists that seek equality for women and men, acknowledging our advantages over men every now and again *will do no harm.*

Thus, a party should take place. Moreover, a Halloween party will likewise display a woman's creativity because a costume will need to be thought of.

In final conclusion there are evidently many, many reasons as to why this Halloween party should take place. Firstly there are the personal uses and the benefits to feminism. As a family unit we should promote the important cause that is feminism because even in today's society, despite the efforts of many courageous women, inequality is still present and therefore we must do everything in our power to amend this inherited discrimination – including having a Halloween party.

Postscript: The Halloween party was duly approved and 30 teenagers and eight adults had a fabulous experience in Shirley, Croydon, virtually incident free – except Tony's fireworks....

In 2013 Frannie submitted another business case for a party for July 13 which was duly approved by the family's CEO, Dr Carolina Marie Yepes.

Frannie was appealing to the mix of agendas for individual stakeholders, particularly her mother. If we look at the tool of stakeholder agenda analysis in Figure 10.1, Frannie had not only reversed any 'turn offs', but appealed to many of the 'turn ons', eg that organizing a large party like this would enhance her organizational and interpersonal skills, be empowering for her as a young woman, be fair, and above all have proven she could influence in a non-grabbing way, and as a reward for her producing a small-scale work of art in that proposal: game, set and match. A redrawn stakeholder agenda analysis would be a no brainer.

FIGURE 10.1 Stakeholder agenda analysis – Halloween party

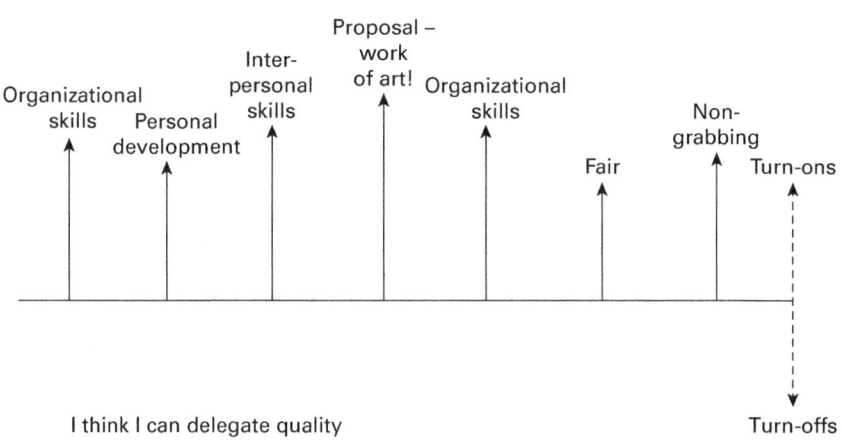

You might gather by now that I take strategy very seriously in my life, and strategic thinking in particular. Finishing a course in Dubai at the time of completing this book (a programme on strategic thinking) my participants said things like this at the end:

> 'I really like the fact that strategic thinking is applicable at every level: corporate, business and individually.'

'It is refreshing that far from being primarily conceptual it is most practical and applicable to everyday issues like time management.'

'For the first time I have a structured process for dealing with complex issues step-by-step as a design specialist, but now I have the business strategy pictures to communicate my ideas' (staff from the Prime Minister's Private Office, UAE).

When I left these guys to take their careers forward there was a sense of transmitting a precious gift (of which I happened to have been the fortunate messenger), so it was a truly emotional ending to three days of intensive 'mini-MBA' work with them.

Vision and thinking differently: an experience of Dubai

My book draws to an official close as I leave Dubai for London in June 2013. Dubai is a wonderful place and is full of amazing design, thoughtfulness and some of the friendliest people on the planet. I would like to thank the staff of the Four Points Sheraton Hotel, for the friendliest, most helpful and most proactive service ever. Their world-class service is the personification of the 'unique resource' that resource-based theory of competitive advantage is all about. I would like to include a little of that experience to illustrate the importance of vision in strategic thinking. Vision guided the design of the (then) tallest building in the world and also what I got to do at the top of it, and on the flight back home as well.

During the daytime I ran a mini-MBA course. In the evening it was lovely and hot so after the gym I went to the bar on the roof of the 43rd floor. I often like to stretch in the evening, and was just attempting a headstand near the pool when a rotund security guard stopped me on the grounds of 'safety'. As some readers will remember from *Demystifying Strategy*, one of my 55 ways of thinking in a cunning way is to think about the 'joy of constraints': following the constraint set by the security guard on the hotel roof I set myself the challenge: 'To do a headstand at the highest place I can find!'

So on the last day of my stay in Dubai I decided that I must go up the top of the highest building on earth, the Burj Khalifa. I set off with not very much time to see if I could do a headstand at the very top without being grabbed by security. When I arrived at the adjacent Dubai Mall I looked at the enormous shimmering, silver spire against the purest blue sky and marvelled at the strategic vision behind the inspiration for that amazing construction, that work of art. This was no product of incremental strategic thinking, riddled with compromise as most buildings are: this was a designer strategy, built with exact purpose, the very clearest strategic vision.

My ticket was for 8.30 am, but a man at the Mall said I couldn't get in and I should come back at 10, which meant that I would have missed the slot I had booked. I didn't believe him, fortunately, and I ran round the Mall like Tom Cruise in a 'Mission Impossible' film and ended up being almost the first person up the top of the Tower, which is over 2,500 feet high! I often play the music and opening scene from 'Mission Impossible 2' where Tom Cruise is mountaineering and hanging upside down from a rock, to send the message that the strategic thinker must have a head for heights – as an energizer on strategic workshops. Also, I use that to send the message that searching for the ideal set of strategies demands the total focus and determination of Tom Cruise embarking on a 'Mission' – and also that the harder it is the more creative, determined and tenacious he is, as strategic thinkers should be.

The lift journey to the top of the Burj Khalifa was itself an amazing experience – the lift was dark and when we started to ascend and accelerate, a light show and music began and became more and more exciting. It took nearly two minutes to rocket up almost 200 floors to the top. Its motion was impeccably smooth, as if designed using alien technology.

The view at the top is simply gobsmacking. The considerable buildings of Dubai are dwarfed by its stature. If you ever need a metaphor for helicopter thinking then this was embodied in this engineering feat. If you ever needed a model for a vision this is it too (our CEOs were all very fond of vision in the heart of this book). In the entrance hall there was a statement of the vision that had guided this magnificent silver construction that shone like a star reflecting the Middle-Eastern sun:

> I am the power that lifts the world's head proudly skywards, surpassing limits and expectations.
>
> Rising gracefully from the desert and honouring the city with a new glow, an extraordinary union of engineering and art, with every detail carefully crafted and beautifully crafted.
>
> I am the life force of collective aspirations and the aesthetic union of many cultures. I stimulate dreams, stir emotions and awaken creativity.
>
> I am the magnet that attracts the wide-eyed tourist, eagerly catching their postcard moment, the Centre for the world's finest shopping, dining and entertainment and home for the world's elite.
>
> I am the heart of the city and its people, the marker that defines Emaar Properties' ambition and Dubai's shining dream.
>
> More than just a moment in time, I define moments for future generations.
> I am Burj Khalifa.

Strategic Thinking: Visioning

As a strategic thinker one should look at all everyday life experiences, like wanting to chill out in a hotel, to go to high spots to do yoga, to look at shopping malls and the tallest spire on the planet as strategic phenomena, as opportunities to practise strategic mindfulness.

A while ago I had decided that I would do some yoga in the most challenging spots that I could find on all of my travels (my strategic vision) and not be put off by being told that 'you are not allowed to do that here', or 'you might fall over and hurt yourself'. I have been practising the yoga headstand since I was 17 – that's 42 years ago; it is very safe. I invert for up to three minutes and afterwards have an extremely clear mind; an ideal space for strategic thinking. (Keeping yourself physically fit I believe significantly enhances one's ability to do strategic thinking especially as one gets older. Meditation, as I have said, also helps.)

When I got to the very top of the Burj Khalifa, I saw to my delight that there was the back-end of a yoga class in the open area where you could look down and enjoy the 38 degree heat; I was ecstatic. I had planned to do a yoga headstand regardless, although I was apprehensive that I would be stopped. But now I had my green light, and I was able to get a total inversion half a mile into the sky. Many photographs were taken by willing observers. I also became a model for the other yogis who all ended up trying to copy me!

An important message from this experience is that if you occasionally do something out of the ordinary it gives you a lift to think differently about things generally; it cultivates playfulness, an essential ingredient in strategic thinking. One of the biggest impediments to strategic thinking is that experienced senior managers are set into their routine ways of working to the point where their thought processes follow the most linear tramlines of just 'processing work'. They really struggle to think outside their mindsets. There is no harm in being different. There is no harm in thinking different, either. In Paulo Cuelho's words, in the *Manual of the Warrior of Light*:

> The warrior of light does not worry that, to others, his behaviour may seem quite mad.
> He talks out loud to himself when he is alone....
> At first, he finds this very difficult. He thinks that he has nothing to say, that he will just repeat the same meaningless twaddle. Even so he persists....
> One day, he notices a change in his voice. He realizes that he is the channel for some higher wisdom.
> The warrior of light may seem quite mad but this is just a disguise.

Strategic thinking is about being playful with your mind and at times being disrespectful to institutional thinking: sometimes it has to be about *thinking in a different way*. It is about being in the flow, which might sometimes means challenging convention and staying with a vision.

Hopefully the dialogues with six leading CEOs and with some further ideas and encouragement and stories from me about how I have looked at everyday experiences as mini-strategic cases, will inspire you to engage in a career as a strategic thinker and also in your life generally. Dare to imagine not just the possible but what may seem the impossible, the unachievable, even things that may seem a little crazy.

I hinted earlier that my vision was about not only doing yoga on a very tall building but in high places generally. In Chapter 1 I talked about having a 'cunning plan' then trying to outdo it with and even better plan, as Blackadder did when he half-drowned Baldrick rather than submit himself to the torture! Far sooner than I had ever hoped I found a second opportunity to do a headstand in a very, very high place!

On my flight back from Dubai on Emirates Airlines, I was having a chat with Matilda, one of the very friendly stewardesses. I told her my laptop battery had died and that I couldn't finish my book. She provided me with an adaptor so I could carry on. I told her that I loved Dubai and had done a headstand on the top of the Burj Khalifa. I also said that on occasion on long flights I sneaked a headstand: once a British Airways stewardess had discovered me doing one, which freaked her out. I showed her this last case study and said: 'Dubai is a model of what a vision can really look like: the buildings, the people, the facilities, and of course, Emirates Airline, the food – down to the free home-made cup-cakes. However good all that is you (those who run Dubai) just seem to want to get even better.'

She said to me: 'But doesn't everyone want to get better?'

I said; 'I don't think so – in the UK I think they often just can't be bothered. Things are just so average or even worse. Take Croydon for example. We had riots and some fires: if something had fully destroyed the place then we could have rebuilt the whole lot; even our own Burj Khalifa.'

'Oh yes,' she said, 'I lived near East Croydon for five days – I see what you mean.'

'Well,' I said, 'I have this vision of Croydon just like Dubai – all the buildings – imagine a tower like the Burj Khalifa in East Croydon – and the malls too.'

'I think you are having a fantasy,' she said, implying that was on the border of madness.

'No,' I replied, 'I am just having a vision.'

Why can't Croydon become more attractive? My vision for Croydon is that it becomes a place where tourists might visit, for example tourists going to Brighton would get off the train at East Croydon and look around. A Dubai-style shopping mall would be good for a start (I believe that there are some plans – but are they truly visionary: do they stretch as the whole setting of Dubai does? Is there much in Dubai that is average? I don't think so).

Just 48 minutes before landing at Gatwick Matilda whispered in year: 'Would you like to have a very special surprise, a present'. She invited me to the galley and said that I could do some yoga, and my headstand; she wanted to take pictures of me. It was very tricky to pull off because the galley was cramped and ran orthogonally to the direction of flight of the plane. As aircraft fly at a slant of several degrees the ground isn't actually level; there is also the slight movement of the plane and less oxygen than normal to contend with.

After some trial and error Matilda got some great pictures of me in the full inversion and also squatting on one leg and in a 'toe stand'. Matilda trusted my competence, so that day I became a member of the five-mile headstand club: my vision was complete. I truly got what I really, really, really wanted. In a period of 24 hours I had overcome the constraints and, through strategic visioning and sheer determination, had realized not only a cunning plan but a stunning plan. A strategic thinker always has that light on in his or her head and applies it to all things in life.

Postscript

I have alluded in this book to the integration of quite disparate cognitive and sensing faculties that are involved in strategic thinking, and that these need to be brought together in an effortless state of flow. While mastery of these disciplines requires application and practice there is also a more intangible ingredient of subtle mastery, to truly light it all up with a deeper and richer intuition. Such mastery requires allowing yourself to see beyond the self-evident to *just sense*. To illustrate the absence of slavish dependency, I end with a story from the Zen warrior whose dream is to have effortless mastery, like our vision of being a true strategic thinker (*Soul Sword – The way and the mind of the Zen warrior*, Vernon Taylor):

> A young warrior gloried in his skill. He could out-shoot everyone in his province... he was told of an old man who was said to be the greatest archer of the region.... The young man, full of himself, sought out the old man to challenge him. He found the old man sitting in a hut in the mountains.
>
> When the old man heard the young man had come he was inclined not to give him a contest. He had nothing to prove. The young man was insistent.

So the old man finally agreed to demonstrate his skill. He took the young man to a high place on the mountain, where the two of them stood on a precipice.

'Stand on the log and shoot at the geese above,' the old man directed.... Balancing himself precariously, he sought a target in the sky and steadied his arm... three birds were pierced by a single shot. He came back to safety, smug in the belief that the old man could not beat his performance.

'You call that archery,' the old man teased. Then, with no bow or arrow visible, he vaulted onto the log and stretched forth his naked arm. Concentrating on his imaginary bow, he released a shot. A bird plummeted from the air. The mouth of the young man fell open with shock.

'How can you practise archery without a bow?' he asked.

'How can you call yourself an archer when you still need a bow,' he responded.

For further amplification on any of the issues in and thoughts in this book, contact: **tony.grundy1@virginmedia.com**, or see **www.tonygrundy.com**. A director- and CEO-level strategic coach, I currently run strategic workshops and three-day mini-MBA courses on strategic thinking with Euromoney, in the UK and globally.

APPENDIX 1
Rethinking and reinventing Porter's Five Competitive Forces

Introduction

In each of the case studies of the six CEOs interviewed in this book there were issues of competitive pressure, or the intensity of the competitive forces within an industry. Even in the case of the Samaritans – a charity – the organization needs to compete for funding against other charities and for 'mind-share' of consumers' constrained disposable incomes. The IPC competes for attention against other sporting and non-sporting spectacles, and while it is closely associated with the Olympics it also implicitly seeks to have a greater share of attention in the athletics world generally. APIL has to justify the funding by its members who are under severe pressure from strategic and regulatory change.

In terms of the more mainstream commercial companies we examined, Moonpig managed to thrive with a 'blue ocean' strategy (ie one that was 'fresh' and was in a context of imperfect competition). While Virgin Galactic is currently where Moonpig was some years ago, with a very enticing market developing, there are always possibilities of a second 'fast entrant' – and as soon as that begins the effects of Porter's Forces can kick in.

In the light of this I decided that I would include in this book some earlier work that I had done to make Porter's model available to a wider audience rather than let it fester in some obscure journal, read only by aging academics in need of what a funeral company that I know well would call the 'Pre-need market'. (Readers who have already consumed the sister book *of 'Demystifying Strategic Thinking' – Demystifying Strategy*, 2012 – would know of my intellectual obsession with that industry. As luck would have it since the earlier book I was lucky to gain very first-hand experience of the industry – and had the great pleasure of visiting facilities!)

Going back to my main plot, then. When Michael Porter came up with the five competitive forces, it put strategic management at the very heart of the management agenda. Porter's framework became a centrepiece of both business strategy and of strategic management (Porter, 1980; 1985). But what has become of his original five competitive forces? Little has occurred since 1980 to develop this thinking (Grundy, 2006). Porter appears to have been more interested in taking his concepts to an even more 'macro' level, particularly the competitive advantage of countries, rather than to micro economics (Porter, 1990). Instead, we only see criticisms that he ignores the basis of 'competing routed in internal competences and resources that are hard to imitate' even though that was the topic of his second book, *Competitive Advantage.*

Porter's model, while it has done extremely well in being taught material on MBA courses for 33 years, and occupying space in every serious textbook since, does not seem to have captured the imagination of other theorists. It seems frozen in time. Also, outside MBA classes, managers have 'vaguely heard about it' but few have got it in their heads so firmly that every shopping foray whether on High Street, out of town or on the internet is a veritable 'Porters five forces experience', as it is for me. Indeed, none of our six CEOs made particular mention of it – although it is clear that in the period up to the sale of Moonpig the CEO there was more than aware that the imperfect conditions of competition in the internet greetings card business might not hold up forever.

If one were to take a sample of attendees on the hundreds of strategic management courses I have run over the last 23 years, one might estimate that between 15 and 20 per cent were vaguely familiar with these early Porter concepts, and only 5 per cent had actively used them at an explicit, analytical level. Less than 1 per cent would use them regularly and maybe 0.1 per cent would use them whenever they buy something in their everyday lives: like a gift card from Moonpig, a ride on Virgin Galactic, a dental plan from Simplyhealth or a coffee at the Paralympic Games. That might seem too obsessive – 'The curse of Porter's five forces' or (Obsessive Competitive Diagnosis – a variant of OCD) but it can come in really useful at times.

CASE STUDY   Buying a car

Last year my wife decided to buy a new car. She had bought a Rover City car five years earlier and although it still had low mileage – less than 30,000 miles – it was clearly falling to bits. The petrol tank leaked, releasing fumes if over a quarter full, and the indicator only worked properly in one direction unless there was a co-driver to hold it in place when turning right. Her son, Basty, usually did that job – the car needed a co-pilot. On 'Top Gear', the TV programme, it was reviewed as 'The worst car that I have ever driven.' The engine sounded as if it had gone to the moon and back and spare parts were extortionate; Rover had of course gone bust in 2005.

Needless to say we didn't over-advertise the deficiencies, we weren't generous with the petrol, and on the test drive the car always turned left. When a punter was interested, we gave in ever so rapidly to what might have seemed a knock-down price. In terms of Michael Porter's five forces, buying a second-hand car is a situation where the seller has far better information about the car so the buyer inevitably loses on a private sale, especially if the car is unreliable or old or both.

I advised my wife to get a Honda – they don't seem to have break-downs and my Honda Civic R had its first ever mechanical repair after 158,000 miles! And that was mainly a cleaning job and a leak. I made sure that we used Porter's forces to maximum advantage. Here is how it works: you only shop on the last day of the calendar month, ideally on a Saturday. You go in at 3.45 pm so there is not much time left. You show interest but not too much. It is 'the first car that you have looked at', so you have just started shopping. Ideally you drive 15–20 miles somewhere and say 'We don't come to this area normally.' Your husband/wife shows a casual lack of interest and asks questions like 'Are you sure that it has got enough power?' That is the softening up process.

Your wife then indicates her budget is 'tight' but you could be tempted to pay £600 less than the price if there was a free year's MOT, etc. It is all take it or leave it. You suggest that the salesman goes and bargains with his boss and just hint, as a half joke: 'You know it is almost the end of the month; we thought you might just want to shift it today; we are busy next weekend.'

That's more or less exactly how my wife managed to get a great deal on a Honda Jazz from a garage in Bromley! It happened to be a Saturday – and the last day in the month – perfect! Whether you are buying a Honda, a jumbo jet or a family all-inclusive holiday to the Canaries, Porter's five forces apply.

Porter was propelled to fame on the back of his five forces model (and other intellectual advances); it seems odd that this valuable model has so little currency amongst practising managers. Why is this? Perhaps it is because:

- Some find the framework somewhat abstract and remote.
- The original framework explained the criteria for assessing each of the five competitive forces, but in the language of micro-economic theory rather than in terms of its practicalities.

- His model was somewhat prescriptive and apparently rigid, leaving managers generally inhibited from being playful and innovative in applying it.
- While the framework does help to simplify micro economics, its structure can be relatively difficult to assimilate. Managers tend to like analytical concepts spelt out in very simple terms, otherwise they find it difficult to integrate them into everyday practice.

I believe that Porter's Five Competitive Forces is a vitally important concept, and one that certainly merits the attention of all practising (senior) managers. I also believe that to operationalize it more effectively requires significant further development. I demonstrate this with a practical example taken from the health club market, which has grown significantly in many countries over the past 10 years, but has been heavily impacted by shifts in competitive pressure.

Let's look at how some really practical value, particularly at the CEO level, can be had out of the five forces:

1 The value and limitations of the model.
2 The interdependencies, both outside and within the five forces.
3 Prioritizing the five forces.
4 The 'micro' competitive forces.
5 Competitive dynamics.
6 Mapping competitive forces, both horizontally and vertically.
7 The way forward.

These will give some valuable insights into how Porter's five forces can greatly improve managers' skills through much more frequent use. Each and every potential innovation in this paper has been triggered by observation of managers' frustration at not being able to use it to its fullest potential. This can then be developed into a far richer system which can be applied to some very real challenges facing CEOs and board directors.

1. The value and limitations of the model

Porter's five forces are depicted in Figure A1.1. His starting point was that he wanted to account for long-term variances in the economic returns of one industry versus another. His genius resided in distilling micro-economics into five variables driving performance:

Appendix 1

a the bargaining power of the buyers;
b entry barriers;
c rivalry;
d substitutes; and
e the bargaining power of the suppliers.

FIGURE A1.1 These forces determine industry profitability

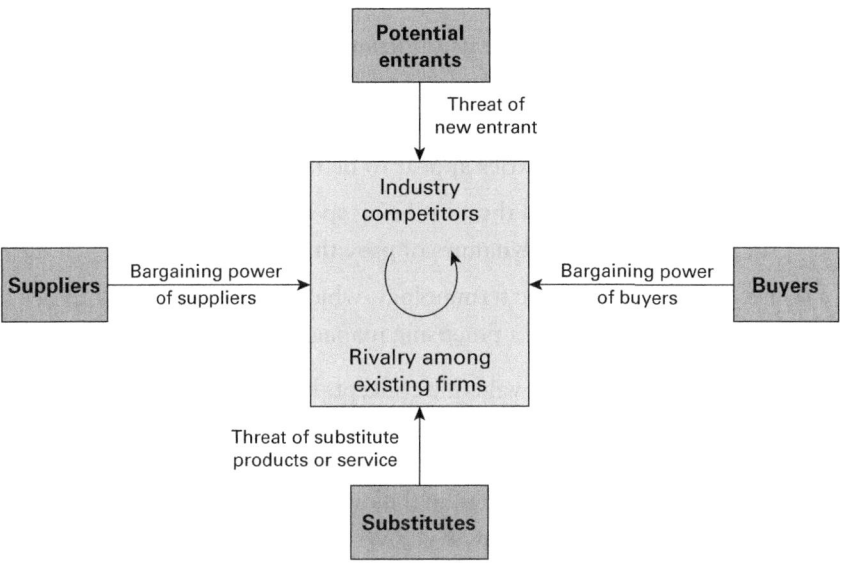

SOURCE: Competitive Strategy, Porter

The value of Porter's framework is that it:

- Simplifies micro-economic theory into just five major influences.
- Shows how 'competitive rivalry' – its central box – is very much a function of the other four forces.
- Helps to predict the long-run rate of returns in a particular industry and goes beyond just market growth rates in defining industry attractiveness.
- Emphasizes the search for imperfect markets, which offer superior returns.
- Emphasizes negotiating power/bargaining arrangements.

The limitations of Porter's framework are that it:

- Places too much emphasis on industry analysis instead of analysis of more specific product market segments at a micro level.
- Oversimplifies industry value-chains, for example 'buyers' may need to be differentiated in terms of channels, intermediate buyers and end consumers.
- Fails to link directly to possible management action: for example, where companies have low influence over any of the five forces, how can they set about dealing with them?
- Looks static, thus an abstraction from timescales.
- Tends to encourage the view of an 'industry' as a specific entity with ongoing boundaries (less appropriate in the present era where industry boundaries appear to be far more fluid).
- Appears self-contained thus not being specifically related to 'PEST' factors or the dynamics of growth.
- Is couched in economic terminology, which may be perceived to be too much jargon from a practising manager's perspective.

Porter's five forces is thus a valuable concept, but one which in its original formulation had some practical drawbacks; it is begging to be developed further. Porter's concept merely scratches the surface of its full potential. Perhaps the very success of the original model led to it not being challenged or developed. This process is now well overdue, and we now look at how:

- The five competitive forces are interdependent with other strategic analysis tools that deal with the external environment, and with each other, and this can be developed into a more comprehensive and coherent 'system'.
- The five forces can be prioritized within a 'force field' analysis format using vector arrows.
- The individual forces can be broken down at a micro level.
- The framework can be transformed into a more dynamic model, at the industry, micro and transactional level.
- The five forces analysis needs to be applied, segment-by-segment, across the business.

2. The interdependencies, both outside and within the five forces

Conventional strategy theory (for example Johnson and Scholes, 1987) highlights the need to think about factors outside the industry. Indeed PEST (political, economic social and technological) factor analysis is possibly the second most widely-known strategy technique after SWOT. But there is a profound gap between PEST and SWOT analysis, and this is only partly met by Porter's five forces. A linking technique is that of 'growth drivers' (Grundy, 1995; Grundy and Brown, 2002a).

Figure A1.2 gives an example of growth driver analysis, helping us to represent the forces which (directly or indirectly) cause or inhibit market growth over a particular time period. (This model will be used in conjunction with the five competitive forces later on, looking at the health club industry.) The key thing to note here is that Porter's framework is part of a bigger system (see Figure A1.3).

Figure A1.3 captures (in a 'strategic onion' model format) the key domains that need to be thought through, within the overall 'competitive climate' beginning with:

a   PEST factors, then, inside that:

b   the growth drivers, and then nested within that:

c   Porter's Five Forces, and only then, at the core:

d   competitive position.

FIGURE A1.2   Growth drivers: dot com market for shares, 2000

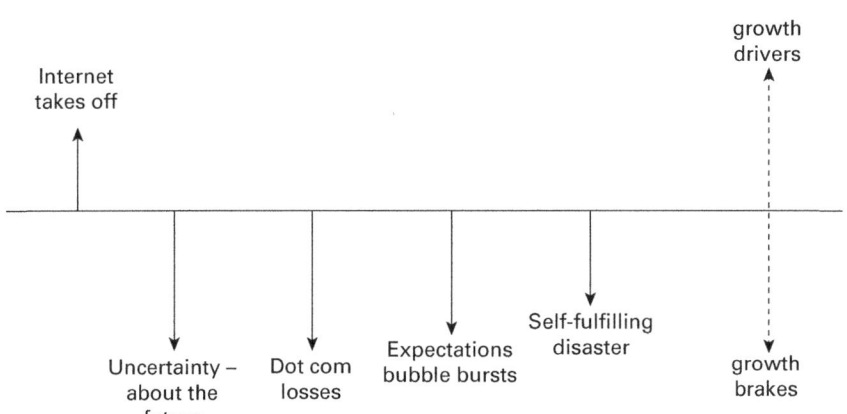

Appendix 1

FIGURE A1.3 The competitive climate

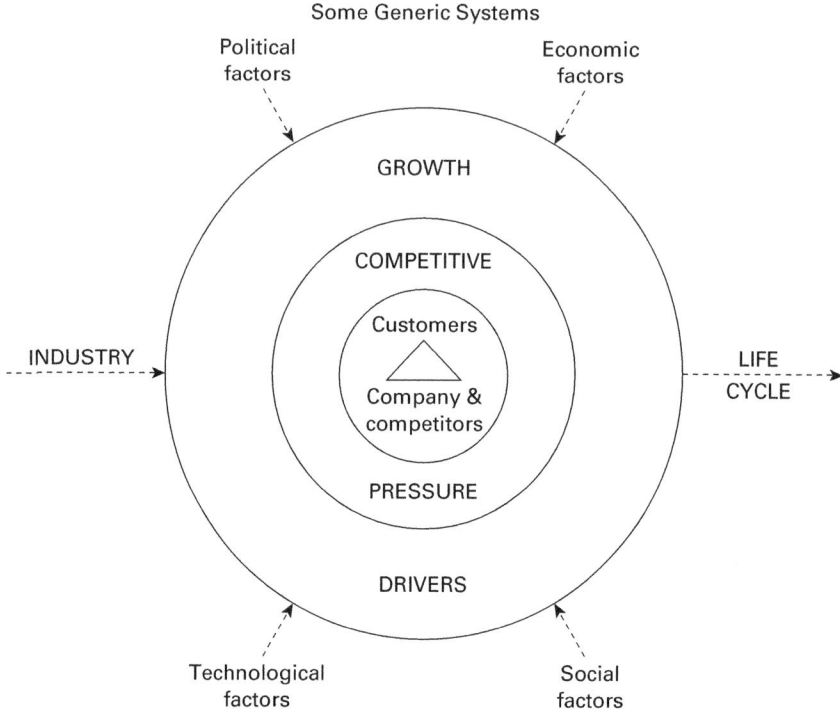

These layers of the 'strategy onion' are highly interdependent, which might be a useful phenomenon for managers to learn about and to apply: for example, where the PEST factors are generally hospitable growth is encouraged, and the full impact of the five competitive forces may not be felt, and may thus be latent. But where the PEST factors become inhospitable, this will clearly dampen the growth drivers. And if the growth drivers within a particular market are themselves tightening, for example due to lifecycle effects, this will put a disproportionate and adverse pressure on Porter's five forces, particularly in the bargaining power of buyers, and upon rivalry. Also, a high growth environment may encourage entrants, and a low one will discourage them. The result can lead a collapse in confidence and in prices, unless there are lots of exits (witness the health club market in the UK in 2002–3, as we will see later). Indeed, it may be helpful to not call it 'Porter's five forces' or even 'five forces', particularly when introducing it to a team or wider organization. An alternative is to call it 'competitive pressure', which is less jargon-laden, implies more of a checklist, and is less intimidating.

Besides these external interdependencies, Porter's Five Competitive Forces are themselves highly interdependent with each other; again something only implicit in Porter and other texts. Figure A1.4 plots the main interdependencies internal to the five competitive forces:

- between bargaining power of buyers and entry barriers: buyers may actively encourage new entrants, thus reducing entry barriers;
- between bargaining power of buyers and substitutes: buyers may actively search for substitutes, thereby encouraging them in a similar fashion;
- between entry barriers and bargaining power of the suppliers: new entrants may seek to enter the market by backward integration, either by acquiring suppliers or via alliances;
- between substitutes and bargaining power of suppliers: suppliers may seek to leapfrog existing industry competitors by marketing and selling substitutes.

The refined model in Figure A1.4 thus illustrates the extent to which each of Porter's five forces needs to be understood as a wider, interacting system rather than as a self-contained unit. While Porter's original concept explains

FIGURE A1.4 Porter's Five Competitive Forces – key internal dependencies

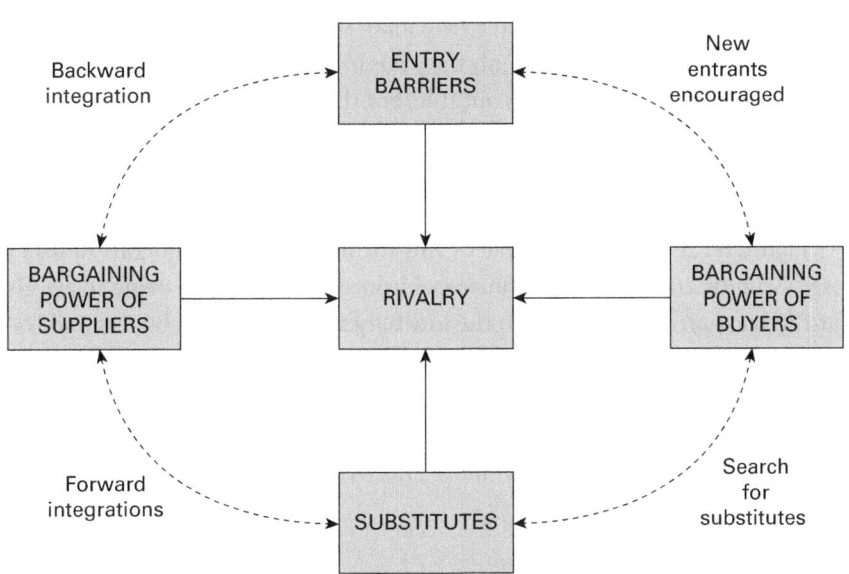

some of these system interdependencies, they are underdeveloped and implicit. Indeed, we can put to one side the conventional input-output/industry boundaries model, which appears to have been the starting point for the five forces. Indeed, if we become playful for a while, some new and quite interesting opportunities open up.

3. Prioritizing the five forces

The five forces need to be prioritized in some way. Porter's teaching methodology (as per his Harvard Business School video cases) involves ticking each force for whether it is favourable, neutral or unfavourable, with three ticks for favourable, two for neutral and one for unfavourable. Unfortunately, because of the original set-up of the model, defined as being mainly about negative strategic characteristics like buyer power, supplier power, rivalry and substitutes, it is quite difficult to apply this scoring method. For instance, where buyer power is high, the model's user needs to think 'that is a bad thing', therefore the score is one tick, or unfavourable. In many instances, especially when first used, the model's scores can come out incorrectly. Porter's model, as it is currently framed, thus presents an immediate barrier to its assimilation. Also, the scoring does not take into account the relative importance and weighting of each score. While two-dimensional grids can do this trade-off (for example, see Grundy, 1995) the approach is still a little cumbersome.

An alternative approach is to borrow from the vector format, originally applied by Lewin (1935) in force field analysis, for enablers and constraints of organizational change. Not only does this model easily separate out whether a force is 'favourable' or 'unfavourable' but the length of the arrows can also be used to show, a) its incidence or severity, and b) its importance. Also, where a force can be split into sub-forces (see the next section) it can depict these sub-forces easily.

Figure A1.5 gives an example of this format within the funerals industry (see Grundy, 2012). Here the funerals business is depicted as being relatively attractive, particularly through the low bargaining power of buyers and less threat of substitutes. With such a visual presentation, it is easy to challenge the judgements supporting these outputs; also, one can do a sensitivity analysis on it. Most important, its visual balance gives immediate interpretation of the industry's overall attractiveness more effectively than by adding together the ticks, as in Porter's approach.

Appendix 1

FIGURE A1.5 Example of format from the funerals industry

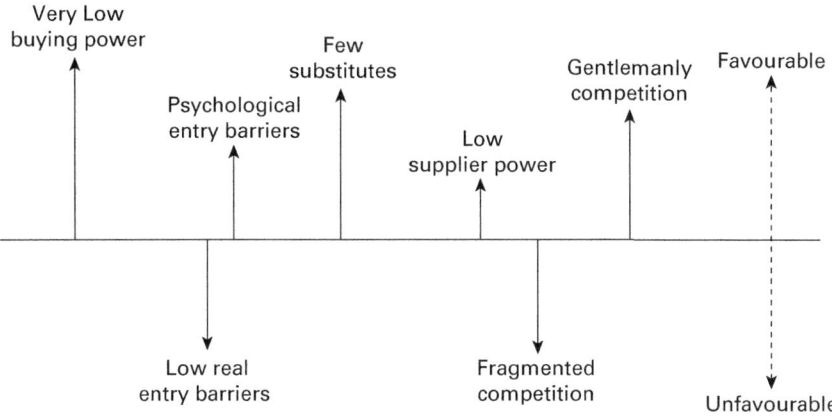

Figure A1.5 thus enables the user to choose which of the five forces is most important, in isolation and in terms of its effects on the system. The forces here are depicted as vector lines, whose lengths depend on, a) perceived importance and, b) perceived favourable influences versus unfavourable influences.

FIGURE A1.6 Bargaining power

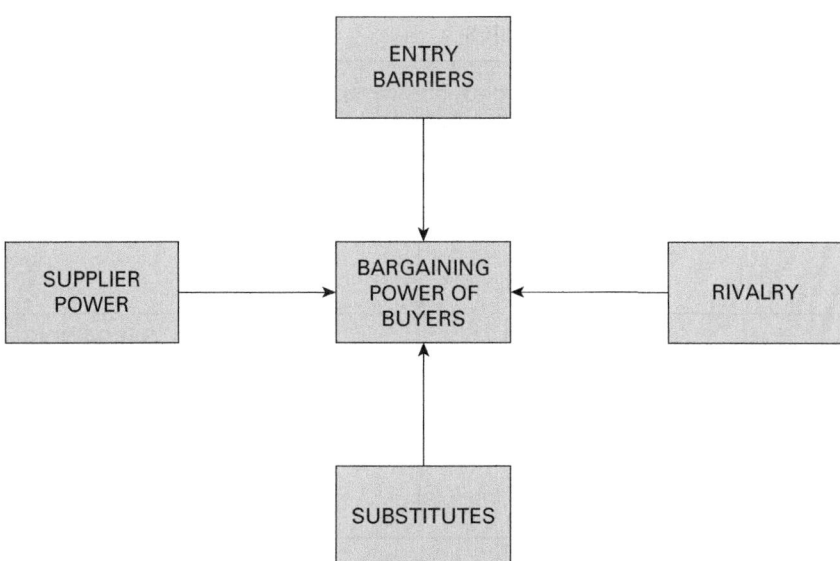

We now look at how each force relates to the other forces; Figure A1.6 explores this. Our first permutation looks at the bargaining power of the buyers in the centre of the framework. In Figure A1.6 the bargaining power of the buyers is increased by competitive rivalry, the availability of substitutes, low entry barriers and low supplier power. 'Bargaining power of the buyers' is thus not an entirely separate element to consider when using the five forces, but needs thinking through in relation to the others. In Figure A1.7, the threat of substitutes (at the centre) is now increased by buyers keen to shop around, and by low rivalry (amongst existing competitors). Entrants may choose to enter via offering substitutes and, once again, suppliers might seek to leapfrog existing competitors via the route of substitutes.

In Figure A1.8, with entry barriers at the centre, buyers may reduce entry barriers or encourage substitutes by their search for better value. Rivalry will of course discourage entrants, as may supplier power. Besides being novel in structure (the five forces model is always presented in the standard Porter format), Figures A1.6–8 give managers far greater flexibility in their use of the model and, hopefully, more insights.

In short, there are many interdependencies both external and internal to Porter's Five Competitive Forces, and these are unlikely to be taught to practising managers, let alone used by them. CEOs would be oblivious – unless they have worked these out at an intuitive level. This means that they are

FIGURE A1.7 Substitutes

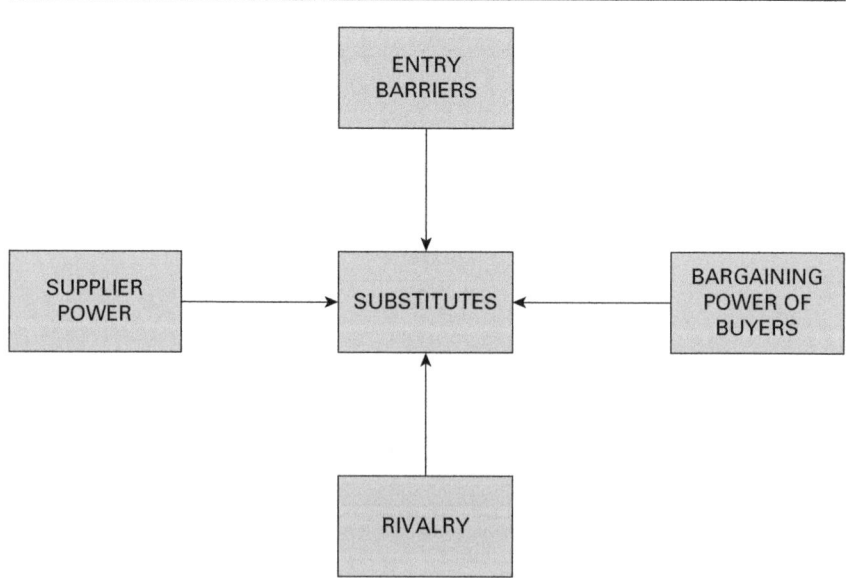

FIGURE A1.8 Barriers to entry

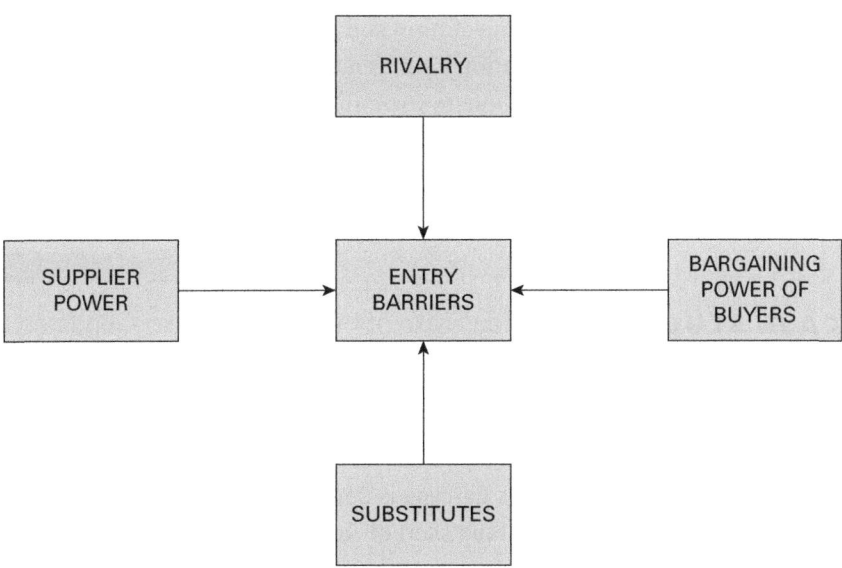

likely to struggle to get deep insights about the structure and dynamics of their external environment purely by using the conventional model.

In the next section we go down a level of analysis, to the 'forces within the forces', or the 'micro forces'. This, I believe, is more helpful and easier to remember than the relatively ad-hoc qualitative considerations in the conventional texts.

4. The 'micro' competitive forces

While Porter (1980) does give some narrative help for assessing the five forces, this is not presented in the very powerfully distilled and visual format of his original model. For example, for 'competitive rivalry' Porter asks us to think about things like the relative concentration of rivals (how many are in the market place, and with what mass), and the number of different 'strategic groups' of similar competitors. By extracting from Porter's text and by observation of the main deliberations that managers actually make, I have distilled a pilot framework to take the five forces down to another level. Also, Porter merely lists these considerations: managers appear often inclined to consider them as 'additive'. However, as we go through the next figures I show how the effects may be 'multiplicative': amplified by each set of micro forces.

Each one of the five forces may have some sub-ingredients that are worthwhile exploring. The following models are potentially viable frameworks put forward for further experimentation and research, to test their resilience and to learn from their application more generally. A particularly interesting application would be to use these to explore how the five forces work at a micro level, possible for individual business transactions. Here's an updated case study from *Demystifying Strategy*.

CASE STUDY The curious case of the wedding cake – updated

My third wedding (and last, I trust) was to Carolina who also had been married twice before. We didn't really want the conventional dress and church scenario – that was out of the question as Carolina is Catholic and the divorced market is not a segment for them. We weren't short of cash but it seemed silly to spray it around like champagne; we wanted something for our money.

I started shopping around and found that some of the really posh venues in Surrey were up to £9,000 before anyone even touched a drink, which seemed absurd. And as soon as you used the word 'wedding' the price seemed to almost double. It struck me that this was due to two things: low bargaining power of the buyers as a wedding is a very emotional thing and the unconscious price collusion by suppliers (low competitive rivalry).

We then enquired about photography. We had quotes from around £300 to £900. In the latter case you had the photographer hanging around for four hours – that's over £200 an hour, which I thought wouldn't be that bad for an independent strategy consultant – it seemed very generous for photography. This seemed pointless so we saved a lot of money by asking a friend with a good camera to do that. It occurred to us that a monkey with a digital camera could get some half decent shots, and a human who we trusted would be even better – do-it-yourself (the 'substitute' was easy).

Next we set about buying the wedding cake, sorry, no, I should say 'the cake': it is very important to get that right. I told my fiancée that she really mustn't say the word 'wedding' – ever – in making the purchase, but she just couldn't help herself and the word slipped out. She had already got a quote of £70 from a deluxe cake shop in South Croydon, which didn't seem massively pricy for only 24 of us (around £3 a slice; still not cheap, although yummy). We were to do the decorations ourselves. Unfortunately I wasn't there in the shop as her strategic minder when Carolina used the word 'wedding' when ordering, and the price suddenly doubled to £140! Carolina said that there must have been some confusion as the price was quoted as £70. The £70 had apparently been for a 'normal' cake. Carolina said that we couldn't do that price and if they wanted to reconsider the price to ring her. She left the shop and just five minutes later she had a call to say that we could have it for £70, sorry but it had been embarrassing as there had been other customers around!

So beware what you call things! I had got it dead right: if it's 'wedding' the same thing doubles in price.

This case just shows the profound influence that emotional value and its skilful manipulation can have on buyer power, on competitive rivalry and the bottom line: price.

The following figures (A1.9–A1.13) can be used either literally (to think through each force visually), or as a convenient and intuitive way of memorizing their underlying drivers. Taking the bargaining power of buyers (Figure A1.9) first, this appears to be a function of:

- importance – in terms of value added;
- urgency – in terms of lead times to consumption;
- discretion; and
- emotion.

FIGURE A1.9 Buyer power – micro forces

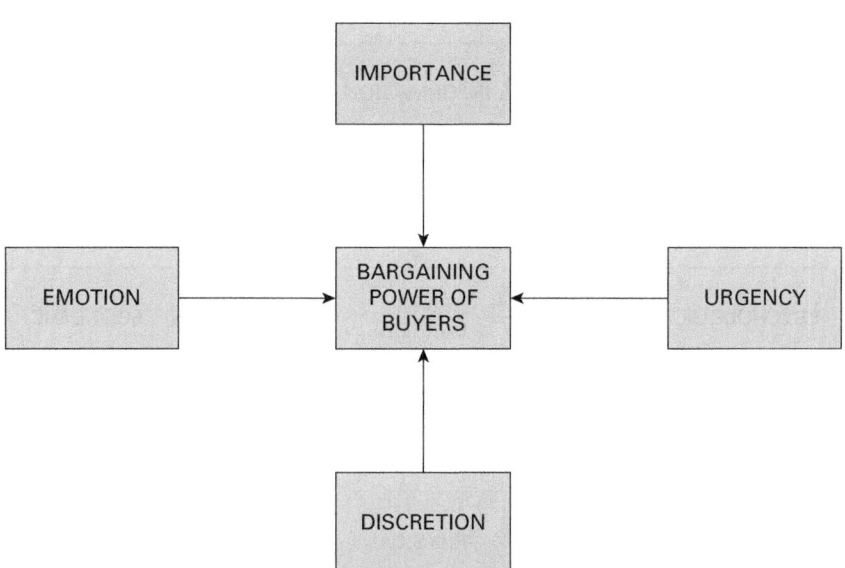

Importance and urgency are derived from conventional prioritization thinking (Covey, 1989); urgency can be measured according to the lead times required to satisfy the need. Discretion is the extent to which you as a customer *have to* fulfil a need. Finally, emotion is a neglected force in management, albeit one that is of relatively obvious significance to customers. The wedding cake example above was high on importance, low on urgency, medium on discretion, but extremely high on emotion.

Another example of this is toothache. It comes on very suddenly and your dentist tells you that he believes the root is nearly dead and advises root canal treatment. This treatment is both urgent and important, and is not discretionary. It is also highly emotional. So should you shop around for the cheapest price for a treatment? Probably not – indeed you would be very happy to pay around £300 for it to be fixed, even if you had to borrow some money. If you did attempt to negotiate a discount with some UK dentists, they may be quite shocked; it runs counter to their usual experience. Their counter strategy is to put you at the end of a long queue.

Coming back to my picture: an astute reader may wonder if the micro forces in Figure A1.9 are interdependent; they are. For example, to some extent discretion may go down if the purchase is highly emotional. Also, importance may tend to reduce the degree of discretion.

Turning back to theory and to the next set of micro forces, or entry barriers, let's examine Figure A1.10. These entry barriers are:

FIGURE A1.10 Entry barriers – micro forces

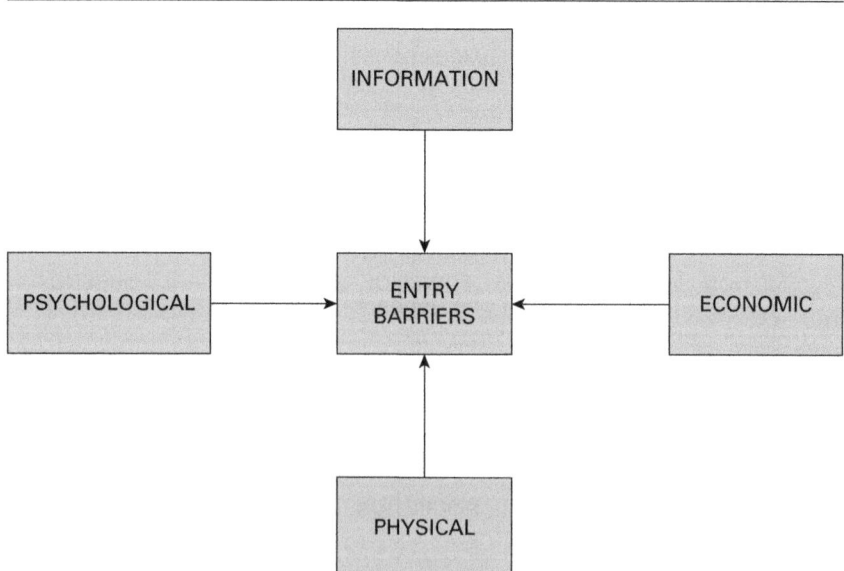

- The physical: can one actually get access to customers or to resources?
- Information: to what extent is it possible to acquire knowledge, not only about the 'what' of the industry but also about its 'how' (the latter being bound up in tacit competences)?
- Economic: what will it actually cost to enter the market?
- Psychological: is this a market I would feel socially and emotionally comfortable being in?

To illustrate the final point, the funeral business appears, using Porter's five forces, to be a highly attractive market. But for the vast majority it would not be a psychologically attractive industry to enter (Grundy, 1995; Gundy and Brown, 2002a).

Rivalry (see Figure A1.11) is a function of:

- commitment to the market (of rivals);
- the number of them;
- their mindset;
- their similarity to one another.

The 'number of competitor refers to the sheer quantity of players in the market. The more similar they are, the more likely head-on competition is

FIGURE A1.11 Rivalry – micro forces

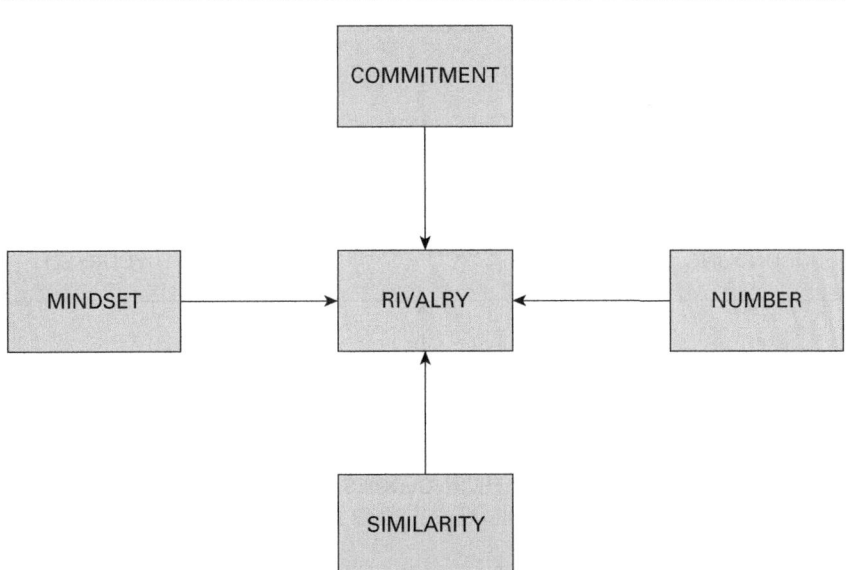

likely to be. (This follows on from Porter's description of 'things to think about'; 1980). Also, the more deeply committed they are, the more severe the rivalry will be. Finally, their mindset will influence the manner of their competition with one another. Clearly these micro forces are interdependent, for example, the existence of a small or large number of rivals might shape their mindset. Their commitment and more general mindset are also clearly interlinked.

Turning next to 'substitutes', Figure A1.12 displays its more micro-level forces. The substitutes are:

- Do-it-yourself – insourcing the activity, for example by making an expensive, sourced-out consultancy service an internal one.
- Other technologies – looking at other ways of achieving the same value (for example, e-learning has substituted a lot of conventional training).
- Emotional – the extent to which the purchase is emotional, or not.
- Bundling or unbundling – the customer's ability to do something either as part of something else, or to take a packaged offering and capture its value by breaking up the value-added activity into its smaller components.

FIGURE A1.12   Substitutes – micro forces

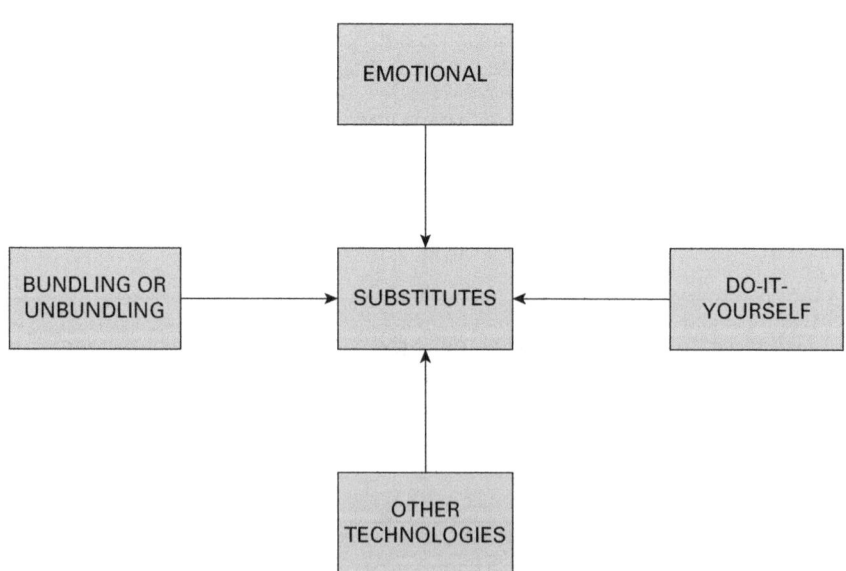

Again, the micro forces may be interdependent: other technologies may facilitate bundling and unbundling and emotional considerations may encourage you to want to do-it-yourself.

Our final picture is Figure A1.13, supplier power. The micro forces can be summarized as follows:

- Unique knowledge: if suppliers has some unique capability, this will obviously enhance their (collective) power.
- Size and number: where there are very few large suppliers, this will increase their power.
- Resource scarcity: where resources are scarce – and preferably permanently – this again will help promote supplier power.
- Forward integration: the suppliers, capacity to integrate forward in the industry chain will improve their competitive power.

Clearly, aspects of this force and of some of the others too suggest linkages and overlaps with the resource-based theory of competitive advantage (for example, unique knowledge). Again, these micro forces are interdependent. For instance, where there are few suppliers *and* high resource scarcity, this will multiply supplier power. Also, where suppliers have unique knowledge, this might facilitate integration, perhaps through strategic alliances.

FIGURE A1.13   Supplier power – micro forces

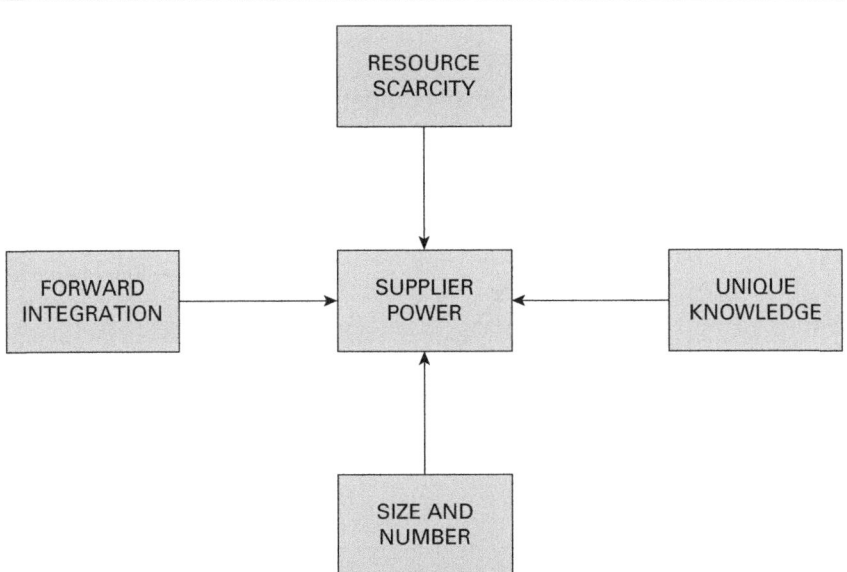

While there may be other ways of grouping the various sub-forces within the framework, these models seem to be both plausible and practical, and go beyond any more fragmentary and narrative approaches found in previous literature. Also, each one contains some rich and insightful interdependencies.

One main benefit is that they encourage managers to think in more depth about each force, rather than at a superficial level. Secondly, they will help managers to understand how these sub-forces interact with each other. (If you aren't comfortable using the diagrams, use checklists.) For example, just as the interdependencies in Figure A1.4, the original five forces were drawn out, we can do likewise for the later figures. For instance, in Figure A1.9, the importance of a purchase is linked with its emotional content, discretion is partly linked to urgency, and urgency needs to be traded off with importance.

5. Competitive dynamics

Porter's Five Competitive Forces is traditionally a static model, diminishing its usefulness. But it can be given a more dynamic perspective, and quite easily. There are some texts such as Warren (2008) and Tovstiga (2010) that deal with the dynamics of changing competitive position over time, rather than with changing competitive pressure externally over time. Porter (1980) looks at shifts in the five forces over an entire industry lifecycle, but as more discrete stages than as a kind of 'strategic ride'. This gap needs to be filled; competitive dynamics at the market level is something that keeps CEOs awake at the night.

FIGURE A1.14 Macro-level competitive dynamics

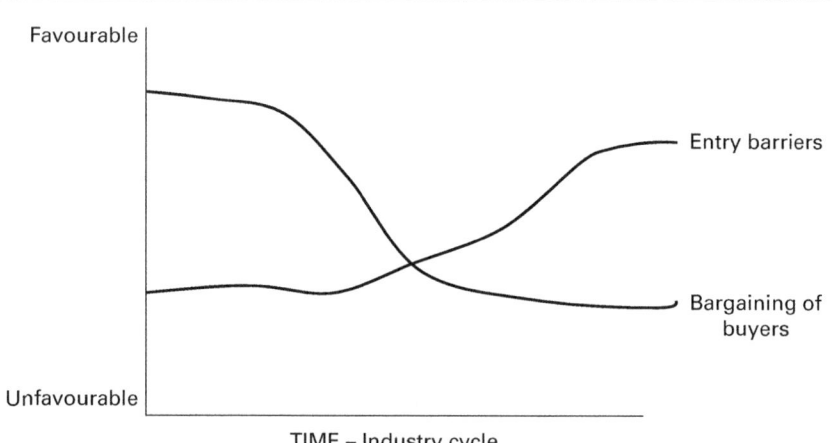

Competitive dynamics can be explored at a macro and a micro level. At a macro level, we can see these impacting dynamically over the industry cycle (Figure A1.14), for example for the bargaining power of buyers and entry barriers. As an industry reaches maturity, entry barriers often increase (favourable) but the bargaining power of the buyers also increases (unfavourable). Each one of the five competitive forces can be plotted individually in an analogous way.

The benefit of the model in Figure A1.14 is that it encourages managers to think about how industry structure may change in the future. It also helps them to reflect on why the industry has changed in recent times. Besides modelling competitive pressure over time, this can also be overlaid by, for example, growth drivers over time (high versus low).

The competitive forces may also vary over time at the level of an individual business transaction (at a micro level). For instance, where a large management consultancy gets involved with a blue-chip client, during the tendering stage the customer's bargaining power might be high. But once the consultants start to do work, it often becomes difficult, if not embarrassing for the client to control variations and the total cost of further stages of work. We therefore see the client's buying power decreasing. Another typical example is that of going into a restaurant where the bargaining power of the buyer diminishes in stages: a) when they enter the restaurants, b) when they sit down, c) when they order, and d) when they have started eating. Of course it is possible to walk out, or pay for the meal eaten so far, but this is psychologically difficult – especially where the buyer is a group of people.

Figure A1.15 allows managers to use the five forces at an everyday level, and to track the impact of these forces (especially bargaining power) over a typical transaction lifecycle. Besides plotting these dynamics (both at a macro and a micro level), it is also important to examine their underlying drivers. These are not only a function of the industry lifecycle effects (Porter, 1980) and the cumulative learning of key players, but also of mindset.

'Mindset' is emphasized by at least some writers (for example Hamel and Prahalad, 1994), yet primarily in a company-specific rather than industry context. The 'industry mindset' has been defined (Grundy, 1997b) as: 'The perceptions, expectations and assumptions about the industry – now and future.' The significance of this concept is that:

- Managers should beware thinking that the structural properties of Porter's five forces are a given. In part, these forces are a reflection of the mindset of the industry, which is often shared between players

FIGURE A1.15 Micro-level competitive dynamics

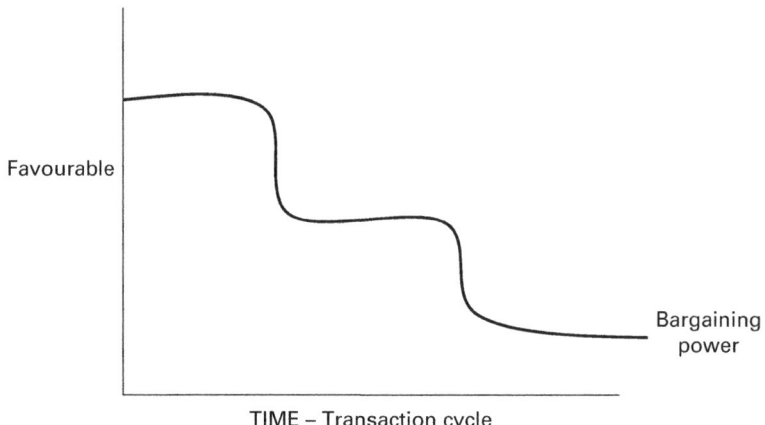

within the industry, and can be disrupted by players who can and will think differently.

- The strength and homogeneity of an industry mindset will reduce the responsiveness of the industry to disruptive change, and facilitate rapid market share build-up by a new entrant. For example, in the UK, Dyson Appliances built a dominant market share of the carpet cleaner market with a bagless model in just two and half years. Its competitors were in a state of shock and denial for a further two years before they imitated the company.

- It helps us to link external analysis/Porterian competitive strategy with the resource-based theory of competitive advantage of the firm (Grant, 1991), by highlighting how mindset can help a company transcend the competitive forces by deploying different marketing and innovative skills.

- By studying the industry mindset and by using the more advanced analysis techniques of competitive forces explored in this Appendix, managers can achieve strategic breakthroughs. For example, the title of an earlier book of mine, *Be Your Own Strategy Consultant* (Grundy and Brown, 2002a), is in part an attempt to deal with the threat of substitutes, or particularly of 'doing it yourself', and offering an alternative substitute to strategy consultants by training in strategic thinking and transferring the process to the client organization.

6. Mapping competitive forces, both horizontally and vertically

Porter's *Competitive Strategy* (1980) focused principally on analysis at the industry level. But this might well be too macro a level, particularly as the competitive landscape within a business might be of highly variable attractiveness. For example, if we take the fees for a day's strategy course, comparing rates from independent consultant to a business school, daily rates range from £1,000 to over £10,000 per day. So when Porter posed the question 'Why are some industries more attractive than others', we must answer this question with, 'It depends: which product/market/sector are you talking about?' Industry structures are like a landscape – highly variable in attractiveness – meaning that we must use Porter's five forces in a more discriminating and localized way to describe them. This 'attractiveness' can be represented in two-dimensional space, horizontally (across sectors) and vertically, in terms of the extent to which it is focused on differentiation versus cost leadership.

Simple matrices like Figure A1.16 might help managers considerably. Three ticks means 'favourable', while two ticks are 'neutral', and one tick is 'unfavourable'; the figure illustrates this for different sectors of the funerals industry.

FIGURE A1.16 Porter's five forces – segmentation

	Basic funerals	Deluxe funerals	Pre-need market
Buyer power	✓✓✓	✓✓✓	✓✓
Entry barriers	✓✓	✓✓✓	✓✓
Rivalry	✓✓✓	✓✓✓	✓✓✓
Substitutes	✓✓✓	✓✓✓	✓✓
Supplier power	✓✓	✓✓	✓✓
Overall attractiveness	13	14	11

Appendix 1

Figure A1.17 examines the competitive forces map within the carpet-cleaning market in the UK in 2004. Previously, apart from one or two deluxe models like the Kirby, the vast majority of models were of similar perceived use, value and price. Following Dyson's entry with a bagless, cyclonic, trendy-looking and premium-priced model, the competitive map of the industry was altered. The majority of purchases became cyclonic and premium-priced, which left a void at the bottom of the market. In 2003–4 new entrants and Hoover began to fill the space with light, cyclonic, cheap machines priced between £30 and £50 each. Here the overall competitive shape of the market has moved from a pyramid shape to an eclipse. Pictures like Figure A1.17 thus help managers to explore (and create) competitive changes.

We need therefore to break down our analysis of Porter's five forces on a segment-by-segment or 'mini-strategy' basis. This helps to make Porter's framework far more context-specific and applicable at the organization level. Indeed, Porter's five forces can be applied right down to the project level and to an individual's role (where there may be variable rivalry, substitutes, bargaining power, etc). These less obvious applications are often perceived as higher value by managers.

Next is a case study showing the application of Porter's five forces at a more general level. We can see this in the context of the health club industry in the UK, and how the competitive space at the lower end of the market can be revolutionized.

FIGURE A1.17 Mapping the five forces: the carpet-cleaning market, 2004

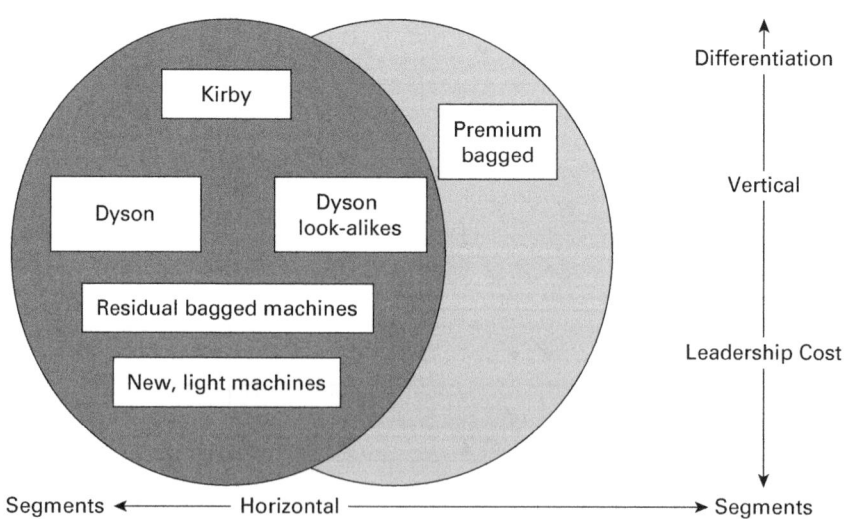

CASE STUDY Competitive pressure in the health club industry, 1995–2013

In 1995 the UK health club industry was at a turning point. The recession of the early 1990s (PEST factors) had inhibited growth, but had also sustained a low(ish) competitive rivalry. Key players in the industry identified considerable latent growth, as the rate of penetration of the potential market was low, both in absolute, percentage terms, and low in relative terms to at least one, service-focused economy, the United States.

As the economy recovered, these conditions triggered a wave of major expansion through new site development. Also, existing players grew by acquisition, creating greater industry concentration (hopefully a positive factor). Many buyers were relatively new to the market, being either newcomers to a gym, or because of industry churn as many people rapidly dropped out of gym membership. This meant that many were unsophisticated in the information they had available, making it easier for companies to charge reasonably high prices relative to what they actually offered.

Current margins were thus good, sites in the industry were available and reasonably cheap, and the industry mindset was very positive: foreseeing easily attainable, and sustainable, profitable growth. In 1996–2001 there followed a major expansion in capacity with players chasing market share and neglecting the 'future' set of five competitive forces, which it was just about to encounter. For just as Hamel and Prahalad (1994) extolled us to think about 'future competitive position' as well as 'present competitive position', so we should anticipate competitive dynamics (see Figure A1.15) by thinking about future competitive forces and the surrounding growth drivers and PEST factors (see Figure A1.3).

One company that took advantage of this opportunity was Topnotch. In 1990s it was a small chain of independent health clubs, with an appeal to the younger market segments and with a theme of excitement, or 'Dare to be different'. Fundamentally, however, Topnotch was a mid-priced operator with a lack of scale and not-so-strong brand awareness – two of the critical success factors necessitated by the 'future' five competitive forces.

In 2001, Topnotch floated its shares on the stock market, and used these funds (after considerable transaction costs) to expand into a chain of over 20 clubs. For reasons of speed, many of these new sites were acquisitions of existing sites. At the time of floatation, financial markets saw this sector at 'very attractive', seeing growth prospects, but not perhaps inquiring into probable trends and discontinuities in both growth drivers and PEST factors. They therefore played a highly encouraging role in this expansion. The effect of 9/11 on the service economy and of economic slowdown generally had a particularly sudden and adverse effect on this industry, and especially on Topnotch.

This can be analysed as follows (using an extended Porter's five forces combined with 'from – to' analysis (Grundy and Brown, 2002a); see Table A1.1. Overall, the 'from – to' analysis represents a negative shift in forces and one significant enough to cause a decline in margins (percentage wise). When combined with volumes being lower than expected, and with over-enthusiastic expansion and the impact on central costs, the effect was, predictably, profit warnings across the industry.

TABLE A1.1 Porter's five forces: 'from – to' analysis

	From	To	Because of
Bargaining power of buyers	Medium	High	Buyers more discerning, experienced and price sensitive
Rivalry	Medium	Very High	Companies desperate to find health club capacity, producing discounting, etc
Substitutes (threat of)	Medium	Medium/High	Buyers can find alternatives thus saving money
Entry barriers	Low/Medium	Medium	Sites now so expensive, hard to enter, but could change again
Suppliers	Low – staff High – sites	Low – staff Medium – sites	Variable

By 2002, Topnotch (like many other chains) was in financial trouble. Yet instead of looking for further ways to adapt the industry mindset, the reactive response of the industry generally was to reduce their largely unnecessary costs. In 2002 Topnotch went into administration, although a major part of it is still in operation today.

Clearly this was a very painful learning experience for all of those involved, particularly investors and many staff, and also for the entrepreneurs who led this growth surge into the teeth of the (future) five competitive forces. If anyone had performed an in-depth analysis in 1996–8 of the future competitive climate for 2001–4, much of this financial pain might have been avoided. As Matthew Harris, CEO of the original Topnotch (and of its remaining, independent sites today) reflects, looking back:

> *I hadn't really heard about the five competitive forces, to be honest. I had absorbed a lot of management theory from various sources – especially the financial stuff – but I just felt, from everything I saw, heard about and imagined, that we could only win through this growth.*
>
> *I first saw Porter's five forces well after we had gone over the precipice. It didn't seem very helpful at the time as I couldn't see what I could really do with it in that situation. And it did seem quite theoretical.*
>
> *Looking back on the experience and reflecting on the competitive situation as we have now, I can see its relevance. Besides the cost reduction which it implied, we are now focusing on how we can turn the buying power of the buyers to our advantage in our marketing strategy. I can certainly see how the forces interplay with each other and with the rest of what is going on – even down to a very specific transaction, like someone joining or leaving us.*

Subsequently Matthew Harris went on to challenge the industry mindset by launching a chain of budget health clubs, Fitness for Less (which of course has been imitated in some respects by others) and created a new 'strategic group' and new competitive space below the medium-priced traditional core of the market. Fitness For Less would face a rather different set of five forces from the other medium-priced operators, effectively an 'industry within an industry'.

In sum, this short case has helped to bring alive some considerations of this Appendix, particularly the dynamic interdependency of the forces with each other, with PEST factors and growth drivers. It also illustrates how operating managers (however senior) can fail to see the full potential of the technique. It certainly highlights how Porter's five forces, combined with challenging the 'industry mindset', can be most fruitful in not only generating fresh competitive strategies but also in reshaping the competitive environment itself and thus sector attractiveness.

You don't have to just accept Porter's forces as substantially 'given' but as a landscape to be explored, challenged and maybe changed. Now that surely must appeal to a strategically thinking CEO.

7. The way forward

I have shown how Porter's Five Competitive Forces model could be developed by:

- combining and interrelating it with other tools (growth drivers, PEST factors, etc);
- looking at its other systemic interdependencies;
- prioritizing it, with the competitive force field-type of analysis;
- examining its sub-forces;
- looking at its dynamics and the impact of the industry mindset;
- segmenting it to examine the variations within competitive landscape.

Porter's model thus offers significant potential for further conceptual development and for practical application. Other areas beyond the scope of this Appendix are its application to:

- Acquisition decision making (see Grundy, 2003b) in terms of the competitive pressure acting on a particular M&A context.
- Alliances, in a simplified way through analysis of 'relative bargaining power'.
- Account management, especially in understanding the industry structure, critical success factors, options and areas of possible (own) company value-added customers.
- Negotiating large contracts. (It would be of considerable help here in decision making and in deal making, eg in outsourcing.)

Perhaps because the technique was born in economics, and perhaps because it was so very successful initially, there have been no significant attempts to apply it across a range of practical management issues or to evolve it further. While many CEOs may not be naturally drawn to doing the 'competitive pressure' diagrams in any comprehensive way, they could really benefit from being able to anticipate and even manipulate the competitive weather ahead of them.

APPENDIX 2
How contingent should strategy be?

Introduction

Strategy development has been characterized by the dichotomy of two major forms of strategy: deliberate and emergent (Mintzberg, 1994). This Appendix argues that this dichotomy is not only too extreme but also limits the ability of academics and managers to think about how organizations cope with the contingent.

The model of contingent strategy outlined here makes a number of contributions to our understanding of strategy, particularly:

- Even where the strategic situation is fluid, it is not necessary to default from a deliberate strategy to an emergent one.
- This entails very careful management of levels of commitment, thus enabling managers not to have to automatically forfeit deliberate (or intentional) elements for pure emergence and the latter's downsides.
- Contingent strategy builds on the helpful framework of contingency theory, on scenarios, and acknowledges the significance of chaos, game, commitment and option theories.
- Various visual tools can help managers to integrate the idea into the strategy process but this raises major issues in managing related organizational processes like communication and strategy.

I now discuss how contingent strategy can be used to inform both theory and practice, first illustrating how contingent approaches to strategy operate in the military context then putting the case for how the conventional strategic management process may need to be adapted to accommodate it. I start with a quote from coverage of the 2003 Iraqi war: a reflection of day four when US troops got bogged down in the south, taken from 'ITV News', 2 March 2003, 09.43):

> The broad thrust of the strategy will be largely unaffected (by the problems of taking Umm Qasr) except that they might want to use these troops somewhere

else. But their strategic intention is to take Umm Qasr, to clear it and to use the port. But they haven't been able to use this yet.

General Tommy Franks will say this is 'no problem' for Professor Prince has just said this is an 'effects-led war' – in other words it is a reactive plan, a multi-faceted, multi-levelled plan, a very complicated plan and it is rather like going into a fishmongers to buy fish – they are waiting – they will pick up that (particular) fish when they want to have that fish, and not only are they thinking of letting it (as it were) run. *(In other words, you might intend to buy a fish of a certain kind, but this is partly dependent upon the catch of the day).*

So mission command works, so that mission commanders get on with their work (in parallel). But equally at a higher level, at the operational level of war, between the tactical, low-level stuff and the strategic stuff, the generals are planning 'what happens next'. They will have a whole range of options to select from. They will have other options to get back to what they do want to do without using these people (at Umm Qasr).

'Inflexible' is not the word which you would use. A principle of war is flexibility, flexibility is the key to planning. Plans don't last, plans are just there, plans are something in the future, and once you start you adapt as necessary.

This suggests that a contingent approach to strategy, so often applied by the military, has perhaps been forgotten by many business managers. Here I put contingent strategy right back onto that agenda.

Strategy is about managing the future: a future that is frequently uncertain. All of strategy is thus a bet about the future, and the conventional response is to try to absorb this uncertainty through some form of business or strategic plan. An entrepreneurial approach to strategy recognizes that all strategies and business plans are bets; but how can we improve the odds of strategic success? And how do we manage strategies that are essentially contingent on aligned future states of the world? A useful approach to adopt is that of the contingent strategy.

Mintzberg (1994) suggests that there is more than one form of strategy: the deliberate and the emergent. But are there other forms that are useful? With a contingent strategy, instead of making a single relatively irrevocable commitment to a course of action, the commitment is as fluid as possible, reducing exposure to the bet. This should, other things being equal, both increase its return and reduce its risk.

While existing theory makes reference to strategic management concepts like contingency theory, scenarios, game theory and options, these appear still relatively remote from many managers' experience. Contingent strategy, in contrast, offers a way of crystallizing these ideas effectively. In a relatively uncertain world, contingent strategy may be a more appropriate model than deliberate or emergent strategy.

Contingent strategy can be defined as: 'A strategy which will be committed to only when certain external and internal conditions are in sufficient alignment and which is then communicated.' Contingent strategy therefore:

- is fluid and extremely flexible;
- holds commitment in suspense; and
- requires fluidity and flexibility within the organization.

Contingent strategy manifests itself in two ways: either as a potential strategy, or as an actual strategy (ie that one is embarked upon). In both cases it has the distinctive feature of preserving maximum flexibility, achieved by managing senior management's commitment to the strategy by not committing prematurely, and not making a commitment either virtually unconditional or hard to change (Ghemawat, 1991).

Deliberate strategy makes it easier and more comfortable to deal with the emotional aspects of making a strategic decision. More open-ended or contingent approaches may prolong ambiguity and uncertainty, perhaps leading to anxiety, making it a more uncomfortable place to be in. Deliberate strategy (which is essentially the model followed in most conventional manifestations of strategy, like strategic plans) can be at least partially substituted in many contexts by contingent strategy. While there may be a small core of business strategies that are 'must-do' in any situation (in effect, deliberate strategies), around that core there may be an important set of existing contingent strategies that one would pursue *only* given certain alignment conditions being in place. Surrounding this set of initial contingent strategies may be a second set, which are currently future and latent (see Figure A2.1). That is, they are strategies that will be triggered only if future conditions are met, effectively focusing on future 'strategic fit'.

The two main forms of strategy, deliberate and emergent, are far too polar and simplistic, and not sufficiently flexible. Contingent strategy is an intermediate form lying between these two extremes. Where the originating external and/or internal environment is even modestly uncertain, a contingent strategy form may be preferable to the two more extreme typologies from Mintzberg. Also, were an organization to adopt a mere contingent mode of strategy for its main business strategies, this will have far-reaching implications for management processes, including business plans, budgets, control and rewards systems, and communications systems.

FIGURE A2.1   Deliberate and contingent strategies

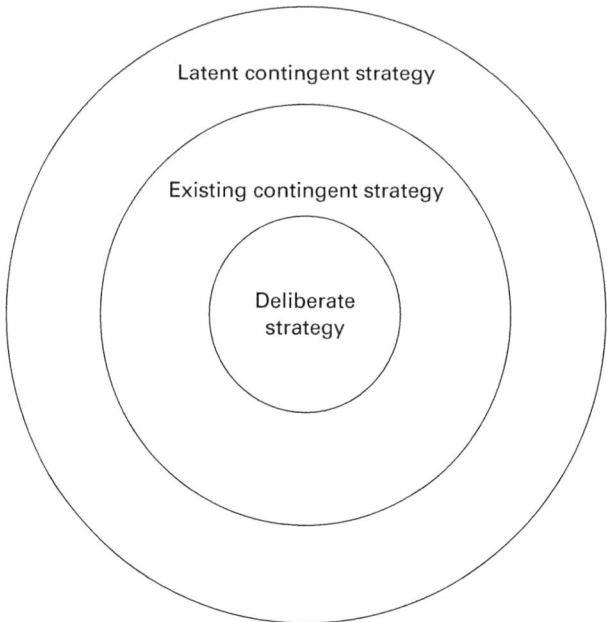

The idea of contingent strategy, which is fundamentally simple, has profound and more complex ramifications for the process of strategic management generally. For instance, it potentially transforms the substance of strategic plans and their optimal communication style throughout the organization, as senior management now need to add caveats to 'We intend to do this, and this is how', by specifying the conditions under which this may or may not happen. It also frees up strategic thinking to be less focused on a single-world view, something which to date has only been on offer via scenario development (DeGeus, 1988; Wack, 1985a, 1985b). It also means that in the mode of 'logical incrementalism' (Quinn, 1980) can become more thought-through while still preserving flexibility in managers' strategic mindsets.

Strategic management in practice is conducted in a manner that is heavily influenced by the mental models that underpin it. The deliberate strategy model (Ansoff, 1965) is still very much in evidence in most managers' mindsets, even when the predominant form of their strategy and its implementation is emergent (Mintzberg, 1994). By allowing some scope for contingent strategy as a form somewhere between the two, both deliberate and emergent forms can play a more effective role in the mix of strategies, which range across a total continuum (Grundy, 2002).

Appendix 2

The argument for a radical shift in the focus of strategic management is presented as follows:

1. existing theory on forms of strategy and context;
2. contingent strategy techniques;
3. the implications for managers;
4. implications for future research;
5. conclusions.

1. Existing theory on forms of strategy and context

In this section we look at:

- Deliberate and emergent strategies and the 'strategy mix', showing there may be more than two useful strategy typologies.
- Contingency theory and contingency planning, which suggests that flexibility to context is important, generally.
- Systems thinking, which emphasizes the impact of interdependencies.
- Scenarios, examining the need to consider alternative futures.
- Chaos theory, which emphasizes that turbulence is an important upsetting factor.
- Game theory, which suggests that there is no 'single right strategy' outside of the intentions of others.
- Commitment theory, which emphasizes the 'strictness' of endured commitment.
- Option theory, which suggests that preserving flexibility (in itself) may help to maximize economic value generally.

In these sections we extract the various contributions from existing theory, which point to the development of this missing form of strategy. Each of these areas is chosen because in one way or another they deal with strategic ambiguity.

Deliberate and emergent strategies and the strategy mix

While Mintzberg's two forms of strategy are most certainly helpful, both at a theoretical and a practical level, they are insufficient. A (earlier) version of the various forms that strategy can take is called the 'strategy mix' (Grundy, 1997b), which distinguishes between:

- Deliberate and emergent strategies (as per Mintzberg, 1994).
- Submergent strategy – where the strategy simply isn't working.
- Emergency strategy – where the logic of the strategy has been lost, and where there is little if any 'pattern in a stream of decisions or actions' (Mintzberg, 1994), and where the consequences for shareholder value creation and organizational morale can be dire.
- Detergent strategy – where the strategy is being revisited with a view to stopping doing things/changing strategic activities and/or resource allocation (Grundy, 2002).

Despite the apparent richness of this framework, one important form of strategy has still been overlooked – contingent strategy. Contingent strategy still implies some form of strategic intent (Hamel and Prahalad, 1994), but what is different here is the implication of a degree of cognitive and emotional detachment from the strategy. This entails spelling out within the strategy, and within all communication of the strategy, that it is not something we can simply expect to happen, in any event and under any conditions.

Figure A2.2 shows us the initial five forms of strategy and where contingent strategy fits in. This implies that deliberate strategy only crystallizes when the full alignment conditions within contingent strategy exist, and that emergent strategies should be screened against the possible courses of action already envisaged within contingent strategy.

FIGURE A2.2 The strategy mix

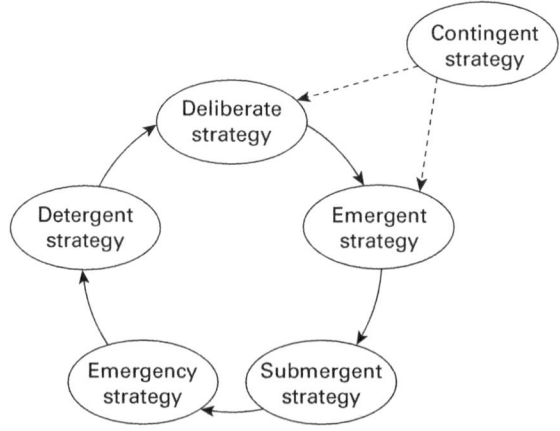

Contingency theory and contingency planning

Contingency theory suggests that prescriptions are applicable depending upon a certain context. In the sphere of strategy in particular, it was contended that strategy should align the organization with its environment (Lawrence and Lorsch, 1967). As a theory of knowledge, this seems to have self-evident plausibility, so what we can do is transfer this idea into the concept of strategy, for a strategy only makes sense because it has some relationship or 'fit' with its environment. Equally, therefore, strategies should only be pursued if they currently reflect and continue to reflect their context.

But while contingency theory has successfully highlighted the need for organizational congruence with changing conditions it is less helpful in enabling managers to cope with this in real time within organizations. The management processes that are bureaucratic organizational responses to changing conditions, such as business plans, budgets, project plans, performance and control measures, and recognition systems, operate within cycles of activity too long to cope with sudden shifts in conditions.

Other than in the simplest of organizations, information, discussion, decision and communication lags prevent the rapid adjustment in plans that would appear to be the hallmark of military-style contingent strategy (as in the extract from ITV). Furthermore, while many organizations have begun to incorporate a degree of contingency planning in their business and plans, this is typically aimed at responding to deviations on a deliberate plan or strategy. Conventional contingency planning thus does not involve holding strategic intent in a contingent, fluid form. This means that far from being unnatural or peculiar, contingent strategy may turn out to be a most helpful form of strategy for many managers.

Systems thinking

Senge (1990) draws our attention to the need to think about how business performance is contingent upon the alignment of internal and external systems. According to Senge, superior business performance (the goal of strategy) is generated by the harmonious interaction between interdependent parts of the business system. Once again, this implies that strategies should only be continuously pursued when the wider system of which they are part is aligned, or can be influenced to line up, suggesting the need for a contingent strategy, rather than a deliberate or closed strategy, or an emergent or totally open one.

This also suggests a need for managers to be adept at learning – and many strategy writers (besides Senge) have emphasized the role of learning in adaptation to strategic circumstances (for example Argyris, 1977; Mintzberg *et al*, 1998). Here contingent strategy may offer a concrete vehicle for managing adaptation through both learning and action.

Scenarios

There is an extensive literature on scenarios (DeGeus, 1988; Wack, 1985a, 1985b) and encouraging managers to 'Think Future'. The basic principles of scenario development are already well articulated in the literature, but their essential focus is on contingency and its impact, just as much as it is on uncertainty. For contingency implies the inter-relationship of two or more events to trigger a particular state of the world. Here one event can cause another, later, stream of events, or two more events can amplify each other through interdependency. But the essential insight from scenario development is that, once again, a strategy should be pursued only *on condition that* a particular future(s) unfolds. It is thus based on assumptions that should be explicitly surfaced and examined (Mitroff and Linstone, 1993).

One of the main potential benefits of contingent strategy is that it is closer to managers' agendas than scenarios. Scenarios may be perceived as more remote from managers' concerns, and to be of a discretionary, 'blue-sky' nature. By contrast, a contingent strategy is one that managers can actually adopt, explicitly, and at an everyday level (Stacey, 1996).

Chaos theory

Chaos theory is also closely linked to scenario thinking. Chaos theory suggests that sometimes a new state of the world can be triggered by very small and apparently marginal events. Drawn from modern physics/mathematics, the idea here is that apparently trivial events can begin to amplify change in the world through destabilizing the status quo (Gleick, 1988; Stacey, 1993).

A favourite story in chaos theory is how the fluttering of a butterfly's wings can cause amplified effects, ultimately a major storm. But while such dramatic escalations of turbulence are perhaps uncertain, there are disruptive situations (for example, ones caused by a sudden piece of bad news in the stock markets) which can have monumentally important knock-on effects elsewhere.

From chaos theory we again see that it could be highly inappropriate to pursue deliberate strategies where the environment may be randomly turbulent. Indeed, contingent strategy would here seem to be more sensible than emergent strategy, which still relies upon a pattern in decisions or action magically coming into alignment. Here, a contingent strategy is a way of managing emergent strategy situations.

Game theory

Game theory (Dixit and Nalebuff, 1991) teaches us that strategies are contingent upon the moves, and intentions, of competitors, rather than primarily focusing on an organization's 'strategic fit' with its customers and with their markets. The important insights for contingent strategy are that there is no single right strategy independent of your competitor's strategies, and your strategy should anticipate, if not pre-empt, the intentions of your competitors.

Given a world of imperfect market information, all strategies must have, it is argued, conditionality attached to them. For instance, a strategy might be embarked on that is conditional on a certain type of competitor response, rather than as a carte blanche to pursue it without pre-set explicit conditions.

Other key players in the context of the game might be customers, suppliers, regulators, etc, and once again conditions of alignment for the strategy may need to be thought through rather than freely given commitment. Game theory thus suggests that contingent strategy could be far more a normal than an exceptional form.

Commitment theory

In commitment theory we see the need to understand how commitment to a strategy is crystallized. Staw (1976) emphasized the importance of escalation in building commitment, a phenomenon observed particularly in acquisitions (Haspeslagh and Jemison, 1991). Ghemawat (1991) went as far as suggesting that commitment is a central dynamic of strategy. Because commitment tends to crystallize prematurely (that is, before managers have learnt enough about it), contingent strategy may be needed to provide a restraint on managers' strategic intent, so that they only continue to pursue the chosen strategy as long as particular conditions are met.

Option theory

Option theory (Morin and Jarrell, 2001) which is drawn from financial economics, can help us to think about the economic value-creating potential or the contingent form of strategy. Option theory teaches us that when we manage a strategy, preserving flexibility as far as possible generates superior economic value in the long run. For instance, where venture capitalists manage a portfolio of investments, their overall return will be maximized if they elect to defer commitment of investment resource until certain successful performance and development milestones are passed by each individual investment. In sharp contrast perhaps, managers who are more intimately involved in their strategies (as they have a vested interest through scenarios), are perhaps less likely to deter commitment to a particular strategy until the necessary conditions are lined up.

While detailed exploration of the quantification of the value of flexibility is outside the scope of this Appendix, suffice it to say that it is possible to put an economic value on flexibility. In the finance sector this is called 'real options' – the management's ability to adopt and to later revise corporate investment decisions in the light of unexpected or risky market developments. Coming back to the real world of most managers, the idea of 'real options' is likely to sound highly esoteric, so again the concept of contingent strategy may well offer a more enticing route in.

This might begin to sound as if we are suggesting managers should wait so long until conditions line up that they are in a 'do nothing' or maintenance mode. But many of the conditions for contingent strategy may be capable of being influenced, either directly or indirectly. For instance, if there is an outbreak of price discounting in a particular market, the company may be able to respond by clever marketing/product repackaging – it does not have to follow suit. Also, while delay may, in some situations, be costly, so too is premature commitment and action.

In conclusion, this brief review of the literature suggests that:

- The existing forms of strategy, whether Mintzberg's forms of deliberate and emergent strategy or the more expanded strategy mix (Grundy, 2002), are still relatively limited in helping managers cope with uncertainty.
- Systems thinking underlines the importance of managers looking at how a strategy nests within its wider system, rather than seeing it as an entity in itself.
- Contingency theory suggests that a strategy only works within its assumed context.
- Scenario thinking highlights that, as there are frequently multiple possible futures, a single strategy, without understanding its conditionality, is likely to be inappropriate.
- Chaos theory underlines this argument even more, suggesting that where the environment is potentially turbulent, a contingent strategy should be the dominant form.
- Game theory suggests we need to always look at strategy in an interactive context and that deliberate strategy (unless it reflects some advanced thinking about potential reaction by competitors, customers, suppliers or regulators) may be inappropriate.

- Commitment theory emphasizes the need for managers to place some emotional distance between themselves and their strategy, to the extent that they can delay full and unconditional commitment for as long as it is economic to do so.
- Option theory suggests that preserving and expanding flexibility will tend to enhance the economic value of a strategy. By making a strategy contingent on certain states of alignment, this flexibility should be maximized.

Redefining strategy as contingent options

There have been many definitions of strategy, for example in terms of competitive advantage (Ohmae, 1992; Porter, 1985), resource-based theory (Grant, 1991) thinking about the future (Hamel and Prahalad, 1994) and deliberate versus emergent strategies (Mintzberg, 1994). An alternative definition of a strategy might be: 'A set of contingent options to deploy resources whose implementation is conditional on future states of the world, both externally and internally.'

This 'set of options' will no doubt be interrelated, closely or loosely. Also, strategy now has the property of contingency. To explore this property a little more, not only might incremental strategies be contingent, but existing ones could be too. In fact, it makes just as much sense to lay down the conditions of continuing with a particular existing strategy as it does for a new one. This will help increase fluidity of resource allocation, and also help to focus on shareholder value creation.

This definition also relates contingent strategy to resource-based theory of competitive advantage (Grant, 1991). Where an organization has a distinctive or unique resource/consideration of resources, it can choose to deploy them 'if, and only if certain conditions are met', to get maximum leverage out of them, and to avoid unnecessary opportunity costs. In military terms, this is comparable to holding one's resources in reserve.

Contingent strategy again reminds us of the entrepreneurial fact that strategy is inevitably something of a bet. Therefore we need to understand how the conditions of the bet are working, and if they change we need to review and adapt our (contingent) strategy for the bet.

2. Contingent strategy techniques

We now look at how managers might take some first steps towards analysing contingent strategies. The various contingent strategy techniques are shown with their full inter-relationships in Figure A2.8 later in this Appendix; these also show their fit with conventional analysis techniques. These include PEST factors, Porter's five forces (Porter, 1985), competitive positioning (Ohmae, 1992), value and cost drivers (Grundy, 2002; Rappaport, 1986), force field analysis (Lewin, 1935) and stakeholder analysis (Piercey, 1989). In addition to wishbone analysis (with its more macro technique of the uncertainty-importance grid), managers will have to think creatively about their strategies, and also to draw in future scenarios.

Contingent strategy can provide a more effective framework for strategy development and execution than alternating between deliberate and emergent strategy. So how can these ideas be operationalized? The next section shows how contingent strategy may require some analytical techniques that differ from the conventional ones.

Earlier I highlighted a practical concern to help managers to cope with more fluid strategy situations. While a number of techniques exist for coping with more determinate views of strategy, for example Porter's Five Competitive Forces, contingent strategy requires some different techniques. This section looks at:

- using the contingent strategy grid;
- wishbone analysis; and
- the uncertainty-importance grid.

These techniques give managers an initial raft of analysis techniques to grapple with a range of ambiguities. We now examine how managers can set about managing contingent strategy.

Using the contingent strategy grid

The contingent strategy grid in Figure A2.3 shows how a particular option looks under a set of evaluation criteria (listed done the left-hand side of the grid) against a number of contingent states of the world. This is a technique for evaluating how this option is likely to fare with different scenarios, and also how it can be refined to be more resilient.

By using this technique managers can appreciate the resilience requirements of a particular option, and then reformulate or adapt that option so that it is more like to hold up in various states. It could also be used to help with their monitoring of corrective action. More generally, it would provide them with a reminder to not see a single strategic route forward as being the only way. This technique is a refinement on a previous one of appraising a variety of strategic options within an existing set of external and internal conditions against these common criteria (Grundy, 2002). The

FIGURE A2.3 The contingent strategy grid

Criteria \ State of the world	State 1	State 2	State 3
Strategic attractiveness			
Financial attractiveness*			
Implementation difficulty			
Uncertainty and risk			
Acceptability (to stakeholders)			

<u>Score:</u> 3 = very attractive, 2 = medium attractive, 1 = low attractiveness.

* Benefits less costs – net cash flows relative to investment

(adapted from: the 'Strategic Option Grid' (Grundy & Brown, 2002)

various options under the old grid, along the top of the figure, are now substituted by different states of the world.

Wishbone analysis

Wishbone analysis helps to:

- Define a desired state of the world (written to the left of the wishbone).
- Identify the alignment factors or conditions, which are both necessary and sufficient conditions of the strategy being successful. These include things over which the organization has either a lot of influence, or low influence.
- Prioritize which of the alignment factors to focus on, either a) in terms of detecting more data or, b) considering where plans can be adapted to improve the chances of full alignment.

Figure A2.4 illustrates this technique with an example from Dyson's successful entry into and subsequent domination of the UK vacuum cleaner market, from 1993 to the present. While many of the alignment conditions held for most of this period, by the late 1990s several, including 'competitors mindset is unchanged', 'premium prices' (sustained at their original) level and 'simple

FIGURE A2.4 Wishbone analysis

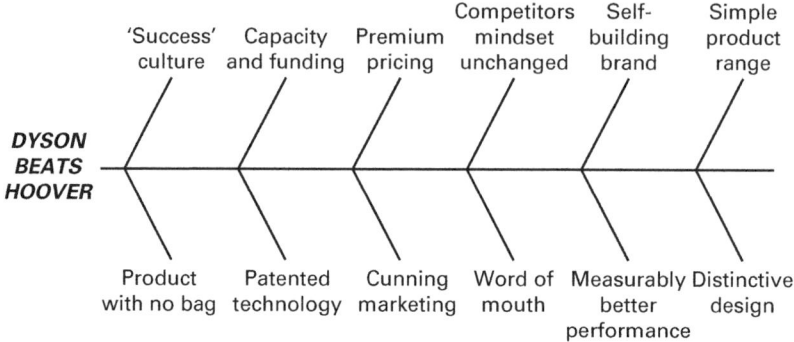

See Grundy & Brown (2002)

product range' began to move out of alignment. This highlights the need to be continually vigilant in monitoring the conditionality of any business strategy as circumstances change.

In many ways a contingent strategy should be drawn up as soon as a strategy begins to look even slightly unsustainable. The merits of focusing on contingent strategy (as opposed to just thinking about sustainability) are that 'sustainable' tends to be thought of in terms of the current state; with a contingent strategy, there is complete alertness and sensitivity to change.

The uncertainty-importance grid

The uncertainty-importance grid helps us to evaluate the wishbone analysis and its individual alignment conditions at a more micro level. The original version of the uncertainty-importance grid, which has been used for scenario development (Mitroff and Linstone, 1993) is seen in Figure A2.5. Using this grid, managers can plot the key assumptions driving the value of any strategic decision. These can be external and internal, and include soft as well as hard assumptions.

Having selected a sub-set of these assumptions, these are prioritized by using the grid. Once assumptions are carefully and skilfully defined, it is possible to debate their relative importance and uncertainty (with a flipchart, the assumptions can be easily moved around using Post-it notes).

These assumptions are defined in terms of 'the future world being ok'. For example, if we were using it to understand the uncertainties of getting to a meeting in London on time, assumptions would be defined as 'the trains will run on time', rather than 'the trains will not run on time'. A frequent mistake

FIGURE A2.5 Example of an uncertainty-importance grid

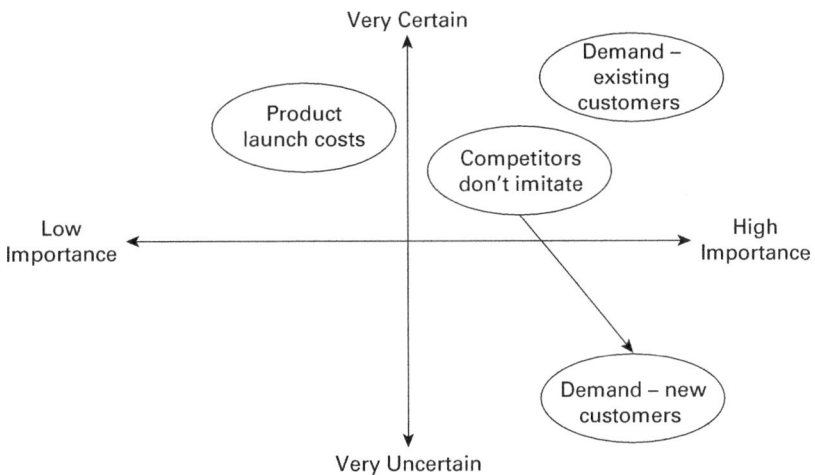

from Mitroff and Linstone (1993)

when first using the grid is to have some assumptions defined positively and some negatively. This makes it impossible to judge the overall downsides to a strategy. An example of this would be 'Kings Cross Station might be closed' (a negative assumption), and 'there will be no London Underground strike that day' (a positive assumption). At the beginning of the appraisal, key assumptions are likely to be mapped in the north and north-east quadrants. Upon testing it is quite common to find one or more assumptions moving over to the danger zone in the south-east.

Figure A2.5 actually relates to a new product launch. The extra sales volume from existing customers is very important, but also considered relatively certain. Sales to new customers are considerably more uncertain (but also very important); these are shown in the south-east of the grid. Product launch costs are somewhat less important and also reasonably certain (shown slightly north-east of the centre of the grid).

The uncertainty-importance grid can be used either before a strategic decision, during implementation, or for post-review. In particular, it can be used to help track whether the conditions pre-set for a contingent strategy are moving so far out of alignment that a fundamental review of the strategy is essential. It can be useful, too, to do a micro-level uncertainty grid (like that shown in Figure A2.6, from Mitroff and Linstone, 1993), and then to break down a particular one of the assumptions using a separate and more detailed uncertainty grid.

Appendix 2

FIGURE A2.6   Uncertainty-importance grid analysed

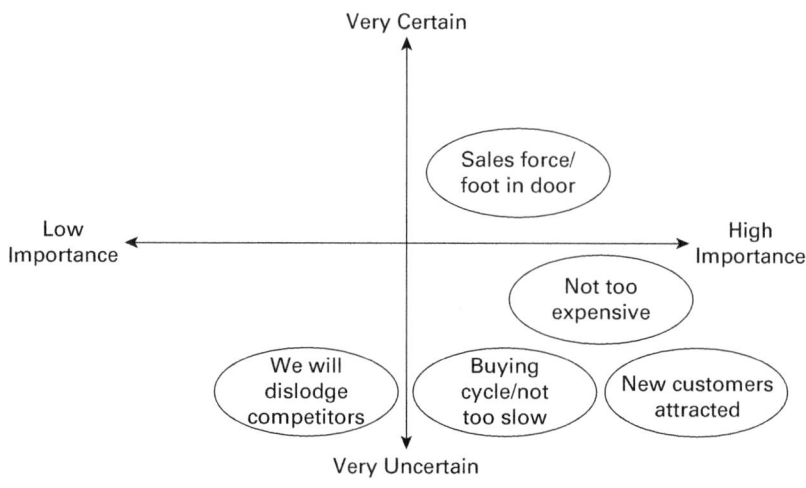

FIGURE A2.7   Wishbone with uncertainty grid overlay

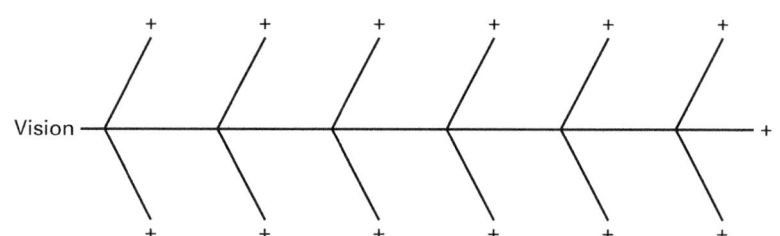

A useful way of representing this visually is to produce a wishbone analysis (Grundy, 2002) and the uncertainty-importance grid as an overlay (see Figure A2.7). Here we see each one of the alignment factors underpinning the contingent strategy being evaluated simultaneously in terms of their relative importance-uncertainty. Note that in Figure A2.8 conventional strategy techniques account for less than one fifth of the process of strategic thinking needed to generate a resilient contingent strategy.

A close variant of this framework is in use at Diageo to develop supply strategies for the group. The practical benefits of this approach (as evidenced by managers at Diageo, noted for its world brands including Guinness and Smirnoff) include the following:

FIGURE A2.8 Contingent strategy techniques

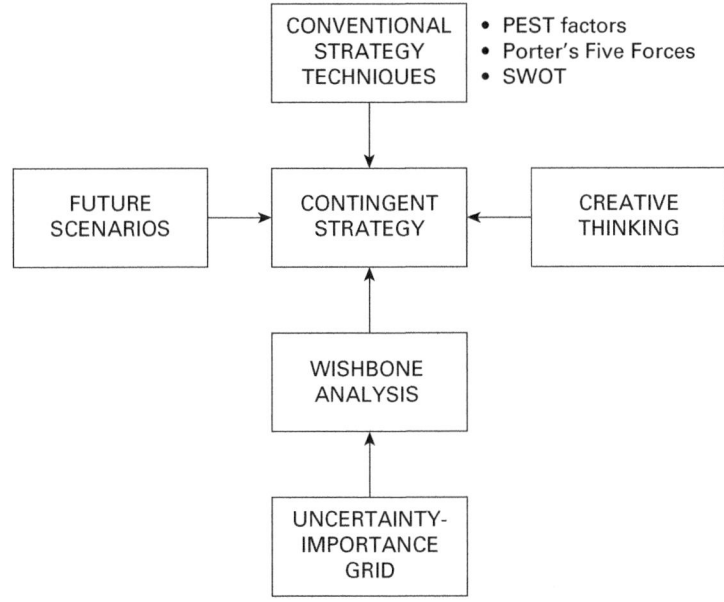

- The contingent option grid brings together a number of disparate analysis techniques (called the 'deep dive' technique) within a more visual framework.
- It facilitates and focuses managers' discussions so that strategic issues can be debated effectively.
- It provides a tangible vehicle for a dialectical process of 'challenge and build' (Diageo's own terms).
- It avoids strategies being seen as 'givens' and provides explicitly for creative input.
- It avoids looking at a single state of the world.
- It provides a total (yet relatively simple) system that managers can build into their strategic routines.

Adrian Green, former Director of Supply Strategy, Diageo (now Director of Quality, Diageo) commented on the utility of this approach, saying that the changes and benefits observed in the supply finance community were both behavioural and practical:

- The structure and format of the strategic options grid provided a model that people were very comfortable with and helped demystify 'strategy' as a rarefied capability.
- Enabled a highly energizing and fun process.
- Gave real clarity to all stakeholders and broke down any parochial positioning.
- Significantly speeded up the strategic process.
- Pushed back the creative barriers on creative thinking, principally from 'too difficult' etc, to 'let's explore these new options'.

To make it effective it is likely that a number of alignment conditions need to be met, namely:

- Managers need to educated and trained to understand why a contingent strategy is needed in the first place, what it is, and how it is to be managed/not managed.
- Rewards systems may need to be softened somewhat so that the business performance which flows on from the contingent strategy is not seen as a 'do-or-die' sort of a plan.
- Without at least some measure of greater flexibility it is possible that a well-articulated contingent strategy could run to ground because of managers being rigidly committed to delivering personal performance goals attached to their own contingent strategy.
- To implement contingent strategy more effectively almost certainly requires improved handling of underlying personal and political agendas as these are more likely to distort and inhibit decision making in times of change (Grundy, 1998).

Having outlined some of the more technical aspects of creating a contingent strategy let's now look at the issues of interpreting it effectively within the management process. Contingent strategy is likely to be especially relevant to incremental strategies (new product/market development, alliances, acquisitions, etc), to divestment options, and to ongoing strategies, which are potentially uncertain.

3. The implications for managers

Contingent strategy has a number of major implications for how managers deal with strategic issues. At present, plans, budgets, monitoring and rewards systems tend to reflect a determinate state of the world, as envisioned in a deliberate strategy framework. Contingent strategy presents challenges in how to apply these processes with greater flexibility and sensitivity.

In particular, the consequence of having a contingent strategy may be that resources earmarked in plans and budgets are allocated and subsequently managed in a contingent and flexible way. Resource availability may thus be contingent on both, a) achievement of key success indicators within the strategy itself and on other alignment conditions surrounding the strategy ie, in the environment, and b) satisfactory alignment of other strategies (and continual achievement of good results) in the company generally. So, in addition to contingent strategies we may also need contingent budgets. This is likely to have radical implications for everyday management of the business. Processes for communicating, monitoring and for adapting specific contingent strategies need to be put in place.

These implications highlight some very significant shifts in management practice comparable to those necessary when implementing other new interventions aimed at changing the management process, for example value-based strategic management (see McTaggart *et al*, 1994). Here, reluctance to adapt control and rewards systems to support changes in management process can prove to be a major stumbling block to effective implementation. In addition, it is likely that managers would need to manage the emotions that coping with the greater fluidity of contingent strategy could bring about. At least with deliberate strategy an emotional commitment is made to a particular path, making it easier for them to relax a little as 'the decision making is done'. However, given the disadvantages of existing approaches (whether these are deliberate or emergent) to strategic management we explored earlier, the overall benefits of a contingent strategy could be well worth the investment in change.

4. Implications for future research

There are a number of potential implications for future research. These break down into two strands. First there is research to explore existing approaches to applying contingent strategy, which is itself contingent upon finding instances where managers have pursued a more contingent strategy style of making and implementing strategic decisions. These might be found more in situations where entrepreneurial management is present and thus be of more limited applicability.

Second there is action research to explore what actually happens when managers attempt to apply a contingent strategy approach, which could focus on:

- Understanding all the adjustments – in processes, behaviours, thinking styles and mindsets, and even the associated emotions – that they need to make.
- Exploring their perceptions of the approach, and why it is/is not believed to be effective.
- Understanding the enablers and constraining influences they experience when experimenting with this approach.
- An appraisal (before and after) of its approximate economic value-added; in other words, what incremental monetary gains could be fairly attributed to its execution.

Given the potentially limited applicability of the first option, as contingent strategy is likely to be found much more rarely in traditional, budget-driven organizations, it may be not only preferable but also more exciting to pursue an action research approach to future strategic decisions. With significant benefits possibly accruing to managers from implementing the process, this may well make it easier to gain access to research sites.

5. Conclusions

To conclude, contingent strategy offers us a potentially very rich avenue for strategy to develop further, in practical as well as theoretical and research terms. This notion helps to recapture some of the fluidity that is found in military strategy (see the extract from ITV). This appears to have been partially lost in the translation of military strategy into commercial strategy, and is only partly captured in emergent strategy.

The idea also helps us to reconcile some of the debate on strategy versus tactics, which often confuses managers. Contingent strategy is adaptable to unpredictable and fluid conditions, without becoming lost in the micro-analysis normally associated with tactics. Contingent strategy integrates a number of more esoteric themes like contingency theory, commitment theory, scenarios, game theory and options in a simple and practical idea. Contingent strategy should help managers to cope better with environmental uncertainties (and more effectively than deliberate and emergent strategy forms). On top of this, it ought to help managers deal more effectively with the relatively 'sticky' pattern of resource allocation characteristic of companies with more mature and perhaps less flexible planning, budgeting, control and rewards systems.

REFERENCES AND FURTHER READING

Ansoff, I (1965) *Corporate Strategy*, McGraw Hill, New York
Argyris, C (1997) Double loop learning in organizations, *Harvard Business Review*, May/June, pp 99–109
Coelho, P (1997) *Manual of the Warrior of Light*, Harper Collins, London
Covey, S (1989) *The Seven Habits of Highly Effective People*, Simon & Schuster, London
Csikszentmihali, M (1975) *Beyond Boredom and Anxiety*, Jossey-Bass, San Francisco, CA
DeGeus, A (1998) Planning as learning, *Harvard Business Review*, March/April, pp 70–74
Dewar, J A (2002) *Assumption-based Planning*, Cambridge University Press, Cambridge
DeWit, B and Meyer, R (1988) *Strategy: Process, content, context*, Thomson, London
Dixit, A and Nalebuff, B (1991) *Thinking Strategically*, Norton, New York
Ghemawat (1991) *Commitment: The dynamic of strategy*, Free Press, New York
Gleick, J (1988) *Chaos: The making of a new science*, Heinemann, Oxford
Goldratt, E M (1990) *Theory of Constraints*, North River Press, Great Barrington, MA
Grant, R M (1991) The resource-based theory of competitive advantage, *California Management Review*, **33** (3), pp 114–35
Grundy, A N (1995) *Breakthrough Strategies for Growth*, Pitman Publishing, London
Grundy, A N (1997a) *Strategic Behaviour*, FT Publishing, London
Grundy, A N (1997b) Strategy mix and the industry mind-set, *Journal of General Management*, **22** (4), pp 16–30
Grundy, A N (1998) *Harnessing Strategic Behaviour*, FT Publishing, London
Grundy, A N (2002) *Shareholder Value*, Capstone Press, Oxford
Grundy, A N (2003a) *Value-based Human Resources Strategy*, Butterworth Heinemann, Oxford
Grundy, A N (2003b) *Mergers and Acquisitions*, Capstone Press, Oxford
Grundy, A N (2004) rejuvenating strategic management – the strategic option grid, *Strategic Change*, **13**, pp 111–23
Grundy, A N (2006) Rejuvenating Michael Porter's Five Forces model, *Strategic Change*, **15** (5), pp 213–30
Grundy, A N (2012) *Demystifying Strategy: How to become a strategic thinker*, Kogan Page, London
Grundy, A N and Brown, L (2001) *Exploring the Inner Energies*, Minerva Press, London
Grundy, A N and Brown, L (2002a) *Be Your Own Strategy Consultant: Demystifying strategic thinking*, Thomson, London

Grundy, A N and Brown, L (2002b) *Strategic Project Management*, Thomson, London

Grundy, T (1997) Strategy mix and the industry mind set, *Journal of General Management*, 22 (4)

Hamel, G and Prahalad, C K (1994) *Competing for the Future*, Harvard Business School Press, Cambridge, MA

Haspeslagh, P C and Jemison, D B (1991) *Managing Acquisitions*, Free Press, New York

James, E L (2012) *Fifty Shades of Grey*, Random House, London

Johnson, G and Scholes, K (1987) *Exploring Corporate Strategy*, Prentice Hall, London

Lawrence, P R and Lorsch, J W (1967) *Organization and the Environment*, Harvard Business School Press, Boston, MA

Lewin, K (1935) *A Dynamic Theory of Personality*, McGraw Hill, New York

McTaggart, J M, Kontes, P W and Mankins, M C (1994) *The Value Imperative*, Free Press, New York

Mintzberg, H (1994) *The Rise and Fall of Strategic Planning*, Free Press, New York

Mintzberg, H, Ahlsrand, B and Lampel, J (1998) *Strategy Safari*, Simon and Schuster, New York

Mitroff, I I and Linstone, H A (1993) *The Unbounded Mind*, Oxford University Press, Oxford

Morin, R A and Jarrell, S L (2001) *Driving Shareholder Value*, McGraw Hill, New York

Ohmae, K (1992) *The Mind of the Strategist*, McGraw Hill, New York

Osho (1990) *Intuition – Knowing beyond logic*, Osho International Foundation, Tokyo

Piercey, N (1989) Diagnosing and solving implementation problems of strategic planning, *Journal of General Management*, 15 (1)

Porter, E M (1980) *Competitive Strategy*, Free Press, New York

Porter, E M (1985) *Competitive Advantage*, Free Press, MacMillan, New York

Porter, E M (1990) *Competitive Advantage of Nations*, MacMillan, New York

Quinn, J B (1980) *Strategies for Change: Logical incrementalism*, Irwin, Homewood, IL

Rappaport, A (1996) *Creating Shareholder Value*, Free Press, New York

Senge, P (1990) *The Fifth Discipline: The art and practice of the learning organisation*, Century Business, London

Stacey, R (1993) Strategy as order emerging from chaos, *Long Range Planning*, 26 (1), pp 10–17

Stacey, R (1996) *Strategic Management and Organisational Dynamics*, Pitman, London

Staw, B M (1976) A study of escalating commitment to a chosen course of action, *Organizational Behaviour and Human Performance*, 16, pp 27–44

Tovstiga, G (2010) *Strategy in Practice*, Wiley, Chichester

Wack, P (1985a) Scenarios: Uncharted waters ahead, *Harvard Business Review*, September/October, pp 73–89

Wack, P (1985b) Scenarios: Shooting the rapids, *Harvard Business Review*, November/December, pp 139–50

Warren, K (2008) *Strategic Management Dynamics*, Wiley, Chichester

INDEX

Italics indicate a table or figure

Acquisitions   149, 150–51
action, translation of strategy into   165–67
Adetula, Samuel   13–14
Admiral   11
Amazon   11
Ann Summers   64
Ansoff grid   34
APIL (Association of Personal Injury Lawyers)   28, 29, 34–35, 67–93
   change management   87–90
   changing business models   72–73
   contingent strategy   82–85
   scenario development   82–85
   stakeholders   77–79
   storytelling   70
   strategic communication   73–75
   strategic leadership   71–72
   strategic thinking in a group context   68–69
   strategic thinking in practice   90–92
   strategic tools   85–87
   strategy implementation   87–90
   the 'time to die' strategically   69
   thinking and decision-making processes   75–76
   time spent on strategic thinking   79–80
   training in strategic thinking   80–82
   uncertainty   79
   value of strategic thinking and decisions   76–77
Ark charity   39
Arsenal Football Club   35
attractiveness/implementation difficulty (AID) analysis   *230*

banks, customer value destruction   13
BBC   148
beliefs and leadership   132–33
Benjamin, Des   130–53, 180–200, 229
Blackadder and the 'cunning plan', case study   15–17
BMW   150
bottom-up versus top-down strategic thinking   125–26
brainstorming   28, 72

Branson, Sir Richard   73, 113–15, 123, 124
breakthrough thinking   101
BT   212
Burj Khalifa, Dubai   243–47
business models
   changing (APIL)   72–73
   link to strategy   20–21
   Moonpig   42–43, 46–48
   Virgin Galactic   119–22
business scope, IPC   163–64
business value system   *41*
buying cycle   *111*

case studies
   APIL (Association of Personal Injury Lawyers)   67–93
   Blackadder and the 'cunning plan'   15–17
   buying a car   250–51
   choice of organizations   34–35
   free cruise as payment for speaking engagement   17–21
   Grand Paraiso Hotel, Cancun, Mexico   12
   Halloween party   237–42
   health club industry   273–75
   International Paralympic Committee (IPC)   154–74
   Moonpig   38–66
   Prudential Ride, London   225–29
   Samaritans   94–112
   Simplyhealth   130–53
   Tesco non-food business   4–8
   Virgin Galactic   113–29
   wedding cake   262–63
CEOs
   and strategic thinking   9–10
   appointment decision   138–39
   dealing with uncertainty and ambiguity   25
   responses to key research questions   202–07
   role as strategic thinker   49–50, 53
   strategic thinking training   235
   time spent on strategic thinking   79–80, 103, 185–87

Champneys Spas   221
change management   87–90
chaos theory   277, 284, 286
charities, measuring the value of strategy   53–55
Clinton cards   27, 42, 44, 46
Coelho, Paulo   208
cognitive behavioural therapy   138
cognitive processes in strategic thinking   229–35
Comet   134
commitment theory   277, 285, 287
communication   194
competition
 and contingent strategy   285
 Moonpig   45–46
 see also Porter's Five Competitive Forces
competitive advantage
 and strategy   10–14
 definition   11
competitive advantage curve   114
competitive advantage over time curve   69
competitive climate   256
competitive pressure over time curve   61, 63
complexity of strategic thinking   23
concentration of focus   195–96
consequences of strategic options   23
constraints of strategic thinking   221–24
context, flexibility of strategy to   283
contingency strategy techniques   287–94
contingency theory   277, 278
 and contingency planning   283, 286
contingent options   287
contingent options grid   293
contingent strategy   277–96
 and the strategy mix   281–82
 and uncertainty   82–85
 APIL   82–85
 definition   279
 existing theory on forms of strategy and context   281–87
 implications for future research   295–96
 implications for managers   294–95
 military context   277–78, 283, 287, 196
 versus sustainability focus   289–90
contingent strategy grid   288–89
core competences   40–41
Cranfield School of Management   39, 40, 63, 75, 212, 229
Craven, Sir Philip   154–55, 156, 158, 159, 161, 163, 165, 168
creative process   187–89
creativity, role in strategic thinking   23, 213
Csikszentmihali, Mihaly   211
Cuelho, Paulo   245
culture   139, 143

cunning checklists   222, 232
cunning plan, strategy as   3, 11, 14–21, 24, 36, 51, 52, 98, 205, 222, 243, 246

decision-making hierarchy   43–44
decision-making processes   75–76
 value of strategic thinking   76–77
deep dive technique   293
deliberate-emergent strategy   19
deliberate strategy   114, 118, 277, 278, 279–80, 281–82
Demystifying Strategy (Grundy, 2012)   1–3, 14, 19, 27, 29, 35, 50, 51, 65, 69, 72, 77, 85, 102, 118, 119, 123, 181, 194, 212, 234
detergent strategy   282
Diageo   292–94
difficulty over time curve   *128*
Direct Line   212
directional policy matrix   61, 222
Disney   3
diversification criteria   143–46
Dragons' Den   60
Dubai experience   242–47
Dyson   272, 289–90

Easyjet   121, 165
economic models   46, 213–14
economic value   183–85
 of flexibility   285–86
 of strategic thinking   223
 of strategy   53–55
economic value added curve   114
economic value over time curve   66
e-mails and strategic conversations   80–81
emergency strategy   282
emergent strategic thinking   102–04
emergent strategy   114, 118, 159, 277, 278, 279, 280, 281–82, 284
emotional advantage and service strategy   134–36
enablers of strategic thinking   221–24
energetic level of strategic thinking   212–13
entry barriers   44–46
evaluating strategic options   23, 29–34
Evans, Deborah   28, 67–93, 178–201, 229
everyday life, applicability of strategic thinking   17–23
evidence-based planning   99–100
evidence-based strategic thinking   199–200
exiting a business, Moonpig   56–57

Facebook   11
facilitation of strategy sessions   151–52
feasibility studies   50–52

Index

Fifty Shades of Grey 3
financial model, Moonpig 46–48
Flannigan Supermarket Direct 48
flexibility
  economic value of 285–86
  of contingent strategy 278–79
  to context 283
flow states and strategic thinking 167–70, 211–12, 217–21
focus, concentration of 195–96
football industry 35, *41*, 137
force field analysis 258
force field-type diagrams 85
formalization of strategy 64–65, 136–37, 166–67
Four Points Sheraton Hotel, Dubai 243
funeral industry 134, 258–59
Funky Pigeon 45, 46
future opportunities, assessment of 127, 143

game theory 277, 278, 285, 286
Gazidis, Ivan 35
GE (General Electric) grid 31–32, 61, 231, 233
Gonzalez, Xavier 155–73, 178–200
Google 11
Grand Paraiso hotel, Cancun, Mexico, case study 12
Green, Adrian 293–94
Greene, Moya 26–28
group context for strategic thinking 68–69
growth driver analysis 255–56

Halls, Monty 18–19
Harris, Matthew 275
health club industry, case study 273–75
helicopter thinking 43–44, 106–07, 194–95, 231
Henley Business School 46, 135, 149
hierarchy of needs (Maslow) 132–33
hierarchy of strategic options 39–40, 104, 178–80
Hoover 272
Hoshin 101
HSA *see* Simplyhealth

Iceland (company) 148
imitation and copying 62–64
implementation 23, 58–60, 87–90, 201
implications of strategic options 23
individual-level strategic thinking psychometrics 217–21
industry lifecycle effects 269
industry mindset 269–71
influencing cycle *112*

innovation, role in strategic thinking 1, 23, 24
inspiration *see* 'light bulb' moments
interdependencies
  in scenario development 284
  systems thinking 283–84
  Virgin Galactic 117–19
International Paralympic Committee (IPC) 35, 154–74
  business scope 163–64
  formalization and measurement 166–67
  lead times for strategy development 161–63
  linking things 164
  mindsets 162
  multi-dimensionality of variables 165–67
  nature of strategic thinking 156–59
  non-linearity of thinking 163–65
  openness to making mistakes 166
  strategic conversations 171–73
  strategic decision-making 165–66
  strategic heart 171
  strategic identity and engagement 170–73
  strategic model 161–62
  strategic thinking and flow 167–70
  strategic thinking process 163–65
  translation of strategy into action 165–67
  use of jargon 157
  vision 157–61
intuition and strategic thinking 39, 233 *see also* 'light bulb' moments
intuitive cognitive processes 70–71
intuitive economic analysis 194
intuitive thinking *see* 'light bulb' moments
Iraq war 277–78

jargon 40–41, 60, 107–08, 157, 200–01, 256
Jenkins, Nick 24, 27, 38–66, 177–200
John Lewis 12, 134–35, 139
Johnstone, Catherine 94–111, 178–201

Keogh, Chris 221
Key Research Questions 175–76
  CEO responses 202–07
key themes of strategic thinking 175–202
Kirby 272

leadership 1
  and beliefs 132–33
  dealing with uncertainty and ambiguity 25
learning
  to do strategic thinking 97–98
  role in managing adaptation 283–84

Index

Legal Complaints Service   67, 76, 83–84
'light bulb' moments   102, 123–24, 190–91, 213
linking things   164

managing adaptation, contingent strategy   283–84
margin manipulation   137–38
Marvel Studios   3
measurement of strategy effects   166–67
Metrobank   13–14
MFI   144
Microsoft   34
military context, contingent strategy   277–78, 283, 287, 196
Miller's Law   101
mindset   162, 269–71
mini-strategy process   76
Mintzberg, Henry   10, 118, 131, 278, 281–82
mission and vision   181–83
modelling, strategic and economic   213–14
  see also business models
Moonpig   24, 27, 34–35, 38–66
  approach to strategy   48–50
  business and financial model   46–48
  business models   42–43
  CEO role as a strategic thinker   49–50, 53
  competition   45–46
  core competences   40–41
  economic model   46
  economic value of strategy   53–55
  entry barriers   44–46
  exiting a business   56–57
  feasibility studies   50–52
  formalization   64–65
  future change   48–50
  hierarchy of decision making   43–44
  hierarchy of strategic questions   39–40
  imitation and copying   62–64
  intuition and strategic thinking   39
  perfect competition and economic value   62–64
  strategic data and evidence   44
  strategic energy   57–58
  strategic jargon   40–41
  strategy implementation   58–60
  strategy tools   60–62
  strategy versus tactics   55–56
multi-dimensionality of variables   165–67

negative energy, impacts on strategic thinking   212–13
Newsom, Susan   115, 116, 119, 122, 125
NHS   144, 146–47
non-linearity of thinking   163–65

openness to making mistakes   166
operational thinking, compared to strategic thinking   24–25
option theory   277, 278, 285–86, 287
options
  consequences of   23
  formulation of   72
  implications of   23
  in strategic thinking   23
  see also evaluating strategic options
Optopus (option generation technique)   32, 33, 34, 85, 114, 119, 145, 174, 232
organizational constraints on strategy   98–100
organizational context for strategy   95–97
organizational identity   170–73
out-of-body experience   77

perfect competition and economic value   62–64
perspectives of strategic thinking   23
PEST analysis   31, 254, 255–56, 293
playful strategic thinking   104–05
Porter's Five Competitive Forces   31, 45, 60–61, 231, 232, 293
  competitive dynamics   268–70
  interdependencies   255–58
  mapping competitive forces   271–75
  'micro' competitive forces   261–68
  prioritizing the five forces   258–61
  rethinking   249–77
  segmentation   271–75
  the way forward   276–77
  value and limitations of the model   252–54
position papers   65, 102
principles and values   138–39, 146–47
process school of strategy   211
Prudential   212
Prudential Ride, London, case study   225–29
psychometrics, strategic thinking capability   217–21

rabbit hole view   43–44
real options concept   286
resource-based theory of competitive advantage   287
right brain activity   70–71
  and strategic thinking   75
Rover Group   144, 150
Royal Mail   26–29, 34

Samaritans   34–35, 94–112
  avoiding jargon   107–08
  emergent strategic thinking   102–04

evidence-based planning 99–100
helicopter thinking 106–07
hierarchy of strategies 104
learning to do strategic thinking 97–98
nature of strategic thinking 100
organizational constraints on strategy 98–100
organizational context for strategy 95–97
playful strategic thinking 104–05
stakeholder involvement 105
strategic excitement 108–09
strategic planning processes 100–02
strategic planning skills 97–98
strategic planning time horizons 97
strategic training 105–06
value of strategic thinking 104–05
scenario storytelling 28, 29, 48, 70, 118, 128
scenarios 82–85, 86–87, 277, 278, 280, 284, 286
Senge, P 283
service strategy and emotional advantage 134–36
Sex Pistols 113–14
shareholder value creation 287
sharing and ownership 191–94
Simplyhealth 34–35, 130–53
    acquisitions 149, 150–51
    appointment of the CEO 138–39
    culture 139, 143
    diversification criteria 143–46
    emotional advantage 134–36
    facilitation of strategy sessions 151–52
    formalization of strategy 136–37
    future opportunities 143
    hiring people 138–39
    leadership and beliefs 132–33
    principles and values 138–39, 146–47
    role of strategic planning 133–34
    service strategy 134–36
    strategic mindfulness 140–42
    strategic vision 131–32, 152–53
    strategy and honesty 146–50
    strategy and teams 137–38
    strategy development and diversification 142
smaller scale strategic thinking 231
Somerfield 48
stakeholder analysis 85, 232, 233, 242
stakeholders 23, 77–79
    involvement 105
Standard Life 234–35
storytelling scenarios *see* scenario storytelling; scenarios
strategic appetite 170
strategic assumptions 124–25

Strategic Behaviour (Grundy, 1997) 211
strategic breakthrough process 229
strategic communication 73–75
strategic conversations 171–73, 189–90
strategic data 44
strategic decision-making 122–24, 165–66
strategic energy 57–58
strategic excitement 108–09
strategic heart 171
strategic identity and engagement 170–73
strategic influencing, Halloween party case study 237–42
strategic intent 10
strategic jargon *see* jargon
strategic leadership 71–72
strategic mindfulness 140–42, 169
strategic models 161–62, 213–14
strategic motives/objectives 74
strategic onion model 128, *129*, 255, 256
strategic option grid 29–34, 77, 85, 143, 174, 231, 232–33
strategic planning
    processes 100–02
    role of 133–34
    skills 97–98
    time scales 97
strategic plans 279, 280
strategic position papers 65, 102
strategic processes and techniques 196–99
strategic project management
    case study 225–29
    process 229–35
strategic questions 24–29
    hierarchy of 39–40
strategic thinking
    as a structured process 23
    asking the right questions 24–29
    compared to operational thinking 24–25
    definition 23–24
    demystifying challenge 1–3
    distinction from routine thinking 23–24
    group context 68–69
    in practice 90–92
    key ingredients 23–24
    key insights 36–37
    key themes 175–202
    mastery and intuition 247–48
    nature of 100, 156–59, 177–78, 201–02
    overview of what we know 210–17
    processes and structures 163–65, 214–15
    psychometrics 217–21
    successful *223*
    the one big thing we have forgotten 15–17, 18–19, 21–23
    value added by 4

Index

strategic thinking recipes 215–17
strategic thinking wheel 233–*34*
strategic training 105–06
strategic vision 131–32, 152–53
   see also vision
strategic workshops 126–27
strategy
   and competitive advantage 10–14
   and honesty 146–50
   as a cunning plan 3, 11, 14–21, 24, 36, 51, 52, 98, 205, 222, 243, 246
   as the 'how' 10
   cutting it down to size 199
   definitions 10–23
   development and diversification 116–17, 142
   existing theory on forms and context 281–87
   implementation 58–60, 87–90
   link to the business model 20–21
   redefining as contingent options 287
   tools and frameworks 60–62, 85–87, 214, 229–35
   typologies 281–82
strategy cognition, role of toolkits 229–35
strategy mix 281–82
study methodology, reflections and lessons 209–10
submergent strategy 282
sustainability of businesses 137–38, 289–90
SWOT analysis 60–61, 231, 255, 293
systems thinking 283–84

tactics versus strategy 55–56
Taylor, Vernon 247–48
teams and strategy 137–38
Tesco 34, 44, 121, 143
   non-food business case study 4–8
themes of strategic thinking *see* key themes of strategic thinking
three Cs (customer, company, competitor) analysis 11
Thursoe, Lord 221
time scale of strategy development 161–63
time spent on strategic thinking 79–80, 103, 185–87
'time to die' strategically 69
toolkits *see* strategy tools
Topnotch 273–75

training in strategic thinking 80–82
transformational change 1

umbrella strategy (Mintzberg) 10
uncertainty
   and contingent strategy 82–85
   dealing with 79, 117–19
uncertainty gap 84–85
uncertainty grid 85–86
uncertainty-importance grid 118–*19*, 290, 291, 292, 293, 94
uncertainty tunnel 82

Value-based Human Resources Strategy (Grundy, 2003) 99
value of strategic thinking 76–77, 104–05, 180–81, 223
value over time curve *121*
values and principles 138–39, 146–47
vicious cycle of strategic thinking *221*
Virgin Galactic 34–35, 113–29
   bottom-up versus top-down strategic thinking 125–26
   business model 119–22
   futures 127
   interdependencies 117–19
   'light bulb' moments 123–24
   strategic assumptions 124–25
   strategic decision-making 122–24
   strategic workshops 126–27
   strategy development 116–17
virtuous cycle of strategic thinking 222
vision 157–61
   and mission 181–83
   see also strategic vision
visionary school of strategy 131
visioning in strategic thinking 237–48
   Dubai experience 242–47
   strategic influencing 237–42

WH Smith 45
Whitesides, George 115–27, 179–200
wishbone analysis 289–*90*, 292–93

Yamaha 143
yoga 86, 142, 211, 212, 245, 246–47

Zen warrior 247–48
Zurich Life 221

Printed and bound by CPI Group (UK) Ltd, Croydon, CR0 4YY
22/03/2026

14847577-0003